Building The Case

Storytelling When Facts Are Fixed and Stakes Are High

Using Story Spine for Winning in Court and in Life

by

Leigh E. Johnson

Forwards by:

Richard Friedman & Kirsten Friedman

Praise for Building The Case:

From a Master Psychodramatist and Pioneer in Trial Advocacy

"'Building The Case' is a journey into the heart of what it means to be a lawyer representing people. Leigh Johnson teaches us that to truly hold our audience, we must first listen deeply—not just to the facts, but to the human story behind them. This book masterfully uses psychodrama to explore how understanding your own story can empower you to effectively tell others' stories. It's a crucial resource for any lawyer who seeks to transform their performance in court and in life.

— Don Clarkson, Psychodramatist, Educator, and Pioneer in Trial Advocacy

From the Creator of Online Action Methods-Tele'Drama

"Leigh E. Johnson's '*Building The Case*' masterfully combines trial lawyering with the transformative power of psychodrama and experiential methods. By integrating the Story Spine framework, this book shows how to turn dry facts into emotionally resonant narratives that connect with jurors on a human level. A must-have resource for trial lawyers and anyone committed to the art of impactful storytelling."

– Dr. Daniela Simmons, Trainer, Educator, and Leader in Experiential Methods

From an Emmy Award Winning Film Director

Leigh Johnson has written what I consider to be an essential book for all attorneys. As we have sadly learned from recent political debates, facts matter very little. Facts are boring, facts are confusing, facts are made up, etc.... But what Leigh points out is that a person who can tell a good story can sway jurors and judges, facts or no facts. So it is essential to learn how to tell a good story, and Leigh Johnson explains how to do that that very effectively in this book. A must read, I think.

–John Jacobsen, Writer/Director/Teacher

From a Seasoned Criminal Defense Attorney

This isn't just a book—it's an invitation to rethink how you communicate. "Building the Case" turns every courtroom argument, every client's struggle, and every personal experience into a story worth telling. The chapter on psychodrama is a revelation—it gave me tools to bring depth and emotion to narratives in ways I'd never considered. And "Juror as Hero"? Pure genius. It's not just about winning cases; it's about connecting, understanding, and ultimately transforming how we see justice. This book will inspire you to find the story in every moment.

– Charles Windon, Esq., 50+ Years of Fighting for Justice

From a Dedicated Public Defender

"Leigh's book is a masterful work that would likely open up the emotions of any reader. Leigh is able to walk you through using the story spine from her own experiences as a human being and a lawyer. It is integrated into a cohesive narrative yet is also full of immediately effective tools. For a trial lawyer, her book led me to feel, immediately, like using the suggestions in the book to work on my cases. I wanted to stop reading the book and do the exercises; they were so clear and compelling, and I immediately knew they would make my work better, more meaningful, and more effective. This book will be a must-have for any trial lawyer or anybody facing any sort of life conflict be they a spouse, parent, child, colleague, or teammate. This book will change lives and storytelling forever."

– Tamara York, Marin County Public Defender

From a Guantanamo Bay Attorney, Jury Consultant, and Educator

Leigh brilliantly constructed a method of creating narratives that permit the client's story to resonate with all audiences in a courtroom. Her brilliance is that she digs deep into her own experiences and powerfully shares with humility her past triumphs and victories to unravel the journey of her expertise. It is this transparency that brings the reader/student to experience the lessons learned and now taught through a compellingly simple structure. The lawyer who embarks on the path of this method, forever committed to learning, and relearning the method that when ultimately mastered become second nature. The bonus is the individual evolves along with the mastery of the craft. Leigh does the superior job of simplifying and explaining the power of storytelling in a courtroom.

– Rosa Alexander Eliades, Emergence Consulting

From a Master Trial Lawyer & Teacher of Trial Skills

This book is a revelation for anyone who needs to tell stories that matter. The Story Spine framework is simple yet profound, offering a roadmap to connect emotionally and logically with any audience. The chapters on psychodrama and inanimate objects brought storytelling to life in ways I never imagined. A must-read for lawyers and storytellers of all kinds.

– Grover Porter, San Bernadino Trial Lawyer

From A Fellow Author & Everyday Person

Leigh Johnson is masterful at teaching the art of storytelling in her book. Building the Case is a fascinating read, not only for lawyers, but also for those wanting to create deeper personal relationships. Leigh's expertise in this unique field shines through as she teaches the concepts and techniques for generating stories that engage your audience. This exceptional book is compelling, beautifully written, and skillfully taught. A must read for anyone looking to strengthen relationships using the art of empathy through storytelling. I highly recommend Building the Case to enhance your communication skills and improve your connection with others.

– Connie Cord, Author of Messages from Love

From a Seasoned Civil Litigator

Building The Case is a tour de force for anyone who crafts narratives, whether in the courtroom or the broader realm of storytelling. Leigh's discussion of personal story spines and psychodrama is a standout highlight. These spines and psychodramatic scenes—focused on personal moments of struggle, resilience, and triumph—offer a compelling framework for organizing narratives. Leigh empathetically encourages readers to strip away pretenses and embrace vulnerability, reminding us that the truest stories are those living with all their messy, beautiful humanity intact.

Seizing the reader's trust, Leigh refreshingly shows hers first with anecdotes and exercises that inspire readers to dig deeper into their own experiences and harness them for storytelling that connects on a soul-deep level. Leigh does not just "tell" the reader to do it. Instead, she lovingly takes her reader's hand and walks with them while "showing" them how. This work is a true victory in training advocacy and storytelling, something that has gone missing in the legal realm. - Thank you Leigh

– Michael Bodey, Esq., Civil Litigator & Lover of Psychodrama

From a World Class Trial Lawyer and Tribal Judge

"Down through the evolution of human beings, stories have been the key to our survival, providing us with information needed for our survival, shared around campfires with other humans who were also making their way across hostile landscapes. Storytelling became the very essence of how we humans organize our experience and share those experiences with others. Very simply put, dramatic experiences of all kinds, from witnessing crimes to car accidents, do not become completely real until the very first time we tell the story of an event to another person.

The story organizes the experience for the participant, and it creates a shared reality for those who hear it and feel the emotional subtext of it. Storytelling is an essential feature of trials, and Leigh Johnson has made it an accessible and understandable process for trial lawyers who often win or lose their trials by virtue of how well they tell the stories of their clients to jurors and judges. The thoroughness of her work is breathtaking in its scope. I have taught and trained with Leigh, she knows the material and has given it considerable thought over the years."

– Charles Abourezk, Psychodramatist, Trial Judge, Appellate Justice and recently retired Trial Lawyer.

From a Poet and a Writer

"Leigh Johnson has not only given us a tool for telling an authentic story, she provides a path for bringing humanity, with all its glory and flaws, into the courtroom. She shifts the question from merely asking whether or not an argument is factual, to asking whether or not the story is also illuminating."

– Cynthia Wold, Poet, Writer, Convener, Founder of Scribble River, Co-Author of The Art of Convening

Building the Case:
Turning Dry Facts into Compelling Narratives

For permission requests, contact:
Leigh E. Johnson
166 Geary Street
Suite 1500 #2658
San Francisco, CA 94108
Leigh@ law4leigh.com

First Edition: 2025

ISBN: 979-8-9923800-0-2

Printed in the United States of America

Edited by Nicole Boccelli-Saltsman

Illustrations by Andy Birkey

Design and Layout by Sharmen Akter

Cover Design Concepts by Kirsten Friedman

Case Story Disclaimer

The case and war stories in this book are **crafted for educational purposes**. They do not depict any specific real-world case, individual, or event. Instead, they are **carefully constructed hypotheticals** designed to illustrate trial advocacy principles and storytelling techniques.

Over decades as both a lawyer and trial consultant, I have encountered a vast range of cases, each with its own unique complexities. The scenarios in this book are inspired by **patterns, themes, and lessons** drawn from professional experience, but they are **not direct accounts of any particular case or client**.

While some situations may feel familiar, **any resemblance to actual cases, people, or events is purely coincidental**. If you recognize something from your own experience, it is simply a reflection of **universal advocacy challenges** rather than a direct representation.

These case stories are meant to be **learning tools**, blending elements from multiple sources, reshaped to illustrate key legal and storytelling strategies. They exist to **sharpen your trial advocacy skills**, not to document or disclose real-world litigation.

Enjoy the learning process, engage with the stories, and use them to build stronger, more persuasive narratives in your own work.

Legal Disclaimer

Dedications

For my mother, Pender Precious Thompson.

To the advocates of justice,
who fight tirelessly for truth, fairness, and compassion in every courtroom.

To my mentors and colleagues,
whose wisdom, guidance, and support have shaped my journey.

And to my family,
for their unwavering belief in my vision and their endless encouragement,

this book is dedicated with gratitude and love.

Epigraphs

"Justice is not found in the facts alone but in the stories we weave from them, stories that compel belief and inspire action." — Unknown

"A well-told story doesn't just present the truth—it makes the truth impossible to ignore."

— Anonymous

"The truth is rarely pure and never simple, but through narrative, it becomes unforgettable." — Oscar Wilde (adapted)

Table of Contents

Preface to the Foreword

Welcome to a unique journey that begins right here in the foreword of this book. I am thrilled to present an introduction that itself is a masterclass in narrative structure, penned by a distinguished trial lawyer, Richard Friedman (Rick), who has graciously used the Story Spine to craft his message. This method, pivotal throughout our exploration, breaks down complex narratives into fundamental elements that resonate deeply with human emotion and cognition.

The Story Spine framework is simple yet profound, consisting of key segments that construct a compelling narrative: It starts with "Once upon a time," setting the scene and introducing the norm. "Every day" follows, establishing the regular pattern of life before it is interrupted by "But one day," the moment that changes everything. This leads to a series of "Because of that" statements, each showing the consequences of the change, building momentum to "Until finally," the climax that resolves the tension. The narrative concludes with "And ever since then," where we understand the new status quo.

In this foreword, Rick has artfully applied the Story Spine to encapsulate not just the personal story of our history, but to echo the larger themes we will tackle in the book—themes of justice, choice, and the human condition as viewed through the lens of legal challenges and societal structures. As you read, I invite you to identify these elements of the Story Spine. Note how each part contributes to evolving the narrative and how effectively this structure can communicate complex ideas and stir emotions.

This approach is not just a stylistic choice; it is central to the message of this book. The Story Spine is a tool that reveals the essence of stories, making them relatable and memorable. It is particularly relevant to the field of law, where every case tells a story, and every story has the power to change outcomes. By understanding this framework, legal professionals can craft better narratives that advocate more persuasively for their clients.

As you proceed, keep the structure of the Story Spine in mind, and consider how it applies not only to the foreword but to the real-life stories and scenarios discussed throughout this book. May this method enrich your reading experience and enhance your professional practice by providing a new perspective on the power of storytelling in law and in life.

Enjoy this innovative introduction and the rich insights that follow, as we delve into the intricate dance of narrative and justice.

FORWARD #1 by Richard H. Friedman

Introduction: I am privileged to present a foreword by Richard H. Friedman (Rick), a distinguished alumnus of Harvard Law School and a venerated figure in the legal community. Rick is the author of five groundbreaking legal texts, including *Rules of the Road, Polarizing the Case, Becoming a Trial Lawyer, The Elements of Trial,* and *The Way of the Trial Lawyer*. These books have revolutionized how thousands of lawyers try their cases.

Title: "A Legal Narrative Odyssey"

Scene: We begin our exploration with a foreword penned by Rick, whose expertise in trial lawyering has illuminated many a legal pathway. In this comprehensive narrative, Rick employs the Story Spine to not only introduce our discourse, but to vividly demonstrate how these narrative bones support the flesh and blood of impactful storytelling. As you traverse his historical journey, observe the meticulous way he weaves facts into a storyline that's as instructive as it is compelling.

Story Spine Forward:

Once upon a time I was a trial lawyer, determined to become the best trial lawyer I could be. Over the decades, I have been skeptical of articles, books and presentations about storytelling. For me, trials were about strategy, tactics, and learning the case better than anyone else. To me, "Storytelling" sounded like a gimmick, then a fad, and worse, an appeal to emotion that signaled that the objective facts were not on my side.

Every day I practiced law, taught trial techniques and wrote books about trial techniques and strategies. I recognized that there were some great trial lawyer storytellers, like my hero Jim Perdue, but I knew I could never do what he did with a story, so I stuck to what I knew and felt comfortable with. I exposed myself to "Storytelling" information as little as possible.

And because of that reluctance on my part, I deprived myself of one of the most important tools a trial lawyer can have (I can't believe I am saying this)—storytelling.

Until one day I met Leigh Johnson when we were both participants in a psychodrama group. I came to know her not only as a successful trial lawyer and trial consultant, but also as an extremely intelligent and kind human being with a compelling personal story of her own.

Because of her persistent enthusiasm for storytelling, and my enormous respect for her, I began to soften my negative attitude—but just a bit. Someone is either good at telling a persuasive story or they are not, I thought, this is not something you can teach, right?

Until one day I was facilitating a course I call "Ethos." We bring 45 lawyers together to work with psychodrama, singing, and other modalities to help trial lawyers overcome their internal obstacles to being better trial lawyers. Leigh was one of the participants. For reasons I don't remember, we had a hole to fill in the program, and I asked Leigh to work with the group on "trial techniques." This was not something we usually work on, but we needed to fill the space.

Leigh said she wanted to work with "story spines" or something like that, and I was preoccupied with the rest of the schedule and said that would be fine. I should have known better, but in fact, my expectations were low.

To my amazement, the participants came back after only an hour and a half, excited and energized by Leigh's exercises. Those that seemed to be natural storytellers and those who had difficulty all seemed to benefit.

Because of that Leigh's exercises on story telling have been part of the Ethos program ever since—when she is able to attend as a facilitator.

But I was still confident no one could write a good "how-to" book about storytelling for trial lawyers. I had considered writing something similar myself, but the topic seemed too subjective, complex, and ephemeral to me. What a mistake!

Until one day Leigh asked if I would read a draft of this book. I agreed, with a heavy heart. How would I tell my friend that her book was mediocre and not helpful?

But she asked, and she was a good friend and ***because of that,*** I read her book.

Finally, I have realized the error of my ways. This book is a masterpiece. Leigh has done what I didn't think possible—written a comprehensive, truly helpful book on how to be a better storyteller. I don't care how good you are—or think you are—if you read this book with an open mind, it will make you a better storyteller and a better trial lawyer. I know I am better for having read it. That's all I am going to say about the book, because the sad (for me) fact, is that Leigh does a better job describing what she is up to in this book than I possibly could.

And from now on when the subject of storytelling comes up, I will say, "there is a book you ***must*** read…"

Rick Friedman-Bremerton WA

FORWARD #2 by Kirsten Friedman

Introduction: I am equally honored to include a second foreword written by Kirsten Friedman, an Internal Family Structure (IFS) Certified Therapist and a Psychodrama Trainer Educator Practitioner (TEP), whose dual expertise in law and counseling enriches her approach to legal advocacy and client support. Kirsten holds a Juris Doctorate alongside a Master's in Counseling, and is a licensed mental health counselor (LMHC) and a seasoned trial lawyer, making her uniquely qualified to bridge the realms of legal practice and therapeutic storytelling.

Title: "Insights at the Intersection of Law and Psychology"

Scene: "Following the expansive narrative journey set forth by Rick, Kirsten, not only a seasoned lawyer but also a gifted psychodramatist and psychologist, offers a potent distillation of what the book is about. Her foreword, though briefer, strikes at the heart of our subject matter with precision and profound insight. Her dual expertise casts a unique light on the psychological dimensions of legal storytelling, providing you with a multi-faceted understanding that enriches the foundation laid by Rick."

Forward:

If you are already an effective storyteller, this brilliant book will up your game. If, because of your overly-protective left brain, or because of your shyness or self-doubt, you believe you are not a storyteller, Leigh Johnson will convince you that you need to be and will show you how to get there. Leigh, a gifted and experienced trial lawyer, uses neuroscience, case examples and personal narrative to build a spell-binding case for the power of experiential storytelling, not just in the courtroom, but throughout client intake and trial preparation.

What she teaches is not a gimmick, a tactic, or a tool. It is a learnable craft, the practice of which not only significantly improves client outcomes but takes trial preparation and practice to a level of deep connection with your clients, your work, and your own humanity.

This book is a treasure for your practice and food for your soul. Spoiler alert, Leigh's own story, which she shares in the book, will move you to tears. Even better, it will help you appreciate and understand *how* you were so moved.

Kirsten Friedman-Bremerton WA

Story Spine Product Safety Warning

Warning: Highly Addictive Storytelling Power Ahead!

This book is not for the faint of heart—or for those content with telling dull, uninspiring stories. Side effects may include, but are not limited to:

- **Life-altering epiphanies** about your personal journey (and maybe a few tears).
- **Unstoppable confidence** in meetings, courtrooms, or the Thanksgiving dinner table.
- **A tendency to narrate everything**, from grocery runs to office dramas, like it's an Oscar-winning screenplay.
- **Heightened emotional connections**, causing friends, family, and even your barista to open up like never before.
- **Verbal superpowers** so strong, they might leave your opponents speechless—and possibly apologizing.

Proceed at Your Own Risk:

By applying the tools in this book, you might just change the way you connect with the world. The emotional depth and narrative brilliance you unleash could revolutionize your career, relationships, and yes, even awkward small talk.

Important Reminder:

- Use responsibly. Unsolicited storytelling can overwhelm unprepared audiences.

- Seek professional guidance for intense psychodrama revelations. This book is storytelling, not therapy.
- Keep out of reach of anyone who thinks storytelling is "just fluff". They won't know what hit them.

"The universe is made of stories, not atoms." – Muriel Rukeyser

Chapter 1
Introduction

"Facts alone inform, but it is the artful weaving of those facts into compelling narratives that inspires action, evokes emotion, and transforms understanding."

Transforming Facts into Compelling Narratives

What do great courtroom arguments and captivating theater performances have in common? Both depend on storytelling to command attention and move their audience. As Steve Jobs famously said, "The most powerful person in the world is the storyteller." And why wouldn't they be? Storytellers don't just share information, they create worlds. They guide emotions, shape perspectives, and inspire action. In the courtroom, being a great storyteller means the difference between jurors yawning through the evidence or leaning forward, hanging on your every word.

Every Great Story Has a Beginning, Middle, and End

Let's start with the basics: stories work because they're structured. Think about your favorite movie or novel—there's a setup that grabs your attention, a middle where everything gets messy, and a resolution that leaves you satisfied (or maybe crying in your popcorn). That's no accident. The human brain thrives on this structure because it creates order out of chaos. In the courtroom, you're not just presenting evidence; you're inviting jurors on a journey. Without structure, your facts are like random puzzle pieces tossed on the floor—good luck getting anyone to see the picture or understand how the pieces fit together.

When you tell a story about your client—whether it's their struggles, their resilience, or the unfair circumstances they've faced—you're engaging the listener's emotions. That's because of mirror neurons. These little brain cells light up when we see or hear about someone else's experience, making us feel as though we're living it ourselves. Want a jury to connect with your client? Don't just tell them the facts; make them feel the story.

Have you ever tried to remember a grocery list without writing it down? You might recall a few items, but chances are, you'll forget half of them by the time you hit the cereal aisle. Facts are like that—they're slippery, especially when they're presented without context. But stories? They latch onto our memory like Velcro. A story gives jurors a way to hold onto the evidence long after closing arguments. It's the difference between saying, "My client grew up in poverty" and showing the jury how your client walked to school every day wearing tattered clothing and raggedy shoes. One is a fact; the other is a story they'll carry with them.

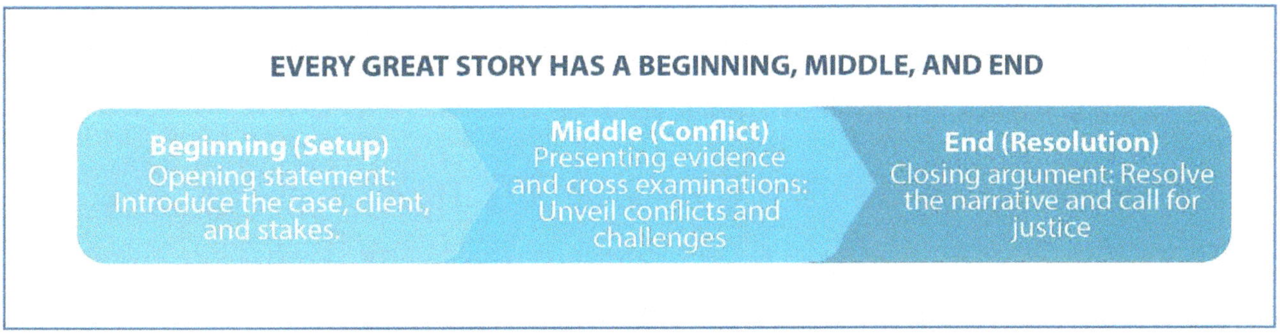

Figure 1: The Three-Act Structure in Legal Storytelling

A Story Puts the Jury in the Driver's Seat

Good stories don't just explain; they offer full immersion. They allow the audience to step into someone else's world, feel their struggles, and understand their choices. In the courtroom, this is critical. A great story puts jurors in your client's shoes, helping them see the world from a perspective they might never have considered. When you show rather than tell, the jurors become participants in the narrative, not just spectators. They stop asking, "What happened?" and start asking, "What would I have done in their place?"

Every trial is a competition of stories. The prosecution has their version of events, and you have yours; same with the civil side of things. Everybody has their story that they believe is truth. The jury won't recall every detail of any story, but they will remember the story that made the most sense, felt the most authentic, and left the strongest impact. That's why crafting your narrative isn't just helpful, it's essential. A strong story answers the jury's questions before they even ask them. It ties together evidence, testimony, and emotion into a single, clear message: justice is on your client's side. And when your story achieves all that? That's when you win.

A cohesive, authentic, and emotionally resonant narrative provides jurors with clarity and conviction. It eliminates doubt, reinforces your key arguments, and positions your client as deserving of their understanding and fairness. The story that best integrates evidence, empathy, and logic will guide the jury toward the outcome you seek.

The Cognitive Science Behind Storytelling

Your brain loves stories. It's practically addicted to them. Why? Because when you hear a story, your brain isn't just passively processing words, it's lighting up like a Fourth of July fireworks display. Stories activate areas associated with sensory experiences, memory, and emotions. Jurors don't just *hear* a story; they feel like they're living it. This is why a well-crafted narrative can transport jurors into your client's shoes and keep them emotionally engaged.

Here's the thing: the human brain is a sucker for patterns. It craves them. Stories satisfy this craving with their natural structure—beginning, middle, and end. This structure organizes information into something meaningful and memorable. Contrast this with raw facts, which often feel like scattered threads with no loom to weave them into a coherent tapestry. A great story doesn't just connect the dots; it paints the whole picture, making it easier for jurors to recall the key evidence. Want your case to stick in their minds? Give them a story they can follow, not a pile of disconnected facts.

The Emotional Power of Stories

For the most part, facts are not naturally charming. They don't flirt with your emotions or tug at your heartstrings. Stories, on the other hand, are emotional rock stars. They activate "mirror neurons" in the brain, the same ones that make us cringe when we see someone stub their toe or make us cheer when the underdog wins. These neurons create empathy and connection, helping jurors care about your client and their case. A story doesn't just deliver information, it builds a bridge between your argument and the jury's emotions. And that bridge is where decisions are made.

In a trial setting, cognitive overload is real, and it's what happens when jurors are bombarded with a barrage of raw information. Without context or narrative, the brain struggles to retain or prioritize those facts. A list of forensic evidence? Forgettable. A story of how that evidence led to the truth? Engaging and memorable.

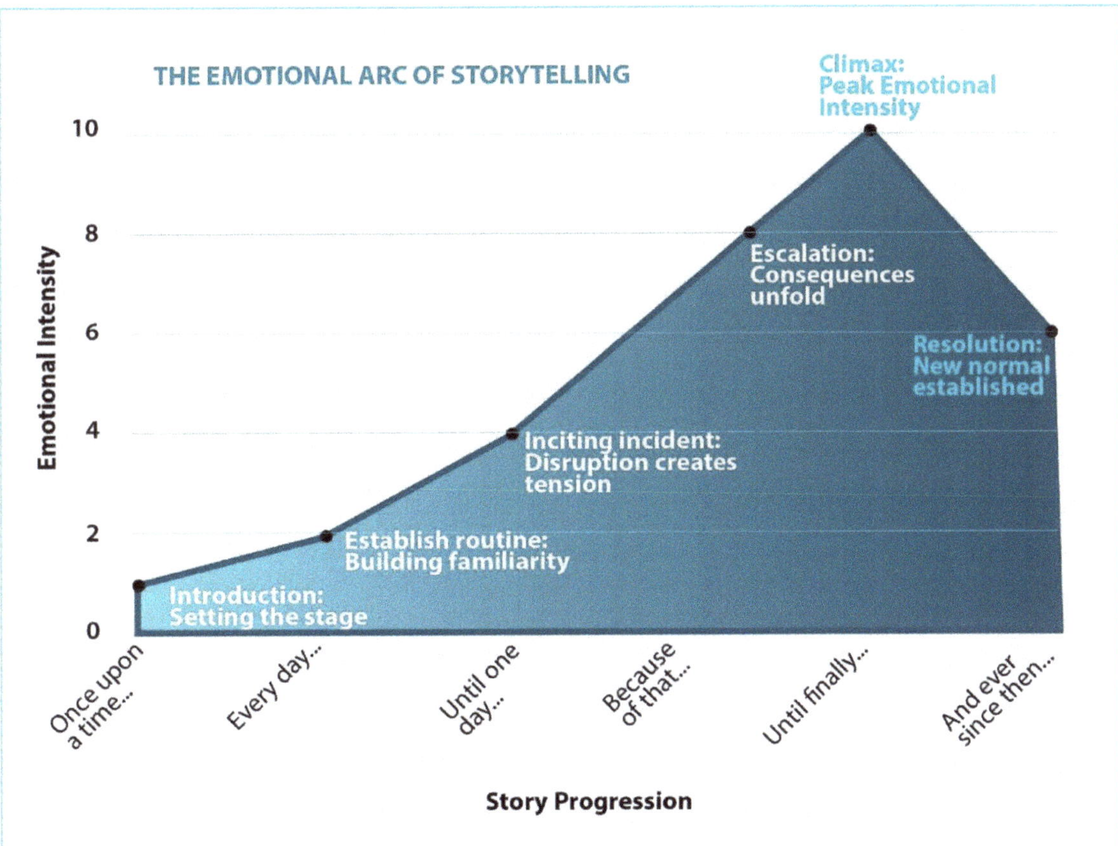

Figure 2: The Emotional Arc of Storytelling

Life Lessons: The Power of A Story

Once upon a time...

A new lawyer stood in court, her case meticulously prepared. The evidence was flawless, the arguments logical, the law firmly on her side. But as she spoke, she saw the jury's focus waver. Her airtight presentation wasn't enough. Facts alone couldn't hold their attention. She felt a gnawing frustration—*what am I missing?*

Every day...

Professionals like her face similar struggles. They rely on expertise, logic, and preparation, believing these will win the day. Yet their messages often fail to land, leaving them wondering why their hard work doesn't inspire, persuade, or connect. What they don't realize is that facts and logic are only part of the equation.

Until one day...

During a trial skills workshop, the lawyer saw something that changed her perspective forever. A colleague shared a raw, emotional narrative—a story that revealed their client's humanity in a way no legal argument could. The room fell silent, and the connection was palpable. For the first time, she understood the transformative power of storytelling. It wasn't just an addition to her work—it was the missing key.

Because of that...

She began uncovering the human stories behind her cases. She dug deep, listening for the emotions and experiences that shaped the facts. Her arguments evolved, no longer just logical but deeply resonant. Juries leaned forward in their seats, listening intently. Clients felt seen and heard. Opposing counsel struggled to counter her emotionally compelling narratives.

And because of that...

She realized storytelling was more than a tool; it was a bridge. Stories shaped perception, built empathy, and created meaning in ways facts alone never could. It wasn't just about winning cases—it was about connection, about helping people truly understand one another.

Until finally...

She saw storytelling as an essential human activity, not just in courtrooms but in every aspect of life. Stories have the power to transform how we see the world, how we lead, and how we influence. She mastered the art of finding and telling stories, knowing they could make the difference between being heard and being ignored.

And ever since that day...

In time, the new lawyer became a seasoned lawyer who was a teacher of stories. She now shows others how to uncover the narratives hidden in their work, how to harness storytelling to connect, inspire, and create change. Every case, every interaction, every challenge holds a story waiting to be told—and she helps others find it.

The Solution: Story Spine Framework

The Story Spine is a powerful framework that transforms raw facts into a cohesive and compelling narrative. It provides the structure needed to ensure every detail serves a purpose, seamlessly fitting into the larger story. The Story Spine organizes information into a clear, logical, and familiar sequence, transforming complex ideas into accessible insights while fostering a powerful connection that holds the audience's attention.

The Story Spine consists of seven simple yet powerful steps:

- **Once upon a time...**: Establish context and characters.
- **And every day...:** Highlight the routine or norm.
- **Until one day...**: Introduce the inciting incident or disruption.
- **Because of that...**: Show the immediate consequences.
- **Because of that...**: Escalate the conflict.

- **Until finally…**: Resolve the core issue.
- **And ever since then…**: Reflect on the new normal or lessons learned.

How It Works

This storytelling framework is going to be your new best friend. It takes your facts and gives them a heartbeat. Starting with "Once upon a time…" and moving through the twists and turns of "Because of that…," the Story Spine creates a natural flow that informs and connects. Whether you're convincing jurors, appealing to a judge, or piecing together your argument during case prep, this framework ensures that every detail serves a purpose. It's the ultimate tool for turning dry facts into a compelling narrative.

Your job as a lawyer is not just to find facts but to shape them into a story that persuades and compels action. To do this effectively, you must start by organizing the overwhelm—a mountain of evidence that needs to be transformed into a clear, structured narrative that jurors can follow. Next, find the humanity in the case. Numbers, charts, and technical details might be necessary, but they don't convince people. Jurors connect with people, so your story must bring your client's experience to life in a way they can feel and understand. Finally, remember to speak to both the head and the heart. Logic may be necessary to win the argument, but emotion is how we make decisions.

Figure 3: The Lawyer's Challenge – Step-by-Step Process Flow

From Air Traffic Control to the Courtroom

I first grasped the importance of translating raw data into actionable communication during my time as an air traffic controller. Every moment involved interpreting streams of data: radar blips, altitude readings, and weather updates. One stormy evening, a flight crew faced severe turbulence while navigating crowded airspace. My job was to take those fragments of data and translate them into a clear, compelling picture the pilots could act on instantly. This experience taught me that **facts alone don't save lives—clarity and connection do**. Just as pilots need guidance to understand their situation, jurors need stories to understand a case. Facts are essential, but without context and narrative, they lose their impact.

In the courtroom, lawyers face a storm of their own: mountains of data, dozens of witnesses, pages of testimony. But without a narrative, all of it remains a lifeless sea of information. It's the story—the clarity, the connection, the humanity—that leads jurors to a verdict. In the courtroom, your jurors are like that flight crew. They're navigating unfamiliar territory, surrounded by a whirlwind of evidence. Your job is to guide them through the chaos—not with random facts but with a story that leads them safely to the right conclusion.

This book is your guide to mastering the art of storytelling using the Story Spine framework. You'll learn how to turn faceless, fragmented facts into narratives that not only inform but move. Together, we'll explore how to use story structures, emotional resonance, and cognitive science to create compelling arguments that stick with jurors long after they leave the courtroom.

Personal Spines, Case Spines, and War Stories

In various parts of this book, I will share life lessons, case stories and personal spines to demonstrate how I handled the presented concepts as hypotheticals in some of my cases. In other chapters I will present war stories, a shorter version of case stories. Each story highlights a unique aspect of narrative-building, from uncovering hidden truths to crafting emotionally resonant moments. By examining these stories, you'll learn how to turn raw facts into compelling narratives that connect with audiences on a deeper level. This is your starting point for mastering the art of impactful storytelling.

A War Story: The Missing Voice

Once upon a time, a young mother named Maria walked into my Family Law office. She carried a manila folder clutched to her chest, filled with documents she thought would speak for her. Maria was going through a contentious custody battle for her 7-year-old daughter, Sofia, against her ex-husband, Daniel—a man with a commanding presence, a well-paid attorney, and a knack for charming people who didn't know him well. Maria, on the other hand, was soft-spoken and overwhelmed, working two jobs just to keep her home.

Every day, Maria tried to prove her worth as a parent through actions that went unnoticed: staying up late to help Sofia with her homework, sewing patches onto her favorite teddy bear, and stretching every dollar to make sure Sofia had what she needed. But in the courtroom, her love and sacrifices were reduced to sterile facts: her income, her work hours, and her lack of family nearby. Meanwhile, Daniel's lawyer painted him as the ideal parent—successful, stable, and, most importantly, present. What the court didn't see were the nights Daniel missed visits or the way his temper frightened Sofia.

When Maria came to me, her story felt buried beneath the paperwork. She thought the documents alone would win her case. But what the system needed to hear—and what Sofia deserved—was the truth of Maria's love, her struggles, and her unyielding commitment.

But one day, I introduced Maria to the power of storytelling. Together, we pieced together her story not just as a collection of facts but as a vivid narrative. Instead of just stating her income and work hours, we described how she spent her mornings braiding Sofia's hair before school and her evenings helping her build science fair projects. Instead of merely pointing out Daniel's absences, we told the court about the time Sofia waited by the window for hours on her birthday, a cake sitting untouched on the table.

Because of that, Maria's voice came alive in the courtroom. The judge saw her not as a file number or a statistic but as a devoted mother fighting for her daughter's happiness and safety. The sterile facts transformed into an undeniable truth about who Maria was and the life she had built for Sofia.

Until finally, the court ruled in Maria's favor, granting her primary custody and ensuring Sofia had the stability and love she needed. For the first time in months, Maria walked out of the courtroom with her head held high, knowing she had been seen and heard.

And ever since then, I've made it my mission to teach clients that the facts of their cases are important, but their stories are what truly matter. Because when the legal system feels cold and indifferent, storytelling becomes the bridge that connects human lives to justice.

Conclusion:

"Storytelling is the most powerful way to put ideas into the world today." ~ Robert McKee

Stories are not merely for fun and entertainment; they are the lifeblood of human connection and understanding. From ancient myths that united civilizations to the narratives that drive today's most powerful movements, storytelling remains our most potent tool for influence and empathy. As we move forward, embrace the reality that a well-told story can change minds, bridge divides, and inspire action in ways facts alone cannot.

Chapter 2
The Power of Story

"Stories are the glue that makes facts stick, the spark that lights up logic, and the bridge that connects evidence to belief."

Why Stories Matter

So, what makes stories so powerful? It's all about *narrative transportation*—that irresistible phenomenon where people get so engrossed in a story that they lose track of their surroundings. When jurors are transported into your story, they stop analyzing isolated facts and start experiencing the narrative. They see the world through your clients' eyes, feeling their struggles, and rooting for their resolution. This emotional investment is what makes your argument land powerfully. Think of storytelling as your courtroom superpower: it disarms skepticism, builds empathy, and guides the jury to your side.

This Isn't About Manipulation—It's About Connection

Just to be clear, storytelling isn't about tricking jurors or spinning tall tales. It's not about manipulation; it's about connection. A well-told story isn't a smoke-and-mirrors act—it's a bridge. It helps jurors understand the human truth behind the facts, giving them the tools they need to see the bigger picture. When you tell a story, you're not distorting reality; you're illuminating it. Your job is to show the jury what's at stake, why it matters, and how justice can be served. It's not just a strategy, it's a responsibility to ensure your client's story is seen, heard, and understood.

When you tell a story, you're inviting your audience to walk in someone else's shoes. You're giving them a front-row seat to the emotions, struggles, and triumphs of your characters. And here's the thing: when people feel those experiences, they care and they act. That emotional connection—empathy—is the doorway to persuasion. You must speak to both the heart and the mind, making your audience feel invested in the outcome. That's the power of a great story—it moves people to believe and act.

Example: Let's compare two approaches to presenting a case:

- **The Fact Dump:** "The defendant's vehicle was recorded traveling 60 miles per hour in a 35-mph zone. The plaintiff's car was struck at the intersection, resulting in $15,000 in medical expenses."
- **The Story:** "On May 5th, Mary Johnson started her morning like any other, driving her kids to school. But at that intersection—the one she passes every single day—a car ran the red light and slammed into her. The crash left her in pain, unable to work, and uncertain how to care for her family."

See the difference? The first approach delivers the facts, but the second makes them memorable.

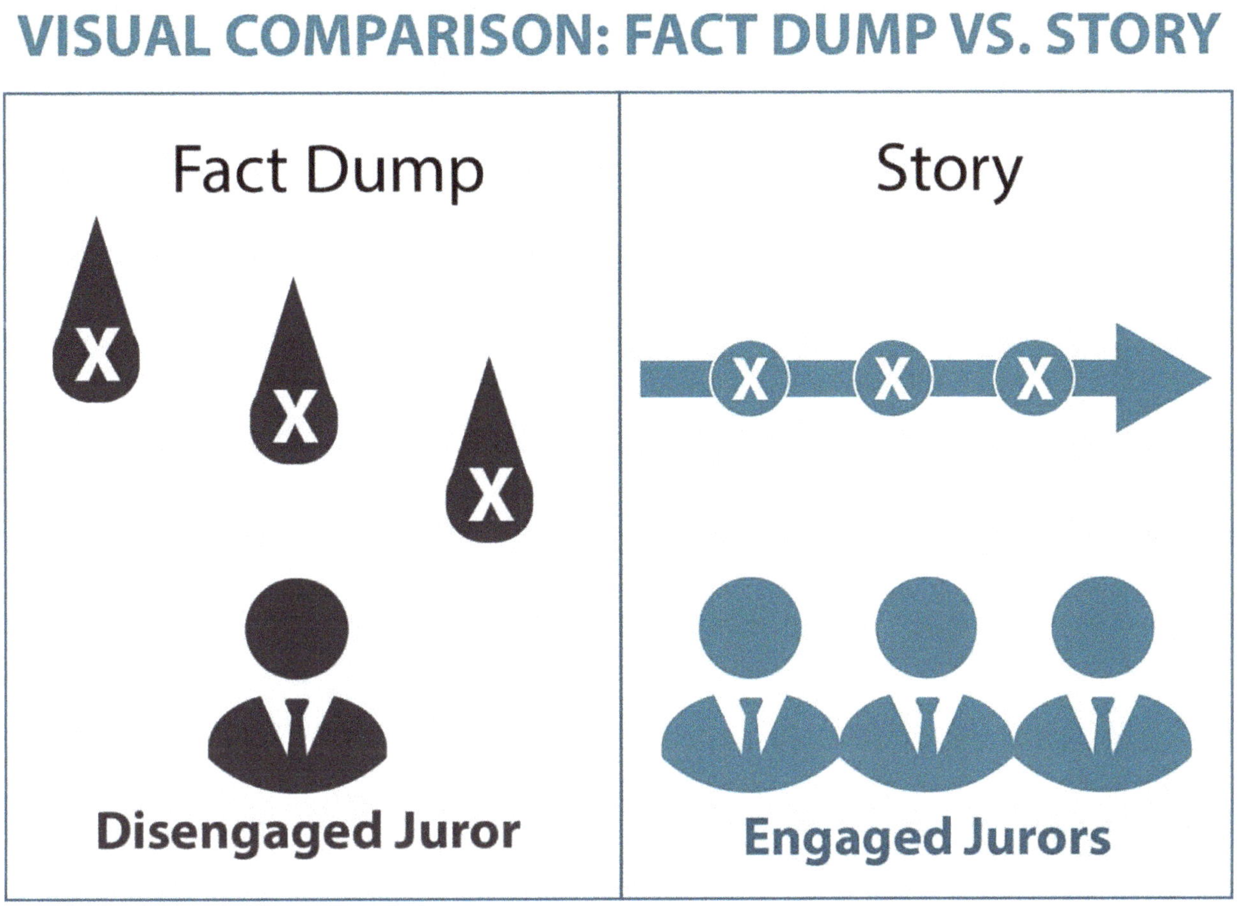

Figure 4: Visual Comparison – Fact Dump vs. Story

The Universality of Stories

Stories are a universal language. No matter the time, culture, or context, they connect with us because they follow patterns deeply ingrained in our psychology. Every great story—whether it's a timeless epic, a blockbuster hit, or a trial argument—has three key ingredients: a protagonist, a challenge, and a resolution. This familiar structure makes stories feel instinctively right. They help us make sense of complex situations by guiding us through the twists and turns. In the courtroom, a well-told story captures the jury's curiosity. They're no longer passive listeners; they're eager participants wondering, "What happens next? Who will prevail? How does it all end?"

In a wrongful death case, you could rely solely on forensic reports to establish fault. Or you could tell the story of the victim's last day, painting a vivid picture of their life, their family, and their untimely loss. The forensic report might prove the claim, but the story gives it heart. When jurors understand the human stakes, they're far more likely to see the justice in your argument.

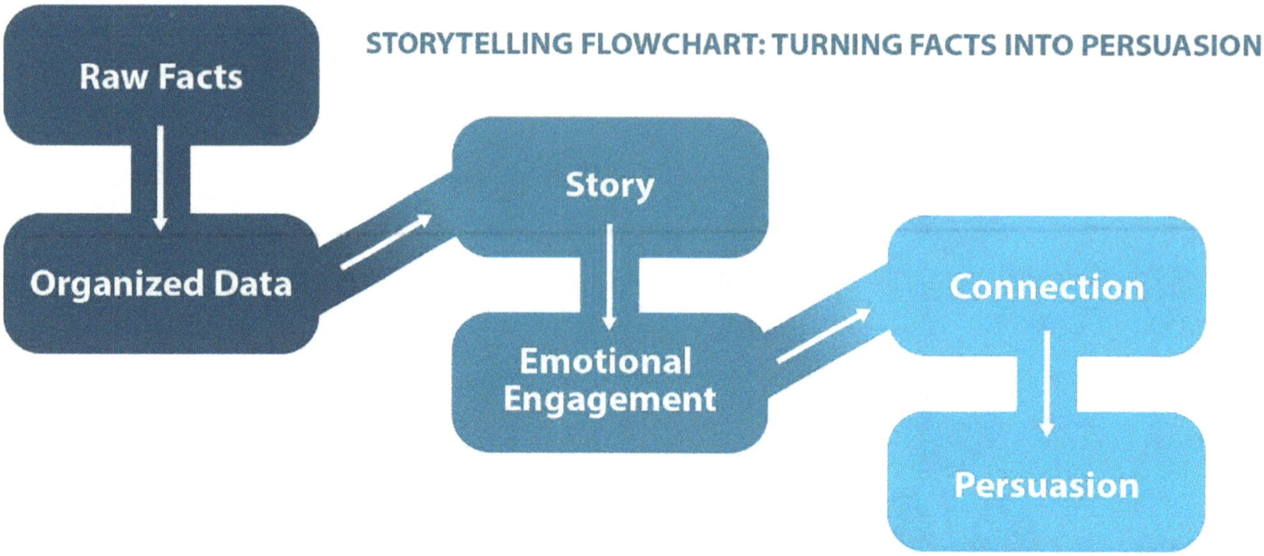

Figure 5: Storytelling Flowchart – Turning Facts into Persuasion

A Case Story: Turning Hopeless Into Possible

Once upon a time, I took on the case of a young man, Jason, accused of an unthinkable crime. He was charged with three counts of murder, allegedly carried out to steal a car he and his friend wanted. The prosecution's story was simple and damning: Jason and his friend lured the victims with the pretense of buying their vehicle, only to kill them in cold blood and take what they wanted. His friend had already been tried, convicted, and sentenced to death. Now, Jason faced life without the possibility of parole—three times over.

Every day, Jason sat in the jail's visiting room, defeated, while we sifted through evidence and prepared for a trial that seemed like an uphill battle. The facts were stark: three people dead, a stolen car, a weapon tied to Jason, and his co-defendant's conviction casting an even darker shadow over the case. His public image was irredeemable, and the system seemed ready to brand him a murderer without a second thought.

But beneath the damning accusations, I saw Jason's truth. He wasn't the mastermind the prosecution painted him to be. His involvement in the crime, while serious, was not what they claimed. The narrative they spun was powerful, but it wasn't the whole story.

But one day, I decided to use the story spine to dismantle the prosecution's case and build a narrative that revealed Jason's role for what it truly was. I started with his background—who he was and how he had arrived at that fateful day. We told the story of a young man who had made poor choices but lacked the intent or malice to commit murder.

We highlighted his co-defendant's influence: a manipulative, dominant figure who had orchestrated the plan and carried out the killings. Jason's role, we argued, was secondary—his actions wrong but not premeditated murder. Through witnesses, forensic evidence, and Jason's testimony, we crafted a narrative that walked the jury through not just the crime but the circumstances that led to it.

Because of that, the jury began to see Jason as more than a criminal record or a mugshot. They saw him as a deeply flawed individual who made a terrible mistake—but not a murderer. The prosecution's neat, tidy story unraveled under scrutiny. The facts couldn't support their version of Jason pulling the trigger with intent to kill.

Because of that, the jury acquitted Jason of the murder charges. Instead, they convicted him of a lesser offense. While it was still a serious conviction, the difference between spending the rest of his life behind bars and having a chance at freedom one day was monumental.

Until finally, Jason faced sentencing knowing he wouldn't die in prison. He understood the gravity of his actions and the pain caused by that day, but he also knew he had a chance at redemption—a chance to live, grow, and one day rebuild his life outside the prison walls.

And ever since then, I've carried this case as a reminder of the power of narrative. Even in the darkest, most hopeless situations, storytelling can uncover nuance, reveal truth, and push back against a system eager for simple answers to complex human stories.

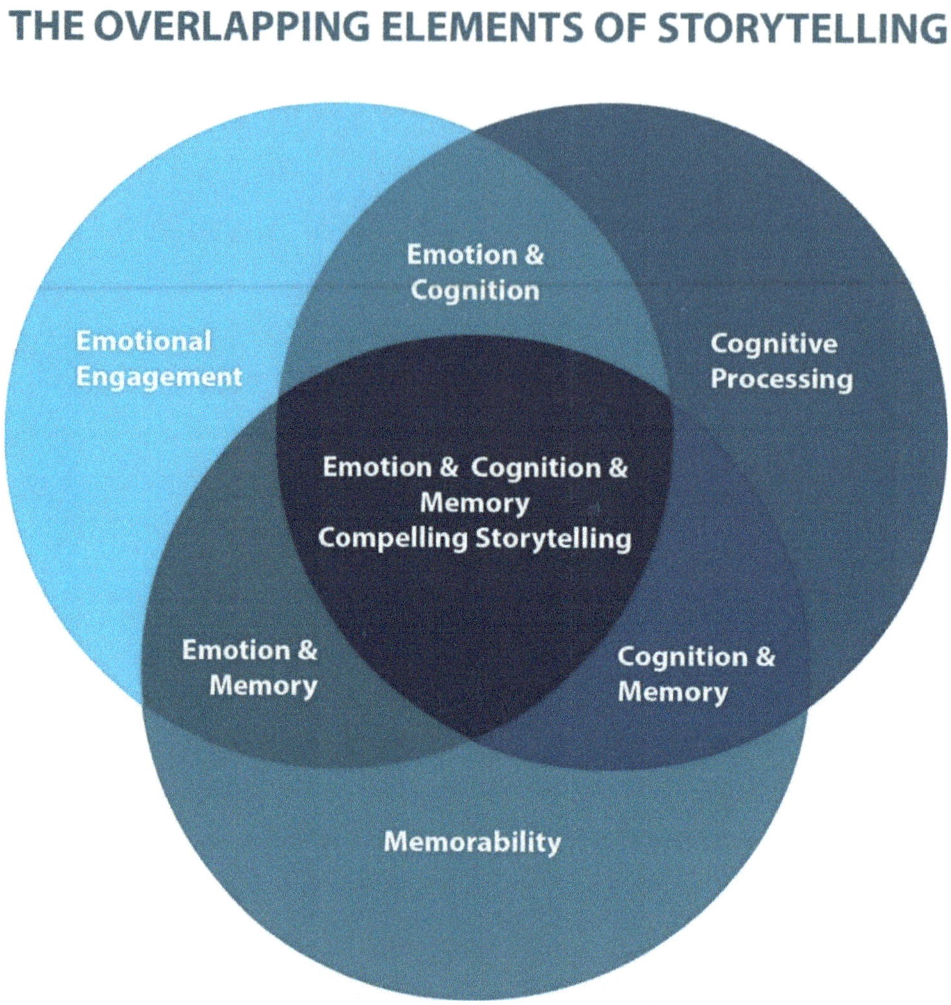

Figure 6: The Overlapping Elements of Storytelling

Conclusion

"A well-told story doesn't just inform—it transforms. It turns information into understanding and listeners into advocates."

Storytelling isn't just a courtroom tactic; it's a human necessity. It connects us and inspires us to act. As you refine your storytelling skills, using the Story Spine, remember that you're not just presenting evidence—you're shaping how jurors see the world. A well-told story can change perspectives, drive decisions, and deliver justice.

Chapter 3
The Story Spine Framework

"The Story Spine is your storytelling GPS, guiding narratives from curiosity to connection, from introduction to impact."

A Roadmap for Narratives

Every great journey needs a map, and every great story needs a structure. Without one, you're just wandering—your audience is left stranded in confusion, or worse, boredom. The Story Spine is that structure, a framework that transforms scattered ideas into a cohesive, engaging narrative. Think of it as your go-to storytelling GPS. It helps you navigate the twists, turns, and occasional roadblocks, ensuring you arrive at your destination with clarity and purpose.

This same principle applies beyond words, as I learned during my time in biotech. There, every plasma batch told its own story—a journey from collection to purification to becoming life-saving products. If one step was skipped or rushed, the whole process fell apart. Storytelling is no different. Each part of the Story Spine—beginning, middle, and end—builds on the one before. Skip a step and the narrative crumbles. Follow the structure, and you end up with something meaningful, memorable, and impactful.

Ever try to follow a story that jumped around too much? One minute it's the beginning, then suddenly the end, then a random flashback in the middle? Frustrating, right? That's what happens when stories lack structure—they lose their audience. The Story Spine solves this by giving your narrative a flow that feels natural and satisfying. It's like taking your audience on a guided tour instead of dropping them in the middle of nowhere with no map. With the Story Spine, every twist and turn has a purpose, every moment builds to the next, and your audience stays engaged from start to finish.

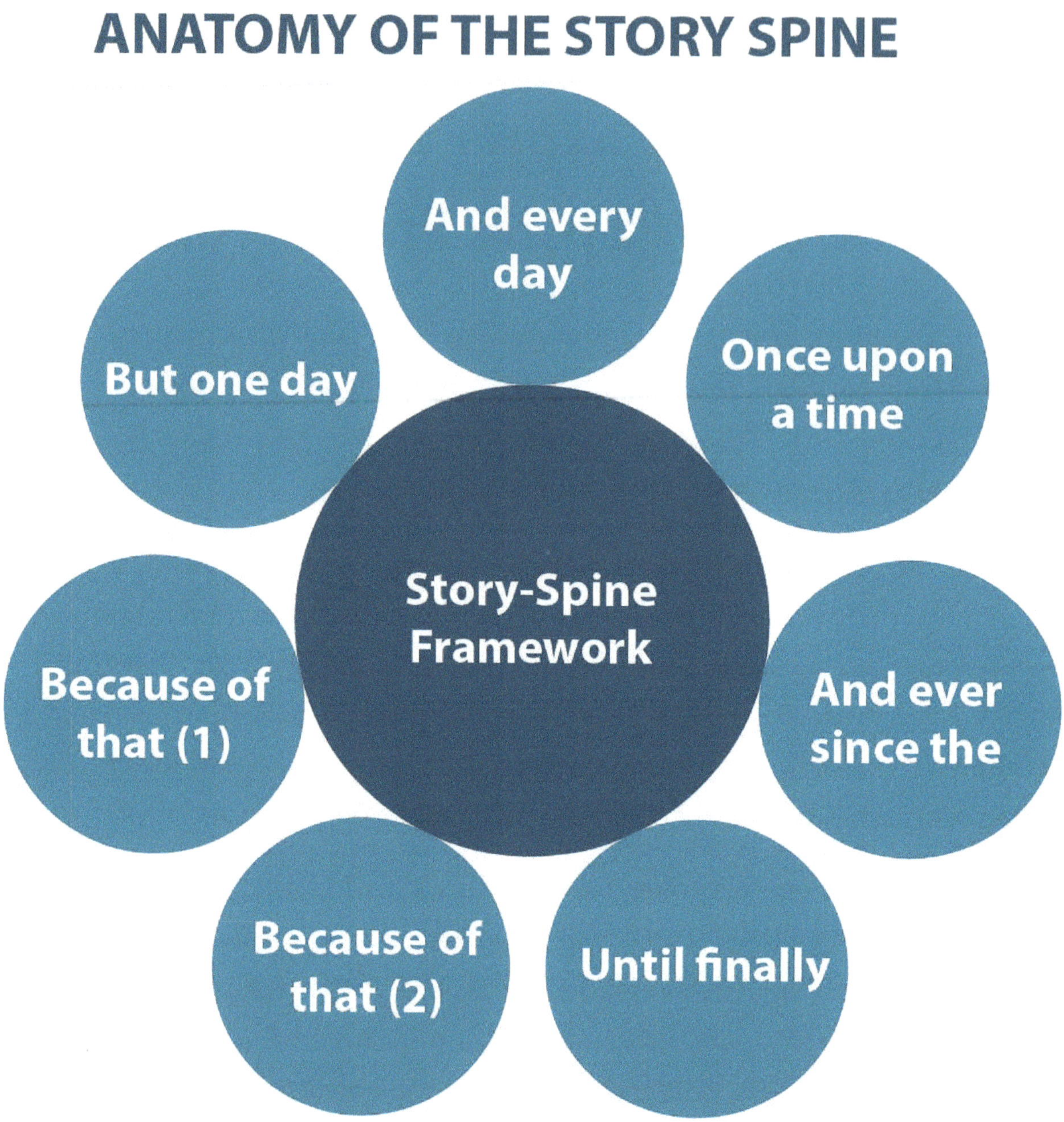

Figure 7: Anatomy of the Story Spine

What Makes the Story Spine So Powerful?

What makes the Story Spine special is its simplicity. It's not a rigid formula; it's a flexible framework that works for everything from Pixar films to courtroom arguments. It helps you turn facts, events, or ideas into something your audience can follow and feel. By creating a natural progression—introduction, tension, resolution—it taps into the universal way humans process and remember stories. Each step builds on the last, creating a narrative that flows naturally and keeps your audience hanging on every word. Why does this work? Because it's rooted in how humans naturally process stories. It creates a rhythm, a flow that feels familiar, even if the story is brand new. Your audience isn't just listening; they're anticipating. They want to know what happens next. Who will overcome the challenge? How will it all end? And as they lean into your story, they become invested. That's the power of structure—it doesn't just organize your story; it captivates your audience.

The Progression of a Story

Every epic adventure begins with describing the character's ordinary world. The Story Spine starts with "Once upon a time" and "Every day," laying the groundwork for what's to come. Think of this as setting the stage. Who are the characters? What is their world like? Why should we care? Without a strong setup, your audience has no idea where they are—or why they should bother listening. A solid beginning gives the story its foundation, anchoring the audience and inviting them in. This is your chance to set the stakes, create context, and make your audience feel invested before the conflict even begins. A great setup isn't just the start of a story, it's the first step to making them care.

Turning Up the Heat: Building Momentum Through Conflict

Now we get to the good stuff: conflict. "Until one day" and "Because of that" are where things take a turn. This is where the stakes rise, the tension builds, and your story shifts into high gear. Conflict is the heartbeat of a compelling narrative—it's what makes the audience lean in and wonder, *what happens next?* In a courtroom, this might be the moment your client's life was thrown off course or when a glaring injustice came to light. These turning points aren't just plot twists; they're the engine that drives your story forward, keeping your audience engaged and rooting for a resolution.

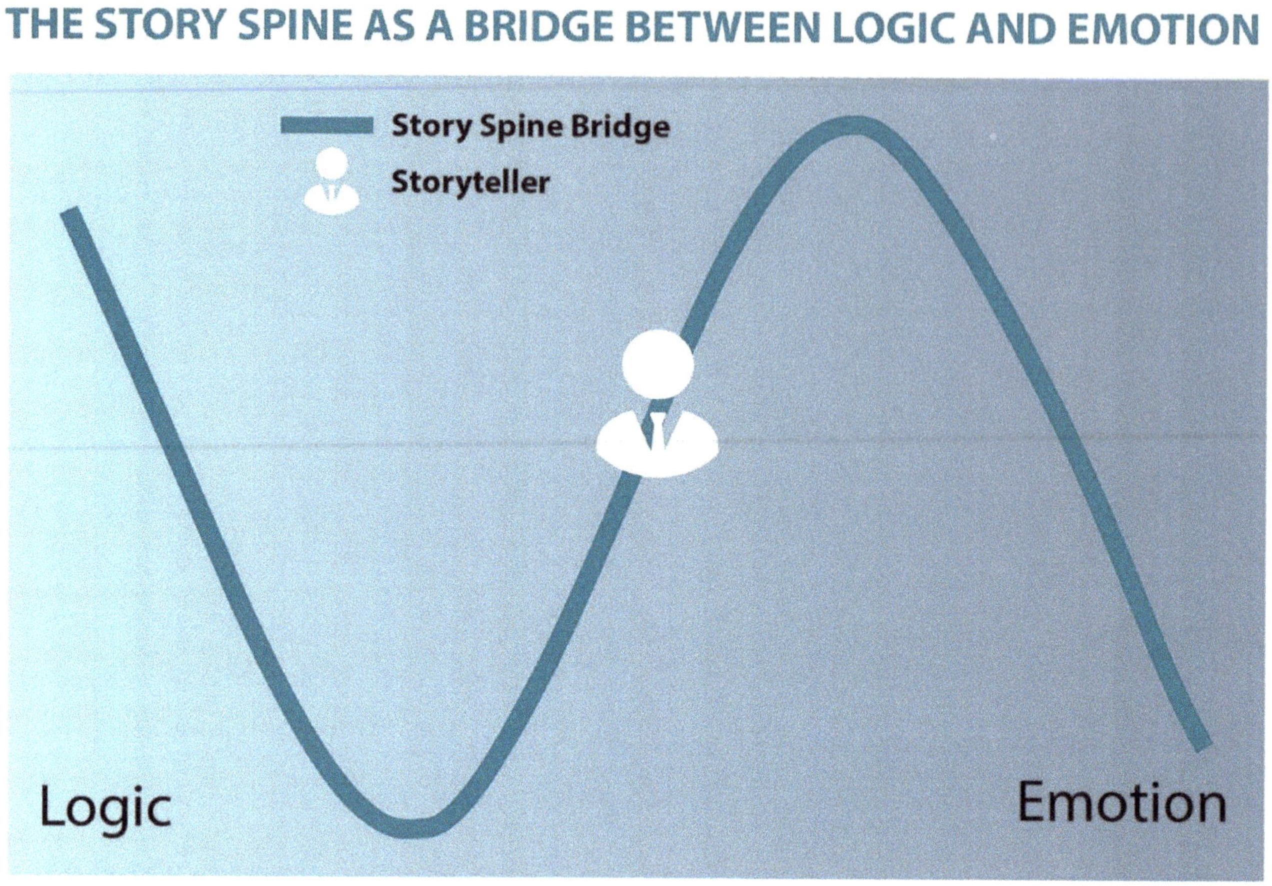

Figure 8: The Story Spine as a Bridge Between Logic and Emotion

The Sweet Satisfaction of Resolution

Every story needs a destination. "Until finally" and "And ever since then" bring the journey to a close, answering the audience's burning questions: What happened? How did it all end? And why does it matter? This resolution is your payoff—the moment when all the threads of the story come together and leave the audience with a sense of closure. Each step builds on the last, creating a narrative arc that feels natural and satisfying.

Example: Using the Story Spine in a Trial

Let's examine how the Story Spine might be applied to a personal injury case:

- **Once upon a time...** *"Once upon a time, there was a 35-year-old small business owner named Michael. He worked tirelessly to provide for his family."*
- **Every day...** *"Every day, he rode his bike to work, enjoyed time with his children in the evenings, and dreamed of expanding his business."*
- **Until** *one day, a careless truck driver ignored a stop sign and collided with Michael during his morning bike ride."*
- **Because of that...** *"Because of that, Michael suffered a traumatic brain injury that left him unable to work, devastated his family's finances, and cost him the joy of playing with his children."*
- **Until finally...** *"Until finally, after months of rehabilitation and a hard-fought legal battle, Michael's family received the resources they needed to rebuild their lives."*
- **And ever since...** *"And ever since, Michael has been an advocate for safe driving practices, determined to prevent others from enduring the pain his family faced."*

Why It Works:

By using the Story Spine, the lawyer transformed a pile of dry facts into a vibrant narrative, one that highlighted Michael's humanity and the real stakes of the case. The jury wasn't just listening—they were invested. But let me tell you, my own journey with the Story Spine wasn't exactly love at first sight.

Flashback to the summer of 2010: I was sitting in a seminar, wide-eyed and eager, hearing about how this framework I first learned about in improv, could create clear, compelling narratives in action. My brain went into overdrive, dreaming up all the ways I could use this to supercharge my work. But when it came time to try it myself? Let's just say my early efforts weren't exactly storytelling gold.

My first attempts were clunky, awkward, and honestly embarrassing. Picture someone sitting down at a grand piano for the first time and banging on the keys, hoping for Beethoven but landing somewhere closer to chaos. That was me with the Story Spine. For a long time, I was intimidated by it. I only dusted it off when I was in narrative trouble—when a trial wasn't clicking, or when my argument felt flat. I treated it like a hammer, hoping it would smash my storytelling problems into submission. Spoiler alert: it didn't.

At some point I realized that if I was going to master this method, then I needed to implement the Story Spine office wide, for all new and existing clients. At the time, I had a thriving Family Law business and a group of very enthusiastic staff. We were committed to creating and updating spines for every client in my office. We put the system in place, and it started with a bang, and ended with a fizzle, because all the spines sounded alike. You couldn't tell one from the other.

The top 3 reasons for divorce in our cases were that someone was cheating, someone had money problems, or someone was being abused. All our spines had only facts and no feelings. We were making spines based on what we needed to remember about the case, and not what the client felt and experienced about the case. We were telling the story of divorce and not the story of the client. Big difference! Once we realized this, we practiced and tried out new ways, until we learned to use it in the way that I'm now presenting to you. So if all your spines are sounding the same, it's likely you are telling the story of the case and not the story of the client.

Here's the thing: the Story Spine isn't a hammer. It's a compass. It's not just a tool for fixing broken narratives; it's a guide to help you build something meaningful from the ground up. But I didn't see that right away. Those early days were frustrating, and I seriously doubted if I'd ever get good at it. I'm sharing this because I don't want you to make the same mistakes I did. Learning something new—especially a skill as transformative as storytelling—can feel awkward and overwhelming at first. It's easy to throw in the towel when your first tries don't match the dazzling results you envisioned. But trust me, that's just part of the process.

With time and practice, I started to see the beauty of the Story Spine. It didn't just shape my courtroom arguments; it changed the way I understood storytelling itself. Eventually, it became second nature—a reliable framework I could use to craft narratives that connected every time. My hope is that this chapter saves you from some of the growing pains I experienced, giving you the clarity and confidence to use the Story Spine effectively right from the start. Because once you unlock its potential, there's no limit to the stories you can tell—or the impact they can make.

A Case Story: A Second Chance for a Lost Boy

Once upon a time, a 13-year-old boy, Malcolm, made a choice that would shape the rest of his life. He had fallen in with a group of older boys who were more street-smart, more daring, and more reckless than he was. One night, their impulsive decisions spiraled into tragedy: a beloved member of the community was killed. The community was devastated and demanded swift justice. Malcolm, the youngest and least sophisticated of the group, became the scapegoat.

Every day, Malcolm sat in a courtroom where he didn't fully understand the gravity of what was happening. The older boys took plea deals, but Malcolm, trusting in the fairness of the system, went to trial. He was convicted and sentenced to life without parole, plus 40 years—a punishment that closed the door on his childhood and his future. At 14, Malcolm was thrown into a world of hardened men and endless walls.

For three decades, he lived behind bars, labeled as irredeemable. Over the years, he built a reputation among fellow inmates as a kind and gentle soul, someone who offered words of encouragement and never sought trouble. But the system only saw his write-ups for minor infractions and the fact that he was transferred frequently. The muscles he'd built to survive and the tattoos he wore to belong painted him as a stereotype rather than the person he truly was.

But one day, a new law declared that sentencing a minor to life without parole without considering mitigating circumstances was unconstitutional. For the first time in over 30 years, Malcolm had a chance to tell his story—not the story of a tattooed, buffed 45-year-old prisoner, but the story of a scared, unsophisticated 13-year-old boy who made a terrible mistake.

Because of that, we faced an uphill battle. The same judge who had sentenced him decades ago would decide his fate today. There was no jury to appeal to, no new evidence about the crime itself to present—only the mitigation evidence about who Malcolm had been and who he had become.

We told the judge about Malcolm's chaotic childhood: the lack of guidance, the peer pressure, the immaturity that made him follow rather than lead. We shared stories from people who had seen his kindness and humanity over the years. We worked to bridge the gap between the boy he was and the man sitting in the courtroom.

Because of that, the judge began to see beyond the surface. The law required that Malcolm's youth and its associated impulsivity and lack of foresight be weighed against his actions. The judge began to consider not just the crime, but the human being Malcolm was, and the man he had become.

Until finally, the life-without-parole sentence, along with the additional 40-year sentence, was rescinded. Malcolm wouldn't walk out of prison immediately, but he had a new sentence that gave him hope—a chance to live life outside the walls before it was too late.

And ever since then, I've carried Malcolm's story as a reminder that no one should be defined solely by their worst moment, especially not a child. The justice system often struggles to see humanity behind stereotypes, but through storytelling, we can help it remember.

Conclusion

"A great story isn't just told—it's felt, remembered, and acted upon. The Story Spine is your blueprint for turning chaos into connection and moments into magic."

The Story Spine is more than a framework—it's a roadmap that transforms scattered ideas into meaningful journeys. By weaving structure with creativity, it ensures that every narrative, whether it's a casual anecdote or a courtroom argument, flows with purpose and resonance. From the spark of curiosity to the final emotional impact, the Story Spine provides clarity without limiting imagination.

Mastering the Story Spine equips you to craft stories that do more than inform—they inspire and move people to action. And the best part? It's not about perfection; it's about connection. As we dive deeper into each element, you'll learn how to add emotional depth, authenticity, and just the right amount of flair to bring your stories to life.

PRACTICE SPINES:

Exercise: Craft Your Own Story Spine

Think of a familiar case, a personal experience, or even a fictional story. Use the Story Spine framework to break it into its seven key elements:

- **Once upon a time...**
- **Every day...**
- **Until one day...**
- **Because of that...**
- **Because of that...**
- **Until finally...**
- **And ever** since...

Write out each part, ensuring the story flows naturally from one element to the next. Focus on making the narrative clear, understandable, and emotionally resonant.

Chapter 4
Crafting "Once Upon a Time" and "Every Day"

"The beginning of a story is where you invite your audience into a world that captures their curiosity and sparks connection."

Setting the Stage

The opening of a story isn't just an introduction, it's an invitation. This is where you welcome your audience into the world of your narrative, setting the stage, introducing the characters, and creating the context that makes the journey ahead worth following. In the Story Spine framework, "Once upon a time" and "Every day" are the cornerstones of this foundation.

These elements provide your audience with the critical "why" behind the story, giving them a reason to care about what's happening and why it matters. When done well, this beginning establishes trust, builds emotional connection, and creates a sense of relatability. It's the narrative equivalent of rolling out the welcome mat and saying, "Come on in—you're going to want to hear this." No matter what kind of audience you're addressing, use those first few moments to set the tone for the entire journey.

A Lesson from the Field

Let me take you back to a time when I thought information alone was enough. During my years as a telecommunications specialist in the U.S. Air Force, I worked under a communications officer who knew a thing or two about storytelling. During one particularly intense combat exercise, I was laser-focused on transmitting data—

coordinates, times, codes. To me, precision was everything. I thought my job was done the moment the information left my hands.

That's when my mentor stepped in. Midway through the mission, he pulled me aside and asked, "Do they know why this matters?" I froze. I'd never even considered that. Sure, the team had the data, but without understanding its context or urgency, they weren't acting with the kind of precision the mission demanded. My mentor showed me how to frame the data with meaning. It wasn't just numbers; it was the lifeline of the mission. He explained how to connect each piece of information to the bigger picture, showing why it mattered and what was at stake. By the end of the exercise, I wasn't just a data transmitter; I was a storyteller. The team didn't just hear the information; they *felt* its importance. And suddenly, everyone was in sync, focused, and unstoppable.

That lesson stuck with me. It's not enough to dump information and hope it lands. Your audience needs context, meaning, and a reason to engage. The opening moments of your story are your chance to set the stage. Without a clear and compelling beginning, your narrative risks falling flat—or worse, losing your audience entirely. But when you take the time to craft a strong "Once upon a time" and "Every day," you lay breadcrumbs that connect the beginning to the eventual resolution, giving the story a sense of cohesion and purpose.

You also draw people in. You ground them in the story's reality. And you make them care. That's the power of setting the stage—it's the spark that ignites the rest of your narrative. So, let's step into your story's world. Because if you can show your audience why it matters from the very first moment, they won't just listen—they'll enter in, ready to follow you wherever the story goes.

The Heart Over the Head: Why Emotion Wins Every Time

Humans are emotional creatures at their core. Our brains are wired to prioritize feelings over cold, hard logic, a handy trait that kept our ancestors alive when split-second, instinctive decisions meant the difference between dinner and *being* dinner. While facts and data are essential for building knowledge, they don't pack the punch needed to inspire action or create meaningful change. Emotional resonance, on the other hand, is like a backstage pass to the brain—it grabs attention, makes information unforgettable, and drives decisions.

Think about it: you've probably heard the statistic, "50% of marriages end in divorce." Sure, it's informative, but it's also… meh. Just another number floating in the vast ocean of data. Now, let's attach a story to that statistic: picture a young couple, starry-eyed and brimming with dreams, who slowly find themselves drifting apart under the crushing weight of financial stress and unmet expectations. The husband works endless hours to make ends meet, while the wife, feeling isolated, juggles the chaos of raising two small children. Their connection frays, arguments escalate, and eventually, they part ways. Suddenly, the statistic isn't just a number anymore; it's a glimpse into the real struggles faced by countless families. The story doesn't just inform; it *connects.*

This is the heavy lifting of emotional resonance. It bridges the gap between understanding and belief. Consider the courtroom: jurors may hear a watertight argument built on forensic evidence or detailed technical reports, but what truly moves them? The plaintiff's story of heartbreak, resilience, or loss. Data provides the backbone of credibility, but it's emotion that forges a human connection. People don't want to hear what's in your head; they want to see what's in your heart.

Life Lessons: Setting the Stage

Once upon a time...

I sat in a quiet conference room, preparing for a critical focus group. The case was heavy—emotional stakes, a client's future hanging in the balance. I stared at my notes, filled with facts and figures. It was complete, but the narrative felt flat, lifeless, dull. I needed to find a way to make it come alive, to pull people into the world of this case and make them care deeply from the very beginning.

Every day...

I worked on cases that carried immense weight—cases where decisions would alter lives, where jurors held more than just verdicts in their hands; they held the essence of someone's story. But no matter how strong the evidence or how well-prepared the arguments, it was clear: if the story didn't start with the right foundation, it didn't stand a chance of holding attention or moving hearts.

Until one day...

I decided to step back and look at the case differently. Instead of focusing on the facts first, I focused on the people. Who were they? What did they want? What was at stake for them? I visualized the setting, the places where these events unfolded—the rooms, the streets, the tiny details that gave their world depth and made it real. Slowly, the story began to take shape. It wasn't just a case anymore; it was a narrative with life and color.

Because of that...

I wove those vivid details into the focus group session. I painted a picture of the characters, their struggles, and their hopes. I described the setting, not just as a backdrop, but as a living, breathing part of their journey. As I spoke, I saw the shift: people sat up, leaned forward, their expressions softened, and they began to ask questions that showed they weren't just listening—they were *feeling*.

And because of that...

The insights from that focus group were transformative. Jurors later connected with the case in ways I hadn't anticipated. They didn't just understand the facts; they understood the people behind them. I then realized the immense power of setting the stage—that by grounding a story in relatable characters and vivid contexts, I could pull an audience into the heart of a narrative from the very first word.

Until finally...

I saw that every story, whether told in a courtroom, a boardroom, or a conversation, begins with the foundation we lay at the start. Characters need to feel real. Stakes need to matter. The setting needs to transport. Without these, the most compelling plot will falter before it has a chance to soar.

And ever since that day...

I've made setting the stage a non-negotiable part of every narrative I craft. No matter what the storytelling task, I always start with the foundation: Who are the people? Where are they in the world? And why should it matter? Because once the stage is set, the story is ready to inspire and transform.

Bringing Stories to Life: Characters, Context, and Emotional Investment

Every great story starts with three main ingredients: characters, context, and a hefty dose of emotional investment. Get this right, and your audience won't just listen; they'll *feel* your story and take their proper places in it.

Characters: First things first—who's the story about? Characters are the beating heart of every narrative, the bridge between dry facts and human connection. People don't relate to abstract ideas; they relate to other *people.* Introduce your characters with enough warmth and humanity to make the audience care. Is your protagonist a single mom juggling three jobs? A young entrepreneur chasing a dream? A 10-year-old dog walker saving for their first bike? Show us what makes them likeable and worth rooting for.

Context: Next up, set the scene. Every story needs a "normal" before it can shake things up. Where does your character live, work, or dream? What does their world look like before the big event flips it upside down? Context is your audience's map, helping them understand the when, where, and why of your story. Paint the picture clearly enough that they can see it, but don't bog it down with unnecessary details—no one needs to know the exact shade of the wallpaper unless it's about to catch fire.

Here's the deal: if your audience doesn't care, your story goes nowhere. You've got to make them feel like your client's story could maybe help them solve a problem or show them how to live better. Most of us seek this; it's why we go to movies and plays and watch television. Great storytelling highlights dreams, everyday struggles, and universal connections like love, family, or ambition. The goal is to identify details that connect with everyone—things that make your audience think, *"that could be me."* Emotional investment ensures your audience isn't just hearing the story; they're living it alongside your characters. Nail these three elements, and you've got a story that grabs attention, keeps the audience connected, and lingers in their hearts long after it's over.

"Once Upon a Time" and "Every Day" in Action

"Once upon a time" isn't just the start of a story—it's your promise that something worth their attention is about to unfold. And "Every day"? That's the calm before the storm, the steady rhythm of normal life that makes the disruption feel inevitable.

Example: A Personal Injury Case

- **Once upon a time...** "Once upon a time, Emily was a 27-year-old nurse with a big heart and even bigger dreams. She loved her job, adored her patients, and felt lucky to wake up every day knowing she was making a difference in the world."
- **Every day...** "Every day, Emily worked long shifts at the hospital, bringing comfort to her patients, assisting doctors in critical moments, and building the future she'd always dreamed of. She was planning her wedding, saving for her first home, and imagining the family she'd one day have."

This opening is more than just a setup—it's an emotional anchor. It paints Emily as someone your audience can relate to and root for. By highlighting her dedication and dreams, you're not just describing a character; you're making her life come alive.

This makes what comes next—the disruption—all the more compelling. After all, when you see the beauty of the "Every day," you can't help but feel the weight of what's lost when it's taken away. That's the power of setting the stage with "Once upon a time" and "Every day." It's not just an opening; it's the heartbeat of your story.

Tips for Crafting Compelling Openings

A great opening is your moment to grab attention, spark curiosity, and give your audience a reason to care. The best openings establish trust and invite people into the world of your story in a way that feels real and engaging. Here's how to make those first moments shine:

- **Be Specific:** Details matter. They're what make characters and settings come alive. Don't settle for vague descriptions like, "John was a teacher." Instead, get specific: "John was a high school science teacher who had a knack for making chemistry come to life with hands-on experiments that left his students in awe." The more specific you are, the more memorable your characters become.
- **Use Relatable Themes:** Tap into universal experiences—family, love, careers, hopes, and struggles. These are the threads that connect us all. When your audience can see themselves in the story, they're far more likely to care. These themes build bridges between your narrative and your listeners.
- **Show, Don't Just Tell:** Vivid imagery and sensory details are your best friends. Don't tell us, "Emily was happy." Show us: "Emily sang along to the radio at the top of her lungs on her morning commute, her smile growing wider every time she glanced at the stack of wedding invitations on her passenger seat." Let your audience see, hear, and feel your story. It's what makes them care. Master these tips, and your openings won't just set the stage; they'll make your audience want to stick around for the entire show.

COMPONENTS OF A STRONG OPENING

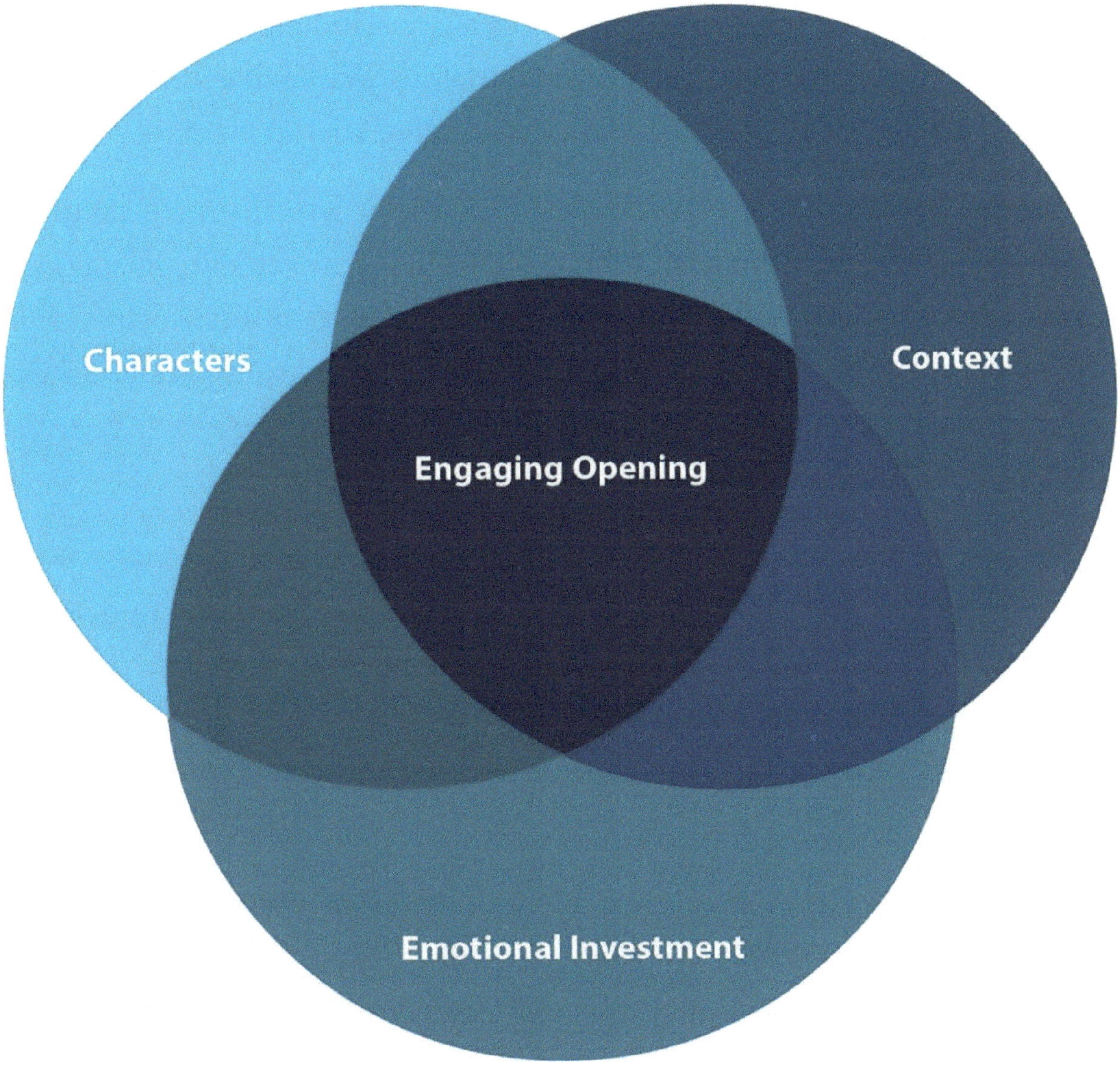

Figure 9: Components of a Strong Opening

A Case Story: The Outsider in the Crossfire

Once upon a time, a skilled and hardworking CFO, Mark, joined a family-run financial fund. He was the only non-family member in the upper echelons of the company, chosen for his financial expertise and unblemished reputation. Mark took pride in his work, ensuring compliance with regulations and keeping the company's finances in order. But beneath the surface, something sinister was unfolding—decisions and schemes that he had no part in and no knowledge of.

Every day, Mark focused on his responsibilities, unaware that the family members he reported to were using the financial fund as their personal playground, engaging in fraudulent practices. Documents were withheld from him, meetings happened behind closed doors, and critical decisions were made without his input. Mark wasn't just out of the loop—he was deliberately kept in the dark.

But one day, the house of cards came crashing down. The financial fund was exposed for widespread financial fraud, and the government swept in with indictments. Mark, along with 13 others, was charged with multiple counts of fraud and conspiracy. The prosecution knew Mark wasn't the mastermind, but they saw him as a valuable pawn—someone they could use to strengthen their case against the family by pressuring him to testify.

Because of that, we were hired to extract Mark from this nightmare. The goal was clear: show the court that Mark didn't belong in the group of 14 defendants. But it wasn't easy. The prosecution painted everyone with the same broad brush strokes, and the sheer complexity of the case—millions of documents, conflicting testimonies, and years of financial transactions—made it hard to separate Mark from the rest.

We dug deep, scrutinizing every piece of evidence and uncovering patterns that proved Mark's exclusion from key decisions. Emails, meeting records, and testimony showed how information was deliberately withheld from him, and how the family had manipulated the system to keep him out of the loop. We built a story that highlighted his isolation, his integrity, and his lack of knowledge about the fraudulent activities.

Because of that, we were able to counter the prosecution's narrative at every turn. When they implied Mark had to know what was happening, we showed how the family deliberately operated behind his back. When they argued he could have stopped the fraud, we demonstrated how he wasn't given the tools or authority to intervene.

Until finally, after a long and treacherous journey through a grueling trial, the truth prevailed. Mark walked out of the courtroom a free man, acquitted of all charges. The other 13 defendants, including the family members who orchestrated the fraud, were convicted.

And ever since then, Mark's case has stayed with me as a testament to the importance of precision in storytelling. In a sea of defendants and damning allegations, a clear and compelling narrative can be the difference between freedom and injustice. It's not just about proving innocence—it's about cutting through the noise to reveal the truth.

Conclusion

"The first lines of a story don't just set the stage—they plant the seeds of empathy and curiosity, paving the way for every moment to come."

The beginning of a story is where facts come alive, and context transforms into the lens through which everything else is seen. "Once upon a time" and "Every day" are the foundation of your narrative. These elements invite your audience into a world they can visualize, introduce characters they can root for, and lay the groundwork for the journey that's about to unfold.

The beginning is where connection starts, where your audience decides whether to lean in or tune out. "Once upon a time" and "Every day" are the gateway to possibility, anchoring your audience in a world they can believe in and care about.

Craft your opening with intention and heart, because it's here that you earn the trust and investment of your listeners. A strong start doesn't just introduce a story—it sets the tone for the transformation to follow, ensuring your audience is with you every step of the way.

PRACTICE SPINES: Crafting Your Opening

Exercise: Write Your Opening

Think of a case or a personal experience. Use the "Once upon a time" and "Every day" frameworks to build a strong, engaging opening.

- **Once upon a time…**

  Introduce the main character(s). Describe who they are and what their life looks like.

- **Every day…**

  Highlight their routines, ambitions, and the stability of their world before everything changes.

Example Prompt:

Write an opening for a trial case where a small business owner is suing a contractor for breach of contract. Focus on the owner's dedication to their business and the role the contract played in their future plans.

Example Response:

- **Once upon a time...** "Once upon a time, Sarah owned a cozy neighborhood café that had become a gathering place for friends, families, and book clubs. For Sarah, running the café wasn't just a job; it was her dream brought to life—a place where every customer felt like family."
- **Every day...** "Every day, Sarah poured her heart into her business. She sourced fresh ingredients from local farmers, greeted her regulars by name, and even stayed late to plan new menu items that would keep her café ahead of the curve. She had big plans to expand the space, bring in more customers, and build a future for her family. And that's where the contractor came in…"

Chapter 5
The Turning Point

"Relatable characters aren't perfect—they're human, and it's their imperfections that draw us in."

The Moment That Everything Changes

Every great story has that one moment—the split second when life as the characters know it is turned upside down. It's the unexpected phone call in the middle of the night, the snap decision that can't be undone, the moment when ordinary turns extraordinary. This is the "Until one day" moment—the turning point that raises the stakes and keeps your audience on the edge of their seats.

The goal is to create a turning point so compelling it leaves the audience hanging on your every word. It's where the audience transitions from passive observers to emotionally invested participants. This is where they begin to feel the weight of the conflict, to see the humanity of the characters, and to understand the stakes at play. It's the spark that transforms the narrative from a series of events into an emotional journey.

In legal storytelling, the turning point is crucial. It's the moment when jurors stop seeing a client as just a name in a case file and start seeing them as a person—someone they can empathize with, root for, or even grieve for. This moment connects the facts of the case to the emotional core that drives decision-making. In every type of case, the turning point is where you have the best chance to make your audience care deeply about the outcome.

The Anatomy of a Turning Point

Every effective turning point has three key ingredients:

1. **Disruption:** Something happens that breaks the character's routine or upends their world. This isn't just a bump in the road; it's a derailment that changes the trajectory of their story.
2. **Emotional Impact:** The turning point isn't just about the event; it's about how the event affects the character emotionally. What do they feel? What is at stake? This is where the audience begins to share their experience.
3. **Set-Up for the Journey Ahead:** The turning point should propel the story forward. It raises questions: How will the character overcome this challenge? What decisions will they have to make? This momentum keeps your audience engaged.

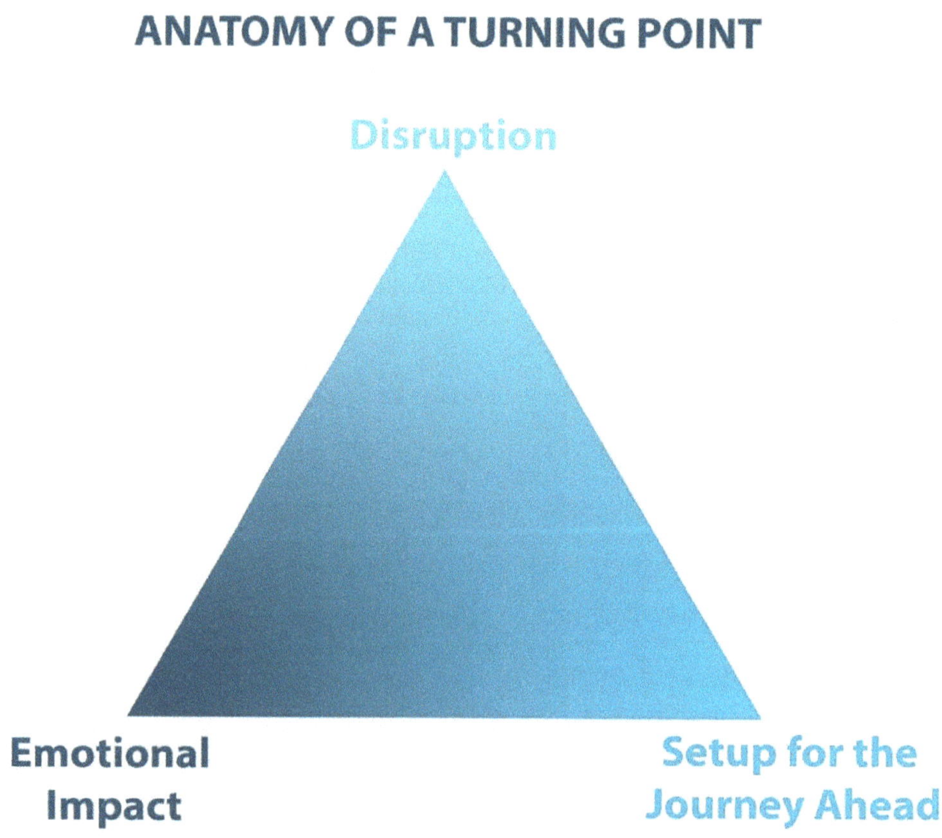

Figure 10: Anatomy of a Turning Point

Life Lessons: The Turning Point

Once upon a time...

I was working on a case that seemed impossible to win. My client was overwhelmed, beaten down by the weight of their circumstances. The facts weren't enough; the jury wasn't connecting with the story we were telling. Despite all my preparation, I felt stuck, as though we were walking a straight line toward a certain loss. Something had to change—but I didn't yet know what.

Every day...

In my work, I see these moments often. A case feels stagnant, a narrative too predictable. The audience—whether a jury, a team, or a group of focus participants—checks out, disengaged from a story that lacks the spark to propel it forward. These moments of inertia demand something bold: a shift, a revelation, a turning point that reignites the journey.

Until one day...

During a psychodrama session, I had my client step into the role of their opponent. At first, they resisted, unsure of how to embody someone who had caused them so much pain. But as they hesitantly began to speak from this new perspective, something extraordinary happened. Tears welled in their eyes as they voiced the emotions of the other side—not justification, but vulnerability. For the first time, they saw the story from a completely new angle. And so did I.

Because of that...

I reframed our entire narrative around this revelation. The turning point wasn't just a plot device; it was a moment of profound truth. It showed the humanity on both sides of the case and shifted the jury's perspective from judgment to empathy. The impact was immediate. Jurors were intently focused, captivated by the complexity and depth of the story.

And because of that...

I began to seek turning points intentionally, rather than waiting for them to appear. I looked for moments of contradiction, places where the story could pivot in a way that challenged assumptions and deepened emotional stakes. I discovered that these shifts were often the difference between a story that merely informed and one that transformed.

Until finally...

I realized that turning points aren't just moments of change; they're the heartbeat of a narrative. They are the places where tension crests, where characters grow, and where the audience becomes fully invested. Crafting them isn't optional—it's essential for creating stories that resonate deeply and endure.

And ever since that day...

I've embraced the art of turning points as a cornerstone of my storytelling process. Whether in a trial strategy, a focus group session, or even in my personal life, I look for the moments where the narrative can pivot, revealing truths that drive the story forward. These are the moments that change everything—the moments where stories, and lives, come together in powerful ways.

Framing the Turning Point

An effective "Until one day" moment doesn't just introduce a change; It captures the audience's emotions and prepares them to fulfill their role in the story. To make it land, you need two essential ingredients: clarity and emotional resonance. The disruption must feel tightly connected to the protagonist's world, goals, and dreams. Use vivid, specific details to illustrate the moment, showing not only what happens but how it upends everything. This is where your audience steps fully into the story, sharing the protagonist's shock, grief, or determination.

Example: A Personal Injury Case

Let's revisit Emily, the dedicated nurse we met earlier:

- **Once upon a time...** Emily was a devoted nurse who found deep purpose in her work, caring for patients and striving to make a difference.
- **Every day...** She worked long hours at the hospital, always putting her family first and dreaming of building a brighter future—a home of her own, financial security, and one day starting a family.
- **Until one day...** As Emily drove home after an exhausting night shift, a drunk driver sped through a red light and slammed into her car. The force of the crash pinned her in the driver's seat, crushing her legs and shattering her dreams in an instant.

This turning point isn't just a plot twist; it's a gut punch. Emily's world is thrown into chaos, and the audience can't help but feel her fear and pain. They're now emotionally invested, wondering how she'll find the strength to navigate the road ahead.

Bringing Your Audience Into the Moment

The turning point is your opportunity to immerse your audience in the story world. Use vivid imagery and sensory details to make the moment come alive. Instead of saying, "She was arrested at the grocery store," bring the scene to life:

"She stood frozen in the brightly lit aisle, her heart pounding as the store manager called her out. Her toddler clung to her leg, wailing, as the security guard approached. All she could think about was the baby formula hidden in her purse—and the overwhelming shame that she couldn't afford it."

Remember, the turning point isn't just a dramatic moment; it's a catalyst for everything that follows. It's the spark that sets the story into motion, forcing the characters to change, adapt, or fight for what matters most. In legal storytelling, this is where jurors begin to see not just the case but the humanity behind it. It's the moment that makes them care about the outcome, not just intellectually but emotionally.

When people see themselves—or someone they care about—in your characters, they connect. They empathize. And most importantly, they care. Relatable characters make the stakes real, the challenges personal, and the journey worth following.

Crafting the "Until One Day" Moment

The "Until one day" moment is the heartbeat of the story. For Emily, it's not just an event—it's the moment her life is divided into "before" and "after." By tying the disruption directly to her dreams and showing its immediate impact, the story becomes deeply personal and relatable. To make your turning point impactful, focus on these techniques:

- **Start with the Ordinary:** Before the turning point, establish the "Every day" world of the character. This contrast makes the disruption more impactful.
- **Show, Don't Just Tell:** Use vivid imagery and specific details to immerse your audience in the moment. Instead of "They were evicted," describe how they packed their belongings into garbage bags and watched as their children clutched their favorite toys.
- **Highlight the Stakes:** Make it clear what's at risk. The audience needs to understand why this moment matters—what's being lost, threatened, or changed forever.
- **Connect Emotionally:** Focus on the character's feelings. Are they heartbroken, furious, or determined? Bring those emotions to life in a way your audience can relate to.

A Case Story: The Little Dog That Exposed the Truth

Once upon a time, a man named Carlos hosted a small gathering at his home—a quiet night meant to bring a few friends together. His loyal companion, a little terrier named Max, curled up at his feet, as much a part of the family as anyone in the room. The evening was filled with laughter and music, a celebration of community, culture, and connection.

Every day, Carlos lived a modest, peaceful life, working hard and keeping to himself. He was proud of the home he had built, a sanctuary for him and Max, a place where friends could come together and feel safe.

But one day, the sound of music and laughter drew the attention of neighbors, and a noise complaint brought local authorities to Carlos's door. What should have been a routine interaction turned into a nightmare. The police stormed in, escalating the situation beyond reason. They beat Carlos and his guests, shouting accusations and asserting dominance. Even Max, a small, harmless dog, became a victim—his teeth kicked out by an officer claiming the dog was a threat.

Because of that, Carlos found himself humiliated and broken. To add insult to injury, he was arrested and charged with resisting arrest, disturbing the peace, and assaulting a police officer. The charges painted Carlos as a violent troublemaker, erasing the reality of what had occurred in his own home.

Because of that, we built a case to expose the truth of that night. At the heart of the story was Max, the innocent dog who couldn't possibly threaten anyone. Max became the symbol of everything that had gone wrong that night—the excessive force, the abuse of power, and the human cost of unchecked authority.

Through testimony, photographs, and witness accounts, we brought the story to life. We showed how Carlos's gathering had been peaceful until the police escalated the situation, how Max had been senselessly brutalized, and how the charges against Carlos were a smokescreen to cover the officers' misconduct.

Until finally, the judge saw through the prosecution's narrative. The criminal charges against Carlos were dismissed, and the court acknowledged the violation of his rights. Carlos walked away free, his dignity restored, though the scars of that night remained.

And ever since then, I've held this case as a reminder of how even the smallest details—like a little dog with a big story—can expose injustice. In the face of systemic power, the truth often needs a voice, and sometimes, that voice comes from unexpected places.

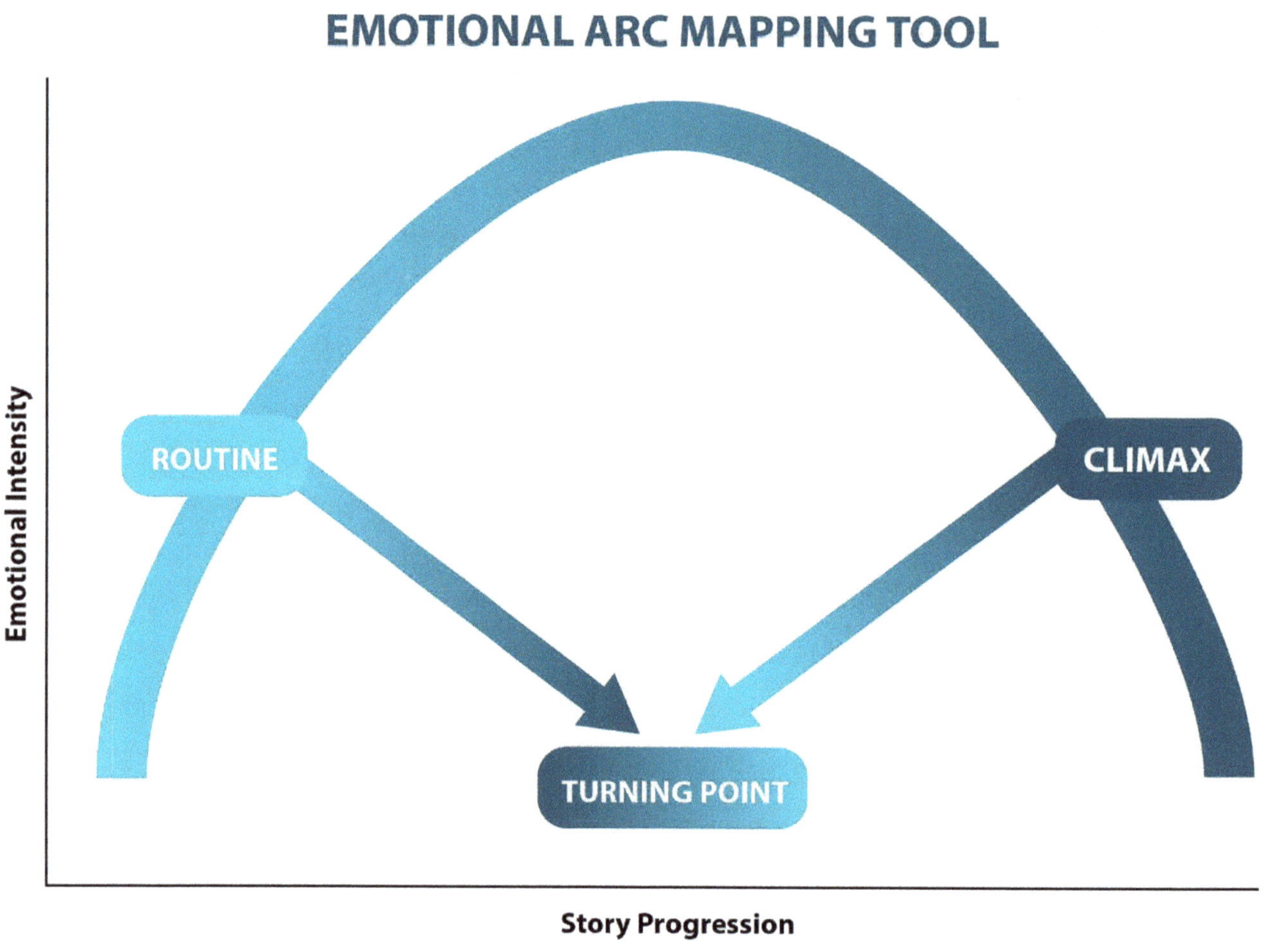

Figure 11: Emotional Arc Mapping Tool

Conclusion

"If you want your audience to care, give them a character they can see themselves in—flawed, driven, and brimming with potential."

The "Until one day" moment is the point where the stakes rise, the conflict takes center stage, and your audience becomes emotionally invested in the journey. A well-crafted turning point doesn't just grab attention; it creates connection, curiosity, and a sense of urgency that pulls the audience deeper into the narrative. As you refine your storytelling skills, remember that the turning point isn't just about what happens—it's about *how* you frame it. The emotional resonance, the tension, and the way you draw your audience into the protagonist's world are what make this moment unforgettable.

Practice Spines

Exercise 1: Choose a case, scenario, or personal story and identify the "Until one day" moment. Write it out, focusing on disruption, emotional impact, and the stakes involved.

Exercise 2: Write the turning point for a case where a whistleblower exposes corporate fraud. Highlight the moment they discover the wrongdoing, their internal conflict, and the consequences of their decision to come forward.

Practical Tips for Crafting the Turning Point

1. **Make It Personal:** The turning point should feel deeply personal to the character, forcing them to confront their vulnerabilities, fears, or limitations. Show how this moment disrupts their world in a way that feels real and specific.

2. **Raise the Stakes:** Conflict drives engagement. Ensure the turning point introduces challenges that feel urgent and significant, not just for the character but for the larger narrative. This is where the audience starts to feel the emotional weight of the story.

3. **Highlight the Emotional Fallout:** Don't stop at the event itself—show how it affects the character emotionally. Does it shatter their confidence? Challenge their beliefs? Strengthen their resolve? The more the audience understands the character's reaction, the more invested they'll become.

4. **Set Up the Journey Ahead:** The turning point should create a path for the rest of the story. What challenges lie ahead? What decisions must the character make? Use this moment to propel the narrative forward, giving the audience a reason to stay engaged.

Chapter 6
Momentum Through Conflict

"A great story isn't smooth sailing—it's a storm. Obstacles are the waves that test the characters and keep the audience on the edge of their seats."

The Power of "Because of That"

Conflict is the engine that propels the narrative forward, creating tension and keeping your audience connected. Without any obstacles, a story risks becoming predictable, dull, and forgettable. Challenges add depth, suspense, and stakes, turning a simple sequence of events into a journey worth following.

Imagine a straightforward case: the defendant has an airtight alibi supported by solid evidence and reliable witnesses. While it resolves neatly, it lacks the twists and turns that make a story memorable. Now compare that to a case where the alibi hinges on a witness who falters under cross-examination. The lawyer scrambles to present new evidence, tension builds, and the audience leans in, wondering how—or if—the narrative will recover. The stakes rise, the story becomes unpredictable, and the audience is now fully engaged. Conflict transforms the mundane into the unforgettable.

Why Obstacles Matter

Obstacles are more than just roadblocks; they are opportunities. They reveal the character's resilience, resourcefulness, and humanity. A legal case without obstacles is like a race without hurdles—it may showcase skill, but it lacks the triumph that comes from overcoming adversity. Challenges force characters to adapt, innovate, and persevere, and it's through this process that the audience forms an emotional connection.

Take, for example, a piece of unexpected contradictory evidence or a witness who suddenly becomes uncooperative. These moments test not only the lawyer's strategy but also their ability to think on their feet. For the audience, these obstacles add suspense and create moments of catharsis when the challenges are resolved. It's these moments that stick in their minds long after the story ends.

Obstacles are what make stories worth telling. They challenge characters to grow, force the audience to engage, and turn simple narratives into unforgettable journeys. The "Because of that" sequence is your chance to create momentum through conflict, building a story that captivates from beginning to end.

Figure 12: Turning Obstacles into Opportunities

Life Lessons: Momentum Through Conflict

Once upon a time...

I found myself in the middle of a contentious trial, the courtroom charged with tension. The opposing counsel was relentless, pushing every point, questioning every motive. My client, visibly anxious, glanced at me with eyes full of doubt. The jury seemed divided, some leaning forward with interest, others retreating behind blank expressions. Every argument felt like a tightrope walk over uncertainty.

Every day...

Conflict was a constant in my work. Cases were built on it, lives were changed by it, and the outcomes of trials depended on how well I could navigate it. I'd learned that conflict wasn't something to be feared—it was the heart of every story. But keeping that conflict balanced, driving the narrative without overwhelming the audience, was a delicate art.

Until one day...

In the midst of that trial, the tension reached a breaking point. The opposing counsel introduced a piece of evidence that threatened to derail our carefully crafted case. My heart raced, but I knew this was the moment I had to embrace the conflict rather than shy away from it. Instead of reacting defensively, I reframed the evidence, using it as a bridge to highlight a larger, deeper emotional truth in our story. The courtroom shifted. The jurors were no longer just spectators—they were engaged.

Because of that...

I realized that conflict isn't just a source of tension—it's the momentum that propels a story forward. When handled with care, conflict doesn't divide; it unites, drawing people into the heart of the narrative. It creates stakes, sparks curiosity, and makes resolutions feel earned rather than handed down.

And because of that...

I began to embrace conflict as an essential tool in every story I told. I stopped avoiding it and instead sought ways to deepen it—finding contradictions, amplifying stakes, and ensuring every challenge felt authentic and meaningful. Conflict, I discovered, wasn't an obstacle to storytelling; it was its driving force.

Until finally...

I understood that the most compelling stories don't shy away from conflict; they thrive on it. Conflict is what makes audiences care. It's the reason they lean in, the reason they hold their breath, and the reason they cheer when the resolution finally arrives. Without conflict, there is no momentum—only stillness.

And ever since that day...

I've leaned into the power of conflict, using it to drive momentum in every narrative I craft. I've learned to wield conflict as a tool—not to create division, but to build tension, stakes, and resolution. Because in the end, it's the conflict that keeps us moving—and the resolution that makes the journey worth it.

Tension: The Driving Force of Engagement

Tension is the magnet that pulls your audience into the story, making them emotionally and intellectually invested in its outcome. The higher the stakes, the more rewarding the resolution. Imagine a high-profile criminal defense case where each new piece of evidence shifts the jury's perception of the accused. Every revelation challenges what they think they know, forcing them to reassess the narrative.

This constant interplay of conflict and resolution keeps the story alive, vibrant, and utterly captivating. Without tension, your audience passively absorbs information; with it, they become active participants, hanging on every twist and turn.

Turning Obstacles Into Opportunities

Obstacles are the fuel that powers a great story. Effective storytellers embrace the challenges obstacles present, transforming them into pivotal moments that deepen the narrative. Here's how:

- **Find the Emotional Core:** What's really at stake for your characters? Uncovering the human element of the conflict—be it fear, hope, or resilience—gives the audience a reason to care.
- **Show Growth Through Creativity:** Highlight how characters respond to adversity with ingenuity and determination. Solutions born from obstacles show transformation, revealing the strength and adaptability of the protagonists.
- **Embrace the Unpredictable:** Let the conflict surprise you. Unforeseen twists can redirect the story in ways that feel authentic and exciting.

In the courtroom, this might mean preparing alternative narratives to address unexpected challenges or adapting your strategy mid-trial to counter an opposing argument. By adapting to obstacles, you don't just overcome them—you make your story richer, more dynamic, and more impactful.

Figure 13: Conflict Analysis Wheel

Keeping the Momentum: The "Because of That" Sequence

Once the turning point disrupts the status quo, the story needs momentum to carry it forward. This is where the "Because of that" sequence shines. In this part of the Story Spine, cause and effect drive the narrative, showing how each event builds logically—and emotionally—on the one before it.

The "Because of that" sequence transforms isolated moments into a cohesive story. In a legal case, it could demonstrate how a single piece of evidence led to new discoveries, how a witness's testimony unraveled under cross-examination, or how the introduction of an unexpected argument turned the tide of the trial.

This sequence not only sustains the audience's interest but also reinforces the emotional and moral weight of the conflict. Every cause leads to an effect, escalating the stakes and guiding the audience toward an inevitable resolution. The story doesn't just move—it gains momentum, compelling the audience to stay engaged and emotionally connected.

Whether you're telling a story in a courtroom, a boardroom, or to an audience of one, these elements ensure your narrative is dynamic, impactful, and impossible to ignore. So dive into the tension, embrace the challenges, and let each moment build on the last—because that's where the growth happens.

Connecting events and escalating stakes, are the driving force of any compelling story. The "Because of that" sequence transforms isolated moments into a seamless journey, one where every twist and turn keeps the audience on edge. It's not just about what happens next—it's about how each moment builds on the last, raising the stakes, keeping the story alive, and the audience tuned in.

Framing the "Because of That" Sequence

To craft an effective "Because of that" sequence, focus on the ripple effects of the turning point. Think of each moment as a domino: the first event triggers a series of consequences that grow in intensity and impact. Ask yourself these guiding questions:

- What immediate consequences followed the turning point?
- How did those consequences affect the protagonist or others involved?
- How did the stakes increase with each event?

Example: A Trial Scenario

Let's revisit Emily, the nurse whose life was upended by a car accident:

- **Once upon a time:** Emily was a devoted nurse who found joy and purpose in her work.
- **Every day:** She worked tirelessly, cared for her family, and dreamed of advancing her career and building a brighter future.
- **Until one day:** A drunk driver ran a red light and crashed into her car, leaving her with life-altering injuries.

Here's where the "Because of that" sequence comes in, showing the cascading consequences of that pivotal moment:

- **Because of that:** Emily was rushed to the hospital, where doctors found multiple fractures and nerve damage, leaving her mobility uncertain.
- **Because of that:** She endured three surgeries and months of grueling rehabilitation, unable to return to her demanding job as a nurse.
- **Because of that:** Her family faced mounting financial strain, falling behind on bills and teetering on the edge of losing their home.
- **Because of that:** Emily's dreams of career advancement and providing for her family were put on indefinite hold, leaving her struggling with feelings of loss and helplessness.

Why This Sequence Works

This "Because of that" sequence reveals the growing stakes and deepens the audience's emotional connection to Emily's story. It transforms the accident from an isolated incident into a series of hardships that demonstrate the long-term consequences of the defendant's actions.

Each step builds on the previous one, showing how the turning point disrupted Emily's life and the lives of those around her. The jury isn't just learning about the case—they're feeling its weight, experiencing the ongoing ripple effects of that one life-changing moment.

Building Your Own Sequence

To frame a strong "Because of that" sequence:

1. Start with the immediate fallout of the turning point. What's the first domino to fall?
2. Show how that event creates new challenges or raises the stakes.
3. Keep the consequences connected and escalating, each one building on the last.
4. Emphasize the emotional toll—how the protagonist and others are affected on a personal level.

By weaving a sequence that's both logical and emotionally resonant, you'll create a narrative that captivates. The audience won't just understand the stakes; they'll *feel* them, staying invested in the story from start to finish.

Case Story: A Healthcare Fraud Trial

This chapter explored the critical concept of momentum through conflict—a lesson we learned in one of the most challenging and emotionally charged cases of my career. This was a healthcare fraud trial that stretched over months, with a mountain of evidence, including secret recordings, strong witnesses for the prosecution, and an overwhelming narrative that painted our clients as criminals. It was a fight not only for their freedom but also for their dignity.

The prosecution's story was sharp and unforgiving. They labeled our clients as schemers, coldly exploiting the healthcare system for profit. But we saw a deeper truth—one that couldn't be reduced to the caricature they presented. Our clients weren't perfect, and we didn't pretend they were. They had made mistakes, but at their core, they were people who wanted to make a difference in the lives of others. We knew we had to show the jury their humanity.

From the beginning, the tension in the courtroom was palpable. Each secret recording played was a gut punch, and the prosecution used them to craft a chilling narrative. But instead of running from this conflict, we embraced it. We dissected every recording, not to deny their existence but to show the context. These weren't the words of villains—they were the messy, sometimes flawed decisions of people trying to navigate the complexities of a broken healthcare system.

Our clients had dedicated their lives to improving access to care, particularly for underserved communities. One of our most powerful witnesses was a nurse who spoke about how our clients had implemented a telemedicine program that allowed patients in rural areas to receive care they'd never had access to before. Her voice brimmed with emotion as she described the elderly patient who cried because, for the first time in years, someone was listening to his health concerns. This wasn't the story of greed—it was the story of people trying, however imperfectly, to make the world a better place.

We carried that momentum into sentencing. The prosecution sought to silence the humanity of our clients by demanding harsh prison sentences of 20-30 years. But we weren't finished fighting yet. We told the judge about a mother who had worked tirelessly to build programs for children with disabilities, about a father who had poured his life savings into creating clinics in underserved areas, and about the countless lives they had touched along the way.

We didn't shy away from their mistakes, but we refused to let those mistakes define them. Instead, we showed their resilience, their hope, and their commitment to making things right. In the end, the sentences handed down were far less severe than the prosecution had demanded. We couldn't erase the verdict, but we gave our clients back their voice, their dignity, and a chance to move forward. It wasn't just about legal strategy—it was about giving the human story its rightful place in the courtroom.

This case wasn't just a legal battle; it was a testament to the power of conflict to reveal deeper truths. Every clash became an opportunity to uncover and amplify the humanity at the heart of the case. And that's the real momentum that moves hearts and gives meaning to the fight.

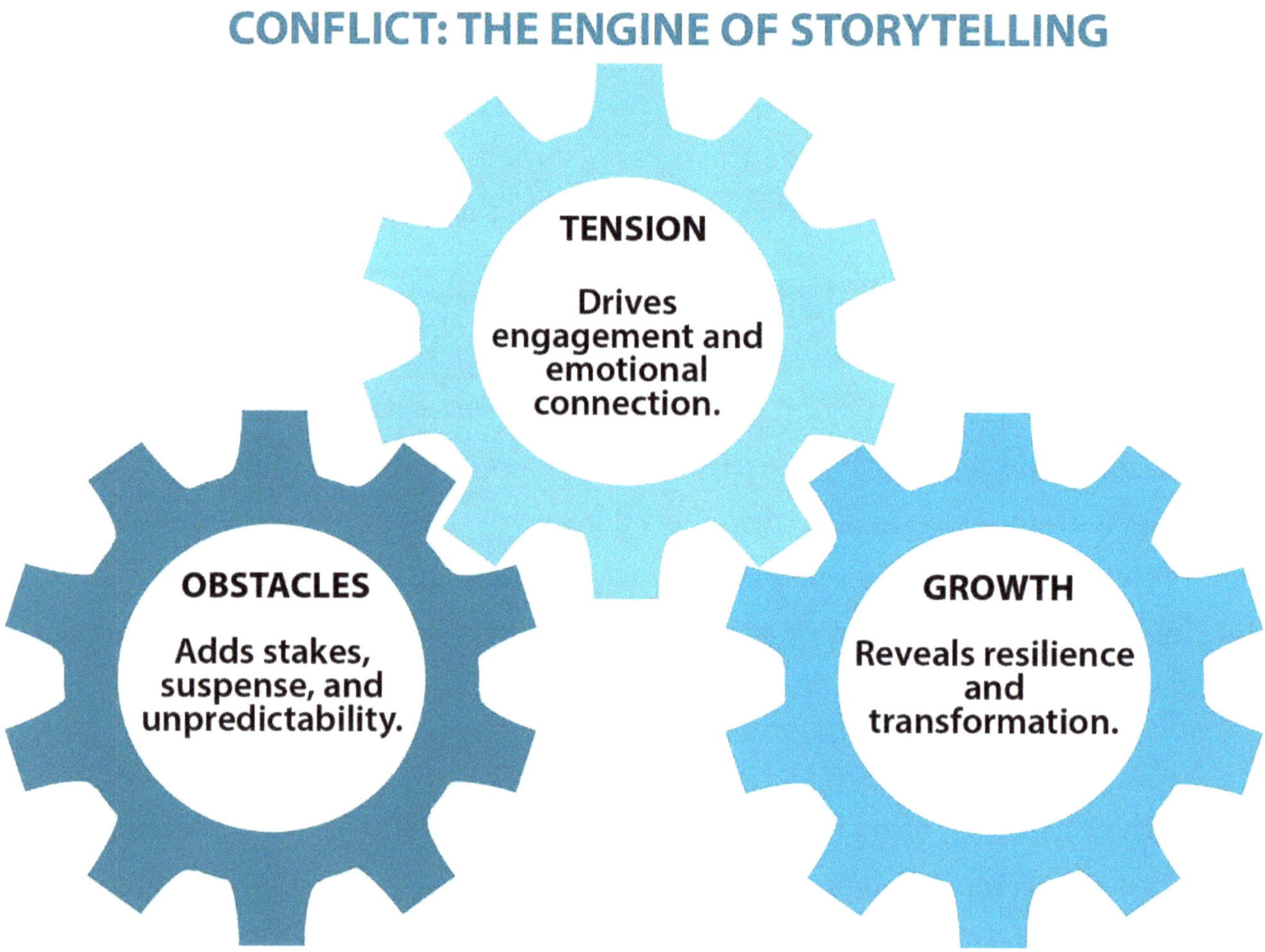

Figure 14: Conflict: The Engine of Storytelling

Conclusion

"An obstacle isn't the end of the road; it's the turning point that transforms an ordinary journey into an extraordinary story."

The "Because of that" sequence is where stories find their rhythm and depth; they are like an engine that drives momentum, builds tension, and adds layers of complexity. An obstacle is the turning point that transforms an ordinary journey into an extraordinary story. The "Because of that" sequence is where the stakes rise, characters evolve, and the audience becomes fully invested.

It's the heartbeat of your narrative, where conflict fuels growth and resolution feel earned. With every twist and complication, you draw your audience further into the journey, keeping them engaged and eager to see what comes next. In the end, it's not just about resolving the conflict—it's about showing how the journey shaped the characters and left an indelible impact.

PRACTICE SPINES

Exercise: Create a "Because of That" Sequence

Choose a challenging case, personal experience, or leadership moment. Use the "Because of that" step to explore the chain of events that followed the turning point.

Steps:

- Identify the turning point that disrupted the norm.
- Write a series of "Because of that" statements, each one logically connected to the previous event.
- Ensure the sequence escalates the stakes and sustains the audience's interest.

Example Prompt: Write a "Because of that" sequence for a legal case where a company's negligence led to a worker's injury, resulting in a chain of consequences for both the worker and the company.

Chapter 7
Wrapping It Up With Meaning

"A great resolution isn't just the end of the story—it's the moment your audience feels it was all worth it."

"Until Finally" and "Ever Since"

Ah, the resolution—the grand finale, the bow on the package, the part of the story that makes your audience sigh, "Ah, now it all makes sense." This isn't just where the story stops; it's where everything clicks into place, leaving the audience with clarity, purpose, and maybe even a tear or two.

In the courtroom, a strong resolution does more than summarize evidence; it seals the deal. Facts alone are fine, but if your closing argument doesn't tie those facts to a moral or emotional takeaway, you risk losing the room. Imagine ending a wrongful death case by saying, "And thanks for coming today." Nope. Instead, you say, "This case is about more than compensation. It's about ensuring no one else has to suffer this kind of loss again." Now, you're not just closing the story—you're giving it meaning.

WHY A RESOLUTION MATTERS

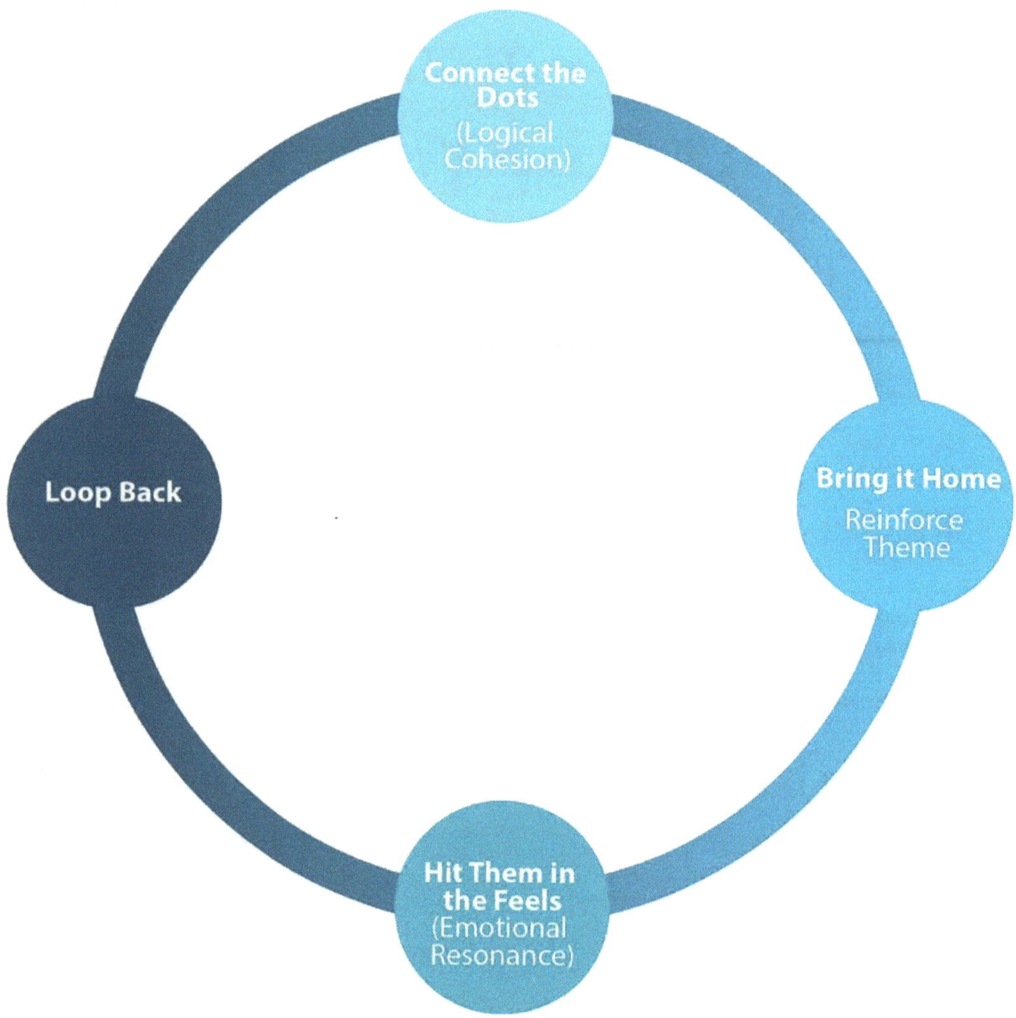

Figure 15: Why a Resolution Matters

Why a Resolution Matters

Think of the resolution as the dessert of your story. You've built the appetite with your turning points, spiced things up with conflict, and now it's time for that sweet, satisfying bite that ties it all together. Without it? The audience leaves the table disappointed and unsatisfied.

When you're wrapping up a courtroom argument, a resolution is your chance to address every lingering question, tie up loose ends, and remind your audience why they cared in the first place. It's the payoff, the emotional and intellectual closure that makes the journey worthwhile.

Crafting a Resolution That Stays

So, how do you make your resolution memorable? Follow these steps:

1. **Connect the Dots:** Take all the key evidence, all the drama, and show how it all leads to this moment. Make it logical and cohesive—no dangling threads allowed.

2. **Bring It Home:** Circle back to your central theme. What was this story really about? Justice? Redemption? Accountability? Hammer it home one last time.

3. **Hit Them in the Feels:** Whether it's hope, anger, or relief, leave your audience feeling something. Emotion is what stays long after the facts fade.

Example: Bringing a Personal Injury Case Full Circle

Let's say you're representing a client who suffered life-altering injuries due to corporate negligence. Here's how you'd tie it all up:

- **Until finally:** After months of medical bills, grueling surgeries, and sleepless nights, we've shown that the defendant's negligence caused this pain and suffering.
- **And ever since then:** While our client is working hard to rebuild their life, they'll carry these scars forever. This verdict isn't just about justice for them—it's about making sure no one else has to endure what they've been through.

You don't just recap the story—you give it meaning. You remind the jury that their decision has a ripple effect, and that they're part of something bigger.

Life Lessons: Resolution and Reflection

Once upon a time...

The verdict had been read, and the case was over. My client's eyes filled with tears—relief, gratitude, and perhaps even a touch of disbelief. As the courtroom emptied, I sat in silence, replaying every moment of the trial in my mind. We had won, but it wasn't just the verdict that stayed with me—it was the journey, the story, and how it had ended.

Every day...

In my work, cases ended with a verdict, but the stories behind them didn't stop there. Clients carried their resolutions into their lives, for better or worse. Juries walked away, reflecting on what they'd heard and what it meant. Every resolution was an opportunity—a moment to close one chapter and leave a lasting impression for the next.

Until one day...

After a particularly emotional trial, I met with my client to reflect on the outcome. They told me, "It's not just about what happened in there. You gave me my story back. You helped me understand it, own it, and move forward." It was then I realized that a resolution isn't just an ending—it's a beginning. It's the point where the audience carries the story into their own lives, interpreting it through their own experiences.

Because of that...

I began to approach resolutions differently. I stopped seeing them as simple conclusions and started treating them as pivotal moments for reflection and transformation. A resolution wasn't about tying everything up neatly—it was about leaving the audience with something to hold onto, something that lingered and inspired thought long after the story was done.

And because of that...

I worked hard to craft endings that balanced closure with possibility. Whether in the courtroom, a focus group, or a conversation, I sought to leave people not just satisfied, but moved—encouraged to reflect on what they had heard, what it meant, and how it could shape their lives. The impact of a story, I realized, lives on in the space after it ends.

Until finally...

I understood that a strong resolution isn't about perfection—it's about resonance. It's about ensuring that the story lives on in the minds of the audience, sparking questions, emotions, and even action. The most powerful endings don't just conclude—they transform.

And ever since that day...

I've made reflection a cornerstone of every resolution I craft. Whether closing a case, finishing a project, or simply ending a conversation, I aim to leave people with more than an answer—I aim to leave them with meaning. Because the true power of a story lies not just in how it begins, but in how it lingers long after it is finished.

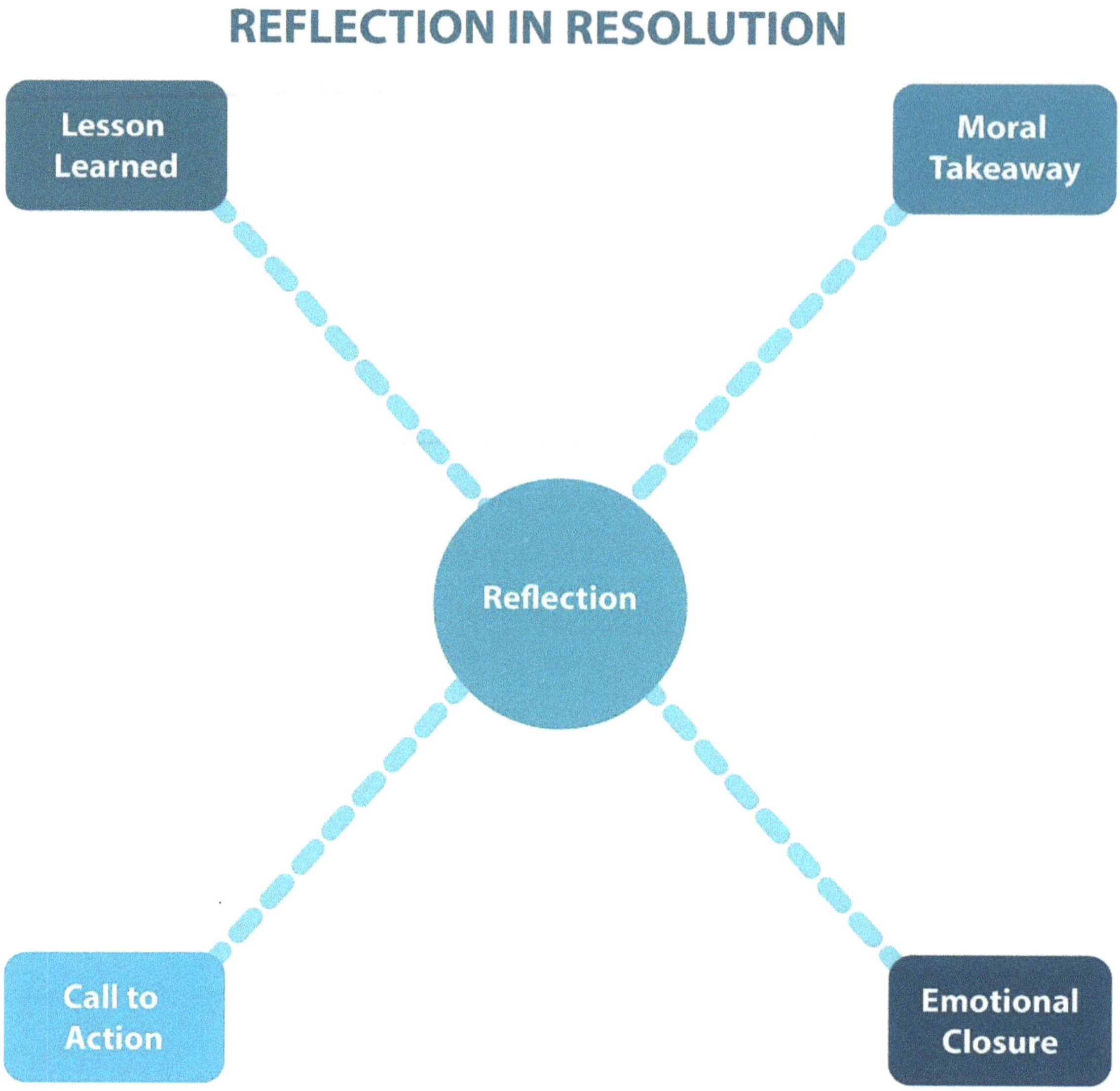

Figure 16: Reflection in Resolution

How to Leave Them Wanting More (in a Good Way)

A resolution should linger, but not because it's unresolved. It should leave your audience thinking, reflecting, and mentally trying on their role in the bigger story. In a trial, this means wrapping your case with a bow that feels both emotionally and intellectually satisfying. Bring them full circle, tie up those loose ends, answer their questions and give them a takeaway they'll remember. Think of it as your mic-drop moment.

It's not enough to summarize the evidence or conclude the events—you must draw out a lesson or message that leaves a lasting impact. In a criminal defense trial, for example, a lawyer might reflect on the idea that people are not defined by their worst mistakes. By emphasizing the potential for rehabilitation and redemption, the resolution shifts from a legal argument to a moral conversation. It invites the jury to consider bigger questions about justice, humanity, and societal values. Suddenly, the verdict isn't just about this one case; it's about the kind of world we want to live in.

Resolving Emotional Stakes

Every story carries emotional stakes, and ignoring them at the end is like closing a book just before the final chapter—you miss the resolution that gives the journey its meaning. If the narrative has been building tension around a victim's loss, the resolution must honor that pain and offer a sense of closure. The resolution should acknowledge the emotional journey the audience has been on.

For example, in a personal injury trial, a lawyer might highlight how a verdict in favor of the plaintiff does more than compensate for their suffering—it ensures that the harm done to them won't happen to someone else. This approach gives the jury a sense of purpose in their decision, showing that their choice isn't just reactive—it's proactive. Addressing the emotional stakes leaves the audience feeling seen, connected, and invested in the outcome.

Building a Satisfying Conclusion

A great resolution feels earned, not plucked out of thin air. The key is to escalate the stakes throughout the story, so the final moment lands with maximum impact. Each piece of evidence, each twist, each reveal should build on the last, creating a narrative that feels inevitable yet satisfying.

In a courtroom, this means structuring your case so that every argument and every piece of evidence leads toward the resolution. Take a negligence case, for example. If your resolution hinges on proving the defendant's repeated failures, you need to show a clear pattern of negligence, each instance adding weight to your argument. By the time you reach the conclusion, the audience should feel the full gravity of the story, and stand ready to deliver a just verdict, not just because it's right, but because it's the unavoidable end of the process.

The Final Bow: Delivering a Resolution That Lasts

The resolution is about delivering the moment that gives and keeps on giving. Consider a lawyer who closes a case with a simple yet profound statement: "This case is about the power of standing up for what's right, even when it's hard." That's not just a conclusion; it's a rallying cry. It transcends the trial, tapping into universal values and leaving a lasting impression on the jury's hearts and minds. It turns the story from a series of events into a call to reflect, to act, or even change.

Delivering on Your Promise

The resolution is your last chance to deliver on the promise you made to your audience when you started telling your story. This is the moment where everything comes together. A well-crafted resolution doesn't just answer questions; it gives the story meaning. It ensures that the audience doesn't just walk away with information—they walk away with the *"why"* that makes it all matter.

In the courtroom, this means leaving the jury with more than evidence. It means giving them a sense of purpose as they deliberate, helping them see their decision as part of something bigger. You're not just asking them to consider the facts—you're inviting them to weigh the story's moral and emotional stakes. These are the moments where your audience finds closure, clarity, and sometimes even inspiration. It's the difference between, "Well, that's done," and "Wow, I'll be thinking about this for a while."

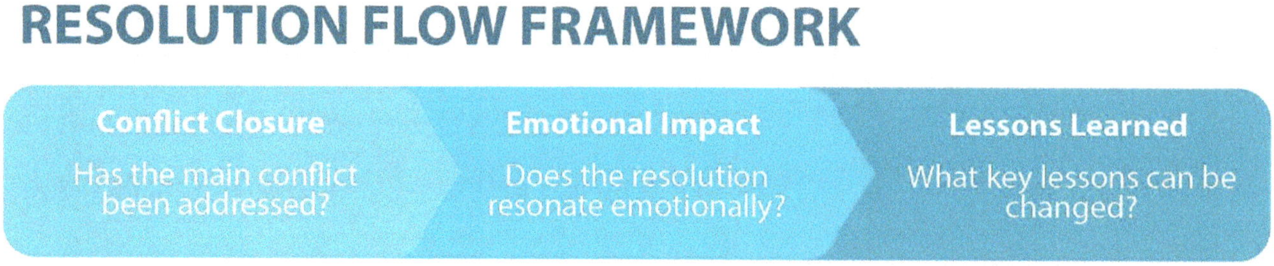

Figure 17: Resolution Flow Framework

Crafting the "Until Finally" Moment

The "Until finally" moment is the story's crescendo—the big resolution that brings it all together. It should feel decisive, emotionally charged, and like the inevitable conclusion of everything that came before it.

Example: A Trial Closing Argument

- **Until finally:** "Until finally, after years of relentless pain, mounting medical bills, and sleepless nights worrying about her family's future, Emily stands before you asking for justice. The defendant's negligence is undeniable, and she is relying on you, the jury, to award her the compensation needed to rebuild her life."

See how that works? The conflict peaks, the emotions hit hard, and the audience is given a clear call to action.

Crafting the "Ever Since" Moment

The "Ever since" moment is the story's exhale—a chance to reflect on the lasting impact of the resolution. It's where you show how the protagonist's life has changed and then tie everything back to the big takeaway.

Example: A Trial Closing Argument

- **Ever since:** "And ever since, Emily has poured her energy into recovery and rebuilding her life. She's found new ways to support her family and has become an advocate for drunk driving awareness, determined to prevent others from enduring the hardships she's faced."

Now the jury isn't just delivering a verdict—they're contributing to a greater story, one with hope and purpose.

A Case Story:
Embracing Humanity in a Personal Injury Case

Our client's case was far from conventional. Struck by a distracted driver while crossing the street, he was left with severe injuries, including a traumatic brain injury (TBI). But the defense wasn't focused on the harm done—they wanted to erase his humanity. To them, he wasn't just injured; he was a "nobody." A gamer who wore furry costumes, they argued he was reckless, immature, and unworthy of millions in damages. They even blamed him for the accident, claiming he ran into the car.

The defense sought to dehumanize him, but we turned their narrative on its head. We leaned into his quirks, showing the jury that his hobbies weren't flaws—they were expressions of creativity, joy, and connection. Friends testified about his humor and kindness, while we revealed how the accident had taken away not just his physical abilities but the vibrant, unique life he'd built.

The defense's condescension only highlighted their bias. We reminded the jury that justice isn't reserved for those who meet societal benchmarks—it's for anyone who has suffered harm. Our client didn't have to be a CEO to deserve accountability. He just had to be human.

The jury saw through the defense's narrative. They recognized his worth and awarded him millions—justice for a man society had underestimated. This case was a powerful reminder that every life, no matter how unconventional, deserves to be valued and defended.

Conclusion

"The best conclusions remind us that stories aren't just about endings—they're about the lessons that stay with us long after the final word."

A strong ending doesn't just tie up loose ends; it leaves your audience with something to think about, feel, or do. The "Until finally" moment provides the closure they've been craving, making the journey feel complete and worthwhile.

Then comes the "Ever since" moment, where you drive home the lesson, the moral, or the key takeaway that ensures your story stays with the audience long after it's told. Together, they transform a story from something that happened into something that matters.

PRACTICE SPINES

Exercise: Write a Resolution and Reflection

Think of a case, leadership moment, or personal story where you reached a resolution and saw its impact. Write an "Until finally" and "Ever since" for that story.

Steps:

- Identify the central conflict and how it was resolved.
- Write the "Until finally" moment, emphasizing the climax of the story.
- Reflect on the lasting impact and takeaway with "Ever since."

Example Prompt: Craft a resolution and reflection for a case where a whistleblower exposed corporate wrongdoing, leading to significant change in the company's practices. Focus on the resolution of the case and the broader impact of the whistleblower's actions.

Chapter 8
Using the Story Spine in the Courtroom

"In the courtroom, a great story isn't just about presenting facts—it's about making the jury see why those facts matter."

Story Spine— Your Superpower

The courtroom is a stage where storytelling and precision collide. Trial lawyers face a unique challenge: facts alone, no matter how compelling, rarely win cases. Jurors don't just need to understand what happened—they need to care. That's where storytelling comes in.

The Story Spine is a great tool for weaving facts into narratives that hit both the head and the heart. Progressing from "Once upon a time" to "And ever since then," gives your case a clear and engaging arc. It simplifies complex legal arguments while emphasizing the stakes and emotional truths that make a case unforgettable.

Think of it like this: the facts are the bricks, but the Story Spine is the blueprint that builds the house. Without it, you're just piling up evidence and hoping it doesn't collapse under its own weight. With it, you're creating a structure that's solid, persuasive, and unforgettable.

Why It Works

Jurors are human beings, not spreadsheets. They crave stories because stories help them make sense of the world. A timeline of events might tell them what happened, but a well-told story shows them *why it matters.* It frames the facts in a way that evokes emotion, forging a connection between the jury and the people at the heart of the case.

For example, presenting a piece of evidence like a signed contract might feel dry and procedural. But if you place that contract within a narrative—"Once upon a time, two partners built a business on trust, until one day…"—suddenly, it's not just a document; it's a betrayal, a turning point, a reason to act.

Using the Spine in Court

Here's how you can use the Story Spine to structure your courtroom narrative:

1. **Once upon a time…** Set the stage. Introduce the characters and establish the "normal" before the conflict. Who are the people involved, and what was their world like?

2. **And every day…** Highlight the routine or the relationship that existed before things went wrong. This is where you make the jury care about the status quo—because they need to understand what's at stake when it's disrupted.

3. **Until one day…** This is your turning point—the event that shatters the normal and propels the case into conflict. Think of this as the heartbeat of your narrative.

4. **Because of that…** Show the ripple effects. Every piece of evidence, every witness, and every detail should connect to the consequences of the turning point. This sequence builds momentum and escalates the stakes. Repeat this sequence as needed.

5. **Until finally…** The climax. This is where you resolve the conflict and tie the story together, delivering the emotional and logical punch your case needs.

6. **And ever since then…** Reflect on the impact. What has changed because of this case? What's the bigger takeaway? This is your chance to leave the jury with something meaningful to carry into deliberations.

Making the Spine Your Own

Using the Story Spine doesn't mean every case becomes a fairy tale. It's about uncovering the human story within the facts and presenting it in a way that connects deeply with the audience. No matter if you're dealing with a complex white-collar crime or a deeply emotional family law case, the Story Spine helps you organize your argument, connect with your jury, and deliver your case with impact. The courtroom may be built on logic, but cases are won on connection. And connection comes from stories. So, the next time you step in front of a jury, don't just present the facts—tell a story they won't forget.

Figure 18: Courtroom Story Spine Framework

Life Lessons: Using the Story Spine in the Courtroom

Once upon a time...

I stood before a jury, my client's life hanging in the balance. The case was complicated, the facts tangled in technicalities and legal jargon. I knew the truth was on our side, but truth alone wasn't enough. The jury needed more than facts—they needed a reason to care, a way to make sense of it all.

Every day...

In courtrooms, I saw the same challenge unfold: lawyers drowning their audience in evidence, hoping sheer volume would tip the scales. But jurors aren't computers; they don't process data in isolation. They connect with stories. Without a compelling narrative, even the strongest case could be lost in the noise.

Until one day...

I began applying the Story Spine to my trial preparation. I used it to map out every case: the setup, the turning points, the conflict, and the resolution. In one particular trial, I reframed the complex facts into a simple, relatable narrative. Instead of starting with the technicalities, I began with my client's journey—the choices, struggles, and consequences that brought us to this moment. The jury didn't just hear the case; they felt it.

Because of that...

The trial took on a different energy. The jury wasn't overwhelmed by details; they were drawn into the story, eager to see where it would go. Each piece of evidence became part of the narrative, every argument another chapter in the journey. By the time I reached closing arguments, the jury was no longer evaluating facts—they were rooting for resolution.

And because of that...

I began using the Story Spine as the backbone of every trial strategy. It clarified my openings, guided my cross-examinations, and gave my closings emotional impact. It became my way of transforming legal complexity into human connection, bridging the gap between the law and the people it served.

Until finally...

I saw that the Story Spine wasn't just a storytelling tool; it was a framework for justice. It helped jurors see beyond the surface, understand the stakes, and feel the weight of their decisions. By turning cases into stories, I gave my clients the best possible chance to be seen, heard, and understood.

And ever since that day...

I've taught lawyers across the country how to use the Story Spine in their own trials. Whether crafting an opening statement or structuring a cross-examination, the framework has proven itself again and again. Because in the courtroom, as in life, the most compelling stories are the ones that connect us all.

Opening Statements: Once Upon a Time in the Courtroom

"The opening statement is your story's invitation—it's where you say, 'Come on in, this is a tale worth hearing.'"

Think of the opening statement as the "Once upon a time" and "Every day" chapters of your case's Story Spine. It's your chance to set the scene, introduce your cast of characters, and establish the world before everything went sideways.

For instance, in a wrongful termination case, you might begin by painting a picture of the plaintiff's life as a hardworking, dedicated employee who genuinely loved their job. You want the jury to see themselves in your client's shoes—to feel their pride, dedication, and dreams. This connection builds the foundation for empathy.

Then, with a well-placed, "Until one day…" you drop the bombshell: their supervisor unjustly accused them of misconduct. The jury is now invested—they want to know what happened, why it happened, and most importantly, how it ends. By starting with a compelling "normal," your opening statement creates an emotional anchor that pulls the jury into the narrative from the get-go.

Cross-Examinations: The Juicy Middle

"Cross-examinations are where the plot thickens, secrets unravel, and the stakes skyrocket."

This is the "Because of that" phase of the Story Spine—the part where conflicts deepen, tensions rise, and the narrative gets its claws into the audience.

Cross-examination is your chance to expose contradictions, poke holes in the opposition's story, and bring hidden motives to light.

Let's say you're working a fraud case. The key witness? Someone who conveniently made a hefty financial gain from the alleged crime. Your questions become the plot points:

- "So, isn't it true you received $50,000 as a result of this deal?"
- "And that transaction was never disclosed to the other parties, correct?"

Each question peels back a layer, creating a ripple effect that builds the jury's understanding—and doubts about the witness's credibility. You're not just asking questions; you're crafting a narrative where every answer adds tension and reinforces your theory of the case. By framing your cross-examination as part of the story's progression, you turn what could be a dry Q&A into a pivotal scene that keeps the jury engaged and invested.

Closing Arguments: The Grand Finale

"This is your big finish—the resolution that ties it all together and leaves your audience thinking, 'Wow, that was powerful.'"

The closing argument is where you hit the "Until finally" and "And ever since then" moments of the Story Spine. It's the climax and the reflection all rolled into one—the point where everything you've built during the trial comes together in a cohesive, compelling resolution.

In a personal injury case, you might conclude with something like this:

- **Until finally:** "After months of pain, surgeries, and mounting medical bills, Mary stands before you today, asking for justice. The defendant's negligence has irreparably changed her life."

- **And ever since then:** "And ever since, she has fought to regain even a fraction of what she's lost. Your verdict isn't just about compensation; it's about accountability and ensuring this never happens to someone else."

The closing argument is where you transform a pile of evidence into a meaningful story. It's where you remind the jury why they cared in the first place and why their decision has real-world consequences. Done well, it doesn't just summarize—it inspires and empowers the jury to take action.

Figure 19: Evidence Integration Flowchart

Why the Story Spine Works in the Courtroom

Using the Story Spine throughout a trial is like handing the jury a roadmap to your case. Instead of overwhelming them with disjointed facts and hoping they find their way, you guide them through a clear, human-centered story. It's a method to organize evidence into a cohesive narrative that engages both emotionally and intellectually. When jurors hear a well-crafted story, they don't just understand the facts—they *feel* their significance.

A compelling story ensures that jurors remember the key points and interpret the evidence through the lens you've carefully crafted. The Story Spine balances precision with persuasion, offering lawyers a powerful tool to engage, guide, and ultimately convince their audience. It's not just about presenting a case; it's about making the jury care deeply about the outcome. It's about inviting them to step fully into the role of decision maker.

The courtroom is where facts meet persuasion. A timeline of events or a stack of evidence might be accurate, but it won't sway a jury on its own. From opening statements to cross-examinations to closing arguments, the Story Spine gives you a structure that connects with jurors on a human level.

Take a medical malpractice case, for instance. Instead of bombarding the jury with timelines and medical jargon, you frame the story using the Story Spine:

- **Once upon a time:** The patient trusted their doctor.
- **Every day:** They followed the prescribed treatment, believing it would help.
- **Until one day:** A preventable mistake changed everything.

With this structure, jurors can easily follow the progression of events, understanding not just *what* happened but *why it matters.* It keeps them emotionally and intellectually engaged, ensuring your arguments sink in.

By organizing your case into a clear narrative, you help jurors make sense of the facts, connect with the people involved, and feel invested in the outcome. So, when you step into the courtroom, don't just present the evidence. Use the Story Spine to craft a narrative that jurors can follow, remember, and care about. Because in the end, it's not the facts that win—it's the story you tell about them.

Connecting the Story Spine to the Jury's Decision

The Story Spine ensures jurors don't feel lost in the details. Instead, they're drawn into a cohesive narrative that gives meaning to the evidence. When the jury steps into the deliberation room, they're not just processing information; they're carrying a story that aligns with their values and motivates them to act.

Think of the courtroom as a stage and your argument as the performance of a lifetime. The Story Spine is your script, keeping the narrative focused, logical, and emotionally impactful. By structuring your case as a story, seamlessly integrating evidence, and reinforcing your key points, you make your argument unforgettable.

A Case Story: Breaking Free from the Golden Cage

This case wasn't one I sought out. In fact, I almost didn't take it. She had gone through four lawyers before finding me, and her intensity was overwhelming. But my paralegal believed in her and set the appointment. What unfolded was a story that read more like a tragic novel than a legal case.

Once upon a time, a young woman dreamed of a life of love and security. At 22, she married a wealthy businessman nearly 50 years her senior. He was a pillar of the community, a man admired for his success and charm. He promised her everything—a marriage of status, a child, a mansion, luxury, and prestige. She had it all, and for a while, the dream seemed real.

And every day, she lived in opulence, enjoying the privileges his wealth could provide. But beneath the surface, her life wasn't her own. He controlled her with gifts and, eventually, drugs. She was trapped in a gilded cage, her personhood exchanged for his control.

Until one day, she found the strength to resist. But her defiance had consequences. When she could no longer be subdued with money or addiction, he used his power to destroy her. He had her committed to a mental institution and took full custody of their child, restricting her to supervised visitation. Alone and broken, she made desperate mistakes, leaving threatening voicemails in her anguish—messages that would later be played in court to paint her as unstable.

Because of that, her case seemed almost unwinnable. The legal system often favors the powerful, and she didn't fit the image of the perfect victim. Her pain was raw, her actions messy, and her life chaotic. But beneath it all was a mother desperate to reclaim her child and her dignity.

Because of that, we worked tirelessly to shift the narrative. This wasn't just a story of wealth or privilege—it was a story of control, redemption, and maternal love. We painted the full picture: while the father held full custody, the child was often left with nannies, neglected despite his resources. We showed how she had been manipulated and broken but was fighting to rebuild her life for the sake of her child.

Until finally, the court saw the truth. We secured primary custody for her, with visitation rights for the father. It wasn't just a legal victory—it was a reclaiming of her humanity.

This case wasn't easy for me. It challenged my assumptions and forced me to confront biases I didn't know I had about wealth, status, and power. But it also reminded me why stories matter. When we look past the surface—beyond the mistakes, the pain, and the messiness—we see the heart of what makes us human. And that's where justice begins.

Conclusion

"In trial advocacy—and in life—the right story doesn't just present facts; it transforms how people feel, think, and act."

The Story Spine is your storytelling Swiss Army knife. In the courtroom, it moves jurors from simply understanding evidence to deeply *feeling* its impact. But the usefulness of the Story Spine doesn't stop at the courthouse doors. In leadership, it's the spark that inspires teams to tackle challenges and chase big goals. In negotiation, it's the bridge that connects interests and builds trust. And in personal storytelling, it's how you forge meaningful connections and leave a lasting impression.

No matter where you use it, mastering the Story Spine empowers you to craft messages that connect and inspire. With practice, it can transform not just your communication but your ability to connect with others in any setting.

Practice Spines

Exercise 1: Create a Trial Narrative

Imagine a wrongful termination case where a single parent sues their employer for firing them after they reported safety violations. Use the Story Spine to bring the narrative to life:

- **Opening Statement:** Craft the "Once upon a time," "Every day," and "Until one day" that introduce the client and set the stage.
- **Because of That Sequence:** Highlight the cascading consequences of the termination to show the stakes.
- **Closing Argument:** Tie it all together with "Until finally" and "Ever since," leaving the jury with a compelling takeaway.

Exercise 2: Spin a Leadership or Personal Growth Tale

Think back to a time you faced a challenge, led a team through a tough transition, or overcame a personal obstacle. Use the Story Spine to map out your journey:

- **Once upon a time/Every day:** Set the scene. What was the norm before the storm?
- **Until one day:** Introduce the challenge. What disrupted your world?
- **Because of that:** Trace the ripple effects. How did the challenge escalate or evolve?
- **Until finally/Ever since:** Share the resolution and its lasting impact. What lessons did you learn, and how did they shape who you are today?

Example Prompt

Write about a time you led your team through a challenging transition or overcame a personal setback. Use the Story Spine to craft a narrative that highlights the struggle, the growth, and the ultimate resolution. Focus on the insights gained and how they've shaped your perspective moving forward.

Chapter 9
Mastering the Method

"A great story isn't just about what you say—it's about how your audience feels. Mastering the method means making every word count."

Common Pitfalls and Pro Tips

Let's face it: storytelling is an art, but it's also a skill—and even the best intentions can lead to missteps. Luckily, with a few tweaks, you can turn common pitfalls into opportunities for greatness.

Pitfall 1: The Overcomplicated Narrative

We've all been there: you've got a case full of juicy details and dazzling evidence, and you're *sure* the jury wants to hear it all. But here's the catch—when you overload your narrative, your audience tunes out. Too much information muddies the waters, and suddenly, your story's clear, powerful message is lost in the noise.

Pro Tip: Simplify, simplify, simplify. Focus on the essentials—characters, conflict, and resolution. Ask yourself:

- "Does this detail move the story forward?"
- "Does it deepen the emotional or logical impact?"

If the answer is no, cut it. A lean, focused story with meaningful details is far more engaging than an overstuffed epic that leaves your audience swimming in confusion. Remember, simplicity is your best friend. I admit that this is easier said than done, but it is worth the effort.

Pitfall 2: Emotion Overload

Emotion is the key ingredient of storytelling, but too much can overwhelm the narrative. When you rely too heavily on sentiment without grounding it in logic, your story risks feeling manipulative or overdramatic. Take the courtroom, for example. A plaintiff's tearful testimony might tug at the jury's heartstrings, but without hard evidence to back it up, that emotional connection won't lead to a favorable verdict.

Pro Tip: Balance is everything. Use emotion to connect and logic to persuade. Craft your Story Spine with this mantra in mind:

- Emotional beats draw them in.
- Logical evidence seals the deal.

For every heartfelt moment, anchor it with a fact. Together, they form a harmonious blend of heart and reason that keeps your audience invested and connected.

Pitfall 3: Forgetting Your Audience

Your story isn't for you—it's for them. If your narrative doesn't align with your audience's values, experiences, or concerns, it won't make an impact.

Pro Tip: Step into their shoes. Think about what matters to them and tailor your story accordingly. If you're talking to a jury, highlight the human stakes. If you're leading a team, focus on the shared goal. Always ask:

- "What does my audience care about?"
- "How does this story align with their perspective?"

When your story meets your audience where they are, it becomes unforgettable. Every detail, every word, every beat in your narrative should have a purpose. Think of your story as a finely tuned machine—if one cog isn't pulling its weight, the whole system suffers.

Life Lessons: Mastering the Method

Once upon a time...

I stood in front of a room full of lawyers, about to present a storytelling workshop. My heart pounding, not from fear, but from the pressure of the moment. These weren't beginners—they were seasoned professionals, skeptical and set in their ways. I knew my method worked, but I also knew that unless I could connect with them in the first few minutes, I'd lose them entirely.

Every day...

Storytelling felt second nature to me in courtrooms and focus groups, but teaching it was another challenge entirely. Each audience was different, with its own biases, expectations, and resistance. Some embraced the Story Spine immediately, while others dismissed it as too simplistic. To make an impact, I needed to adapt—learning to read the room, meet people where they were, and guide them step by step toward understanding.

Until one day...

During a workshop, I asked the group to craft a story about a defining moment in their lives using the Story Spine. One attorney, hesitant at first, stood to share a raw and unpolished narrative about a case that haunted him. The room fell silent as his story unfolded. It wasn't perfect, but it was real. By the end, his colleagues weren't critiquing—they were applauding. In that moment, I saw the power of practice, vulnerability, and spontaneity within the framework.

Because of that...

I embraced the idea that mastery wasn't about rigid perfection; it was about flexibility, connection, and authenticity. I began incorporating feedback loops into every session, encouraging participants to experiment, make mistakes, and refine their stories. I learned to embrace the unexpected, using spontaneity to breathe life into the structured framework of the Story Spine.

And because of that...

The method came alive for those who practiced it. Lawyers who once clung to dry facts began to trust their instincts, finding their unique voices within the structure. Storytelling became less of a tool and more of an art—one that adapted to the storyteller, the audience, and the moment.

Until finally...

I realized that true storytelling mastery is a journey, not a destination. It's about understanding your audience, embracing feedback, and finding confidence in your ability to adapt. It's about using structure as a guide, not a limitation, and discovering the freedom within the framework to let the story unfold naturally.

And ever since that day...

I've made it my mission to teach others how to refine their storytelling skills—not by seeking perfection, but by practicing with intention, embracing vulnerability, and trusting the process. Mastering the method isn't about memorizing rules; it's about learning how to connect deeply, adapt effortlessly, and tell stories that resonate every time.

The Danger of Skipping Conflict

One of the biggest storytelling mistakes made by novices and experts alike-is rushing from the setup to the resolution as if the middle doesn't matter. But the "Because of that" phase of the Story Spine is where things really start to happen—it's where the stakes are raised, the obstacles emerge, and the audience leans in, desperate to know what happens next.

Picture this: a lawyer skips over their client's hardships and goes straight to asking for a favorable verdict. Sure, they might present a resolution, but without the struggle, the jury won't feel the weight of what's at stake. It's the challenges—the sleepless nights, the tough decisions, the uphill battles—that make the resolution satisfying and impactful. So, don't rush. Take your audience on the journey, tension and all.

Stay Flexible: Stories Evolve

Another storytelling misstep is clinging too tightly to a rigid narrative, even when it's clearly not working. Stories need room to breathe, adapt, and evolve. Great storytellers don't just stick to their plan—they adjust and adapt as the story unfolds.

For instance, imagine a lawyer starts with a narrative focused on their client's innocence but new evidence emerges mid-trial. Suddenly, the story shifts: the focus pivots to systemic failures that led to the charges in the first place. By staying flexible, the lawyer crafts a narrative that connects with the jury instead of sticking with one that no longer fits.

Revisit your story often. Ask for feedback, reflect on how it's landing, and don't be afraid to make changes. Good storytelling isn't about being perfect—it's about being adaptable and impactful.

Pacing: The Key To Success

Pacing can make or break your story. Linger too long in the setup, and your audience starts checking their watches. Rush through the resolution, and you rob them of the payoff they've been waiting for. Each phase of the Story Spine should flow naturally into the next, building anticipation without overstaying its welcome.

And don't forget the power of pauses. Strategic pauses and emphasis can highlight key moments, giving your audience time to process the gravity of the story. Practice telling your story aloud—it's the best way to hear its rhythm and pinpoint where you need to slow down, speed up, or punch up the drama.

Storytelling is part art, part skill, and a whole lot of practice. The Story Spine gives you a sturdy framework, but crafting a truly unforgettable narrative requires refinement and awareness of potential pitfalls. Take your time. Explore the conflict. Evolve when needed. Pace it just right. When you master the Story Spine, your stories won't just be heard; they'll inspire, and linger long after they're told. And that's where the real power lies.

Simplification, Audience Focus, and Polishing Your Story

Simplification isn't about dumbing things down; it's about cutting through the noise to reveal what really matters. Imagine your story as a diamond in the rough. Simplification is the chisel that removes unnecessary details, jargon, or tangents, leaving behind something clear, compelling, and impactful.

Whatever the project, always ask:

- Does this detail serve the story?
- Will my audience remember this moment?
- Am I adding clarity or confusion?

When you simplify your narrative, you don't lose depth—you gain focus. And that's what makes your story accessible, engaging, and downright irresistible.

Audience Focus: Speak Their Language

A story that doesn't connect with its audience is like shouting into the void. To truly connect, you need to tailor your narrative to the people listening. Think about it: What do they care about? What keeps them up at night? What inspires them to act?

By aligning your story with their values, emotions, and experiences, you create a bridge of understanding. Suddenly, your message isn't just something they hear—it's something they participate in. Audience-focused storytelling isn't just a nice touch; it's the difference between polite applause and a standing ovation.

Polishing Your Story: Shine Bright

Polishing is where your story levels up from "pretty good" to "wow, that stuck with me." It's about refining the flow, tightening transitions, and making sure every detail serves its purpose. Polishing isn't about chasing perfection—it's about making your narrative clear, authentic, and emotionally resonant.

Here's how to polish like a pro:

- Read your story aloud. Does it flow naturally, or do you stumble over parts?
- Pay attention to tone. Are you balancing emotion and logic?
- Enhance the arcs. Does your story rise, fall, and resolve in a way that feels satisfying?

A polished story isn't flawless; it's memorable. It stays with your audience long after the final word, leaving a lasting impression.

Great storytellers aren't just remembered for *what* they say—they're remembered for *how* their story made people feel. Each time you tell a story, you're shaping your legacy. Every narrative is an opportunity to teach, influence, inspire, or spark action.

Think about it: when you're guiding a jury through a case, your stories carry your voice, your values, and your vision. They become part of how you're known, how you're remembered, and how you make a difference.

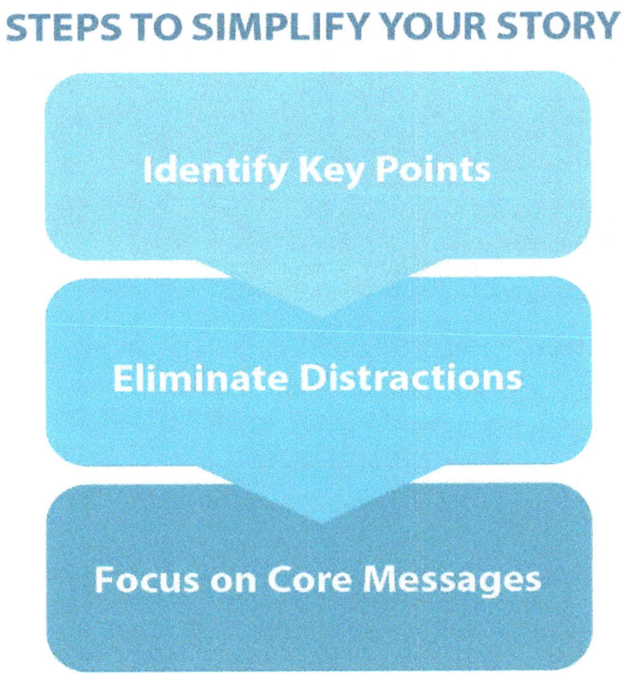

Figure 20: Steps to Simplify Your Story

A Case Story:
Uncovering the Truth Behind a Banking Fraud Scheme

It began with a frantic call. My client, a single mother and bookkeeper for a small nonprofit, was in tears. She'd just been charged with orchestrating a multi-million-dollar banking fraud scheme. To the prosecutors, she was a mastermind, siphoning funds through complex transactions. To her, it was a misunderstanding spiraling out of control. She admitted she'd seen something strange in the accounts—but she had no idea it would lead to this.

The Allegation

The bank alleged that she had knowingly facilitated fraudulent transactions. Suspicious wire transfers and forged documents traced back to her login credentials. To them, it was an open-and-shut case: she had access, she processed the transfers, and she didn't report them. The prosecution claimed she was complicit, profiting quietly while leaving a trail of financial ruin.

But when I met her, the picture wasn't so clear. She was terrified, not defiant. She admitted she'd noticed irregularities but thought they were the result of system errors or simple oversights by her employer. "I didn't want to lose my job by making waves," she said, her voice trembling. "I thought I was fixing mistakes, not committing a crime."

The Defense: Knowledge Without Intent

Our defense centered on intent—or lack of it. Yes, she had processed the transactions, but she hadn't understood their significance. She wasn't a financial expert; she was a bookkeeper earning barely enough to keep her and her daughter afloat. Her "involvement" was the result of following instructions, not a calculated effort to defraud.

We painted for the jury a vivid picture of her reality. She worked late hours, juggling the demands of her job and single motherhood. Her employer, a charismatic but controlling executive, frequently asked her to "fix" discrepancies and process last-minute transfers. She assumed he knew what he was doing—he was the boss, after all. Why would she question him?

Exposing the Real Perpetrator

The turning point came when we dug deeper into her employer's role. Through forensic accounting and expert testimony, we uncovered a pattern: her boss had orchestrated the fraud, carefully funneling funds while using her as an unwitting accomplice. He'd exploited her trust and her reluctance to challenge authority, knowing she'd take the fall if anything went wrong.

Emails revealed cryptic instructions like, "Just handle this; it's above your pay grade," and pressure to meet deadlines without asking questions. A damning audit showed that other employees had noticed irregularities but had been similarly dismissed. It wasn't just negligence—it was manipulation.

Humanizing the Story

In court, we didn't just argue with the facts—we told her story. We brought in coworkers who spoke of her dedication and honesty. We showed how she had stayed late countless nights, trying to balance the books. We called her daughter to share how the charges had turned their lives upside down—how they'd lost their home, how she'd watched her mother crumble under the weight of accusations.

We didn't shy away from her knowledge of the irregularities. Instead, we framed it as a tragic example of misplaced trust. She wasn't perfect, but she wasn't a criminal. She was a hardworking mother, caught in a web of deceit spun by someone far more experienced and calculating than her.

The Verdict

The jury deliberated for hours, and when they returned, the relief was palpable. She was acquitted of all major charges. The court recognized her as a pawn, not a perpetrator. The prosecutor turned their attention to her employer, who would later face his own reckoning.

The Aftermath

My client walked out of the courtroom with her name cleared, but the scars remained. The trial had cost her nearly everything—her job, her savings, her reputation. But she found a way forward, rebuilding her life with the same quiet resilience that had carried her through the trial. And for me, this case was a powerful reminder that justice isn't always about proving innocence—it's about showing the humanity behind the mistakes.

This story wasn't about absolutes. It was about complexity, about intent versus perception, and about how easily trust can be weaponized. It reminded me that the most compelling cases don't just win in court—they resonate in the hearts of those who hear them.

Figure 21: Story Spine Mastery Pathway

Conclusion

"Mastering storytelling isn't about dodging mistakes—it's about embracing them, learning from them, and turning them into stepping-stones for better, stronger stories."

One of the great things about storytelling is its ability to transform dry facts into memorable moments, strangers into allies, and ideas into action. But it doesn't stop there. It can reshape how we see ourselves, deepen our connections with others, and amplify the way we influence the world around us.

The Story Spine will help you harness that power. So go ahead, embrace the stumbles, take the detours, and keep refining your stories. After all, every great storyteller started with a few rough drafts. What matters is that you keep telling—and transforming—one story at a time.

PRACTICE SPINES

Exercise: Revise a Previously Crafted Story Spine

- Choose a Story Spine you've written for a trial, leadership moment, or personal story.
- Identify potential pitfalls:
- Are there unnecessary details? Does the story flow logically? Does it connect emotionally? Is the takeaway clear?
- Revise the story to simplify, enhance emotional resonance, and tailor it to your audience.

Prompt: Revisit the story of a trial where a single mother sued a negligent landlord for unsafe housing conditions. Refine the narrative to focus more on her emotional journey and the impact on her children, ensuring the jury feels the stakes deeply.

Exercise: Your Transformative Story

Think about a time when storytelling helped you create change, connect with others, or overcome a challenge. Craft your narrative using the Story Spine:

- Start with "Once upon a time" and "Every day" to set the stage.
- Introduce the turning point with "Until one day."
- Build momentum with "Because of that."
- Conclude with "Until finally" and reflect on the impact with "Ever since."

Prompt: Share a story about a personal or professional transformation where you learned something that continues to shape your perspective today.

Chapter 10

A Story Spine in Action – Frank's Case

A Case Study

Once Upon a Time

"Every story begins with a moment of connection—a chance to see the person behind the case."

Frank walked into my office, a father clinging to a thread of hope. He had made mistakes—mistakes he didn't deny—but he also had a love for his daughter, GG, that burned brighter than the judgment society placed on him. In his mind, he would always be her father, no matter what the outcome of his case. Sitting across from him, I realized I wasn't just representing a client in a parental termination case; I was stepping into a story about love, loss, and resilience.

These cases were always difficult, marred by addiction, mental health struggles, and a history of neglect. Judges often went with the better parent in termination proceedings, and I knew the odds weren't in Frank's favor. But his resolve to be seen and heard demanded something more than just a standard defense. It called for a story.

Every Day

"The ordinary struggles of everyday life often reveal the extraordinary strength within."

For Frank, life had been a series of uphill battles. Addiction and incarceration had derailed his ability to care for his daughter, and the court had little reason to believe in his capacity to change. But Frank didn't come to me asking for custody. He came to me wanting to maintain a connection with his daughter, to remain a part of her life in whatever way he could.

As he sat across the desk from me recounting his struggles and dreams, I knew that the usual approach wouldn't suffice. That's when I decided to try something different, drawing from the storytelling and psychodramatic techniques in my toolbox.

Until One Day

"Turning points are where we confront the truth, finding clarity amid chaos and conflict."

We began to recreate pivotal moments in Frank's life: the first time he met his daughter, the joy and awe of holding her in his arms, and some of the special times they had shared together. I asked Frank to step into his daughter's shoes and tell me her story, to see the world through her eyes. He became GG and showed me who she is and how she acts when they are together. Then, I asked him to become the adoptive parents—people he barely knew, but whose love for his daughter he respected.

Frank spoke as the adoptive parents, articulating their hopes for GG's future and their fears of allowing him to remain in GG's life, and then he spoke to them, thanking them for the care they provided while sharing his pain at the thought of losing her. When I pushed him to become the judge, he resisted. But with some gentle guidance and lots of support, he bravely became the person he saw as the villain, the person who had the power to take his precious daughter away.

Frank articulated the difficult decision he knew the court would make. In that moment, he found clarity—not just about the inevitability of the outcome but about the ways he could still show love and remain a presence in his daughter's life. Frank's pronouncement in the role of the judge was to terminate rights and not allow any type of visitation. While I hoped the judge would show some mercy and grant minimal visitation, I was also relieved, knowing that Frank was going to be able to handle whatever happened.

Because of That

"The choices we make in the face of challenges define the stories we leave behind."

When Frank and I entered the courtroom, we didn't have control over the outcome, but we did have a voice. In a bench trial, where openings are rarely allowed, the judge granted me five minutes to speak. I used that time to tell GG's story—not through direct evidence but through a narrative that highlighted the bond between father and daughter, a bond invisible to legal standards but one deeply felt by the people involved.

I shared the story of a little girl who saw her father as a giant, whose limited time with him still shaped her world, and whose love for him endured despite his flaws. This was not a plea for custody but a call for the court to see Frank as GG saw him—not as a man defined by his mistakes but as her father, inextricably linked to her identity.

Until Finally

"Resolution doesn't always mean victory, but it can bring understanding and dignity."

The judge ultimately terminated Frank's parental rights, a decision we both knew was likely from the beginning. But something profound had shifted. Frank left the courtroom not with victory but with a sense of dignity and understanding. He hugged me and thanked me, not for saving his rights but for giving him a vision of his daughter that would stay with him forever. For Frank, the process of telling his story allowed him to reclaim a part of himself, and for me, it was a moment that transformed the way I practiced law. From that day forward, I never conducted an intake interview sitting behind a desk again. Frank taught me the power of action.

And Ever Since Then

"Every story leaves a mark, shaping how we see ourselves and the world around us."

The lessons I learned from Frank's case have stayed with me. They taught me that storytelling isn't just a tool for persuasion; it's a way to honor the humanity at the heart of every case. Frank's story, and countless others like it, reminds me of the value of finding the human heart in my work. The courtroom is where I discovered that truth—not just for myself but for the clients I've had the privilege to represent. Through using the Story Spine and Psychodrama, I've learned that even in loss, there can be dignity, and even in silence, there is a voice waiting to be heard.

GG's STORY SPINE:

These are the words I spoke for Frank and GG in court that day. There wasn't a dry eye. And Frank felt heard and understood. Though he lost his parental rights, he knew he would always be GG's dad. His acceptance and grace in the face of such a great loss was inspiring. He taught me the meaning of bravery that day.

A story about a little girl and her dad:

Once Upon a Time:

When I was a little girl, my dad was a giant to me. He was the strongest, kindest, smartest, and best dad in the whole wide world. He didn't live with us, but he used to come by and see me sometimes. I didn't understand then, as a kid, why my mom always seemed to be mad at him. But I understand now, it's because kids and adults see things differently.

Every Day:

You see, my dad told me I was the most important thing in the world to him, and I believed him. He told me he loved me more than life itself. He said that I was his perfect work of art, and that I was the best thing he'd ever done; the only thing he'd ever done right. Sometimes, he would promise to come see me, and then he wouldn't show up, but I knew he must have had a good reason. My mom would get mad. She said he was a liar and couldn't be trusted. But even when he showed up late, I was so happy to see him. I was so glad he was there that I forgot all about him being late.

Until One Day:

My mom said he was no good and would never amount to nothing. I couldn't understand why she hated him so much, so I didn't tell her how much I loved him. I sometimes wondered if she hated me too, because I was a part of him. I now know that my mom just wanted what was best for me. She wanted my dad to be the man she knew he was capable of being. She wanted him to be responsible and reliable. She wanted him to help her and to provide financial support. Me, I just wanted him to be my dad, because kids see things differently.

Because of That:

Throughout my life, my dad never came around much, but the times when he did are some of my best memories. I always wanted to see him no matter how long he had been gone. My time with him, as limited as it was, helped shape me into the person I am today.

Until Finally:

As I grew older, I came to understand that kids and adults see things differently. My mom's anger was born out of hope and disappointment. My dad, despite his failings in society's eyes, gave me something priceless—the belief that I was loved, special, and worthy.

And Ever Since Then:

Though my dad never lived up to society's standards, he remains a giant to me. Those fleeting moments with him, however imperfect, helped make me who I am today. Kids see things differently, and that perspective taught me how to hold onto love even when life gets hard.

If GG were here today, this is what she might say to you. It is in this vein, Your Honor, that I am asking you to protect GG's rights and allow her to keep her relationship with her dad. We are not asking for custody. We are just asking to continue the relationship because kids see things differently.

Reflecting on Connection and Empathy

Frank's case taught me that the power of storytelling lies not in its ability to win every battle but in its capacity to create understanding and connection. Through psychodrama and the Story Spine, Frank found a way to express his love for GG, his gratitude to her adoptive parents, and even his acceptance of the court's decision.

The court may have ruled against Frank, but the process gave him something no verdict could take away—a voice. GG's story was told, Frank's love was validated, and an emotional bridge was built between him and those who now care for his daughter. We ordered the transcripts of the hearing for Frank so that he would have a permanent record showing that he fought for his little girl. This case was a reminder that storytelling is as much about healing as it is about advocacy.

The Power of Giving a Voice

Frank's story revealed the transformative power of giving someone a voice, especially in situations where they feel powerless. By stepping into the roles of GG, the adoptive parents, and the judge, Frank was able to articulate emotions he hadn't yet processed and see perspectives he hadn't considered. The act of storytelling didn't just prepare him for court—it prepared him for life after the trial, giving him the tools to move forward with clarity and purpose. And in telling GG's story, we gave the court a glimpse of her voice, even though she wasn't physically there to speak.

This case reminded me that vulnerability is not a weakness; it's a powerful tool for connection. When Frank shared his love, fears, and regrets, it was raw and imperfect, but it was also deeply human. That authenticity struck a chord with everyone in the courtroom, including the judge. Even though the outcome wasn't what we hoped for, the process of telling the story allowed everyone involved to see Frank not just as a "defendant" but as a father and a person. It's a lesson I carry with me: that the courage to be vulnerable can transform even the most difficult narratives.

The Imperfect but Necessary Resolution

Not every story ends the way we wish, but that doesn't mean it lacks meaning or impact. Frank's parental rights were terminated, but his story didn't end there. He left the courtroom not as a defeated man but as a father who had spoken his truth and fought for his daughter's voice to be heard. GG's story lives on, not just in that courtroom but in the hearts of everyone who heard it. The resolution was bittersweet, but it was a resolution nonetheless—one that allowed Frank to continue loving his daughter, even from a distance.

Frank's case is more than one man's struggle; it's a testament to the broader power of storytelling in law and life. It shows that even in the face of seemingly insurmountable odds, stories can illuminate truths, foster empathy, and pave the way for healing. Frank's journey and GG's story were not just legal arguments; they were human experiences that brought clarity and connection to an otherwise dry procedural process. This case reinforces why I use and teach the Story Spine: because it transforms facts into narratives that matter, allowing justice to be seen through the lens of humanity.

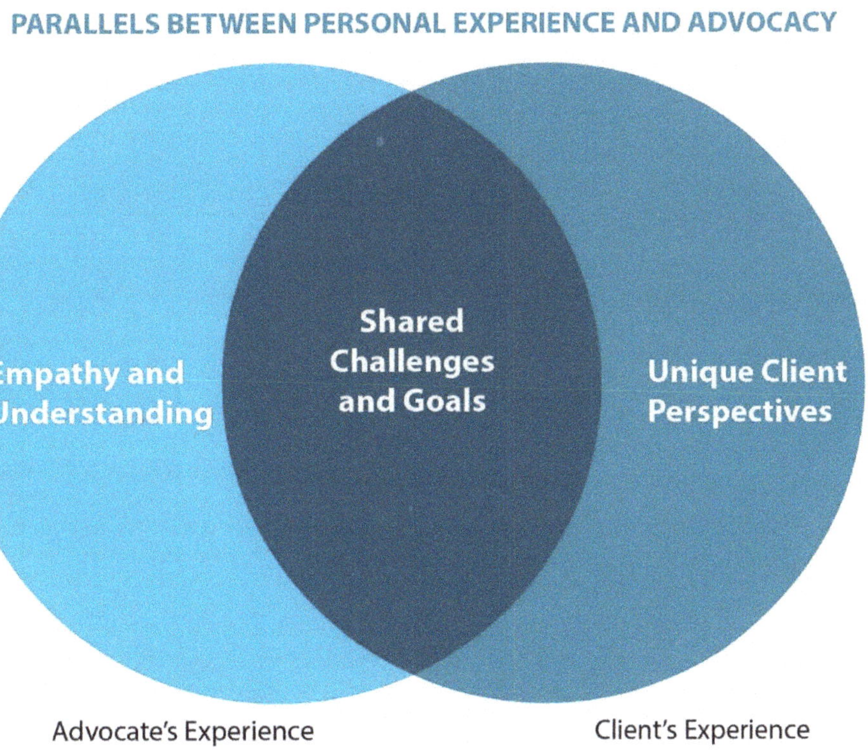

Figure 22: Parallels Between Personal Experience and Advocacy

PRACTICE SPINES

1. Role Reversal Exercise

Objective: Build empathy and uncover new perspectives by stepping into the roles of different stakeholders in a case.

Instructions:

1. Choose a case you're working on and identify the key stakeholders (e.g., your client, the opposing party, the judge, a juror, or a third party impacted by the case).
2. Assume the role of one stakeholder and describe the events from their perspective. Use first-person language to articulate their thoughts, feelings, and motivations.
3. Switch roles and repeat the exercise with a new perspective.
4. Reflect on how this exercise changes your understanding of the case or influences how you would tell the story in court.

Impact: This exercise deepens your ability to see all sides of a story, making your narrative more nuanced and relatable.

2. Personal Story Spine Mapping

Objective: Connect emotionally with the case by creating a personal story spine that parallels your client's journey.

Instructions:

1. Think about a personal experience where you felt powerless or had to advocate for something important to you.
2. Write your story using the Story Spine structure: "Once upon a time," "Every day," "Until one day," and so on.

3. Identify parallels between your story and your client's experience (e.g., shared emotions, struggles, or resolutions).
4. Use these insights to craft a more empathetic and compelling narrative for your client's case.

Impact: This exercise helps you connect emotionally with your client's journey, making their story more authentic and heartfelt.

3. Visualizing the Stakes

Objective: Clarify the stakes of a case by visually mapping out the story's emotional and factual elements.

Instructions:

1. Create a chart with three columns: Facts, Emotions, and Stakeholders.
2. For each key event in the case, write down:
   - The facts (what happened).
   - The emotions involved (how people felt or reacted).
   - The stakeholders affected (who is impacted and how).
3. Review your chart and pinpoint the elements that will have the strongest impact on your audience. Use this visual tool to refine your Story Spine, ensuring it emphasizes the stakes that matter most.

Impact: This exercise ensures your story balances factual clarity with emotional resonance, creating a compelling and complete narrative.

Chapter 11
Using Psychodrama to Bring Story Spines to Life

"Psychodrama transforms storytelling into an experience, where the audience doesn't just hear the story—they feel it."

Breathing Life Into Stories

I first encountered the transformative power of psychodrama at the Trial Lawyers College, founded by the legendary Gerry Spence. It was there that I began to understand the profound connection between storytelling, empathy, and advocacy. Through Gerry's vision and the College's innovative approach, I learned how psychodrama could unlock deeper truths, not only in the stories we tell as lawyers but also in the lives of those we represent.

Gerry's groundbreaking work has forever changed the way lawyers connect with their clients, their juries, and even themselves. His passion for justice and his commitment to teaching generations of advocates have left an enduring legacy, and for that, I am deeply grateful. Thank you, Gerry Spence!

My first personal psychodrama was at Thunderhead Ranch, in the Johnson Barn, with the esteemed Don Clarkson as my director. Don was a skilled guide able to take anyone into the most devastating stories and help them create better ones. I cried as I told Don that my mother didn't love me, and he showed me, powerfully, in action that she did, scene after scene, in the only way she knew how. I was forever changed that day.

John Johnson, John Ackerman, Don Clarkson, and perhaps some unnamed others, were all there with Gerry when he first began experimenting with psychodrama and lawyering. Since then, thousands of lawyers have been trained how to represent people using these methods.

Psychodrama is where storytelling meets action. This experiential technique invites participants to step into the shoes of characters, dramatize pivotal moments, and explore emotional conflicts in a safe, supportive environment. Think of it as storytelling in 3D—it takes the abstract and makes it tangible, turning narratives into dynamic, living experiences. When paired with the Story Spine framework, psychodrama takes your narrative to the next level. Suddenly, "Once upon a time" isn't just words; it's a moment you step into, see, and *feel.* This powerful blend makes stories more authentic, more emotional, and pretty unforgettable.

The Roots of Psychodrama: A Journey of Creativity and Connection

Psychodrama was born from the genius and heart of Dr. Jacob L. Moreno, a psychiatrist and sociologist, and his wife and collaborator, Zerka T. Moreno. In the early 20th century, they saw the transformative power of stepping into a role—how spontaneity and creativity could unlock emotions, solutions, and even healing.

Jacob Moreno believed that dramatic enactment wasn't just play-acting; it was a pathway to discovery and connection. Zerka Moreno added structure and refinement, ensuring that psychodrama wasn't just a burst of creativity but a methodical tool for exploring inner conflicts, relationships, and growth. Together, they created a practice that brings stories to life in ways that words alone never could.

Life Lessons: Using Psychodrama to Bring Story Spines to Life

Once upon a time...I was leading a focus group for a particularly emotional case. My client had been wronged, but they struggled to articulate their story, their emotions buried under years of frustration and pain.

Every day... Clients like this walk into courtrooms, their truths muted by the weight of their experiences. Lawyers often fail to tap into the raw, emotional heart of a case, relying instead on logic that doesn't reach the audience's core.

Until one day... I introduced a psychodrama exercise, asking my client to step into the shoes of their opponent. At first hesitant, they soon spoke with startling vulnerability. The shift was transformative—not only did they unlock their own feelings, but the legal team gained a richer understanding of the case's emotional resonance.

Because of that... The narrative we crafted was layered with authenticity, its emotional power undeniable. The courtroom became a stage for human connection, not just legal argument.

And ever since that day... I've used psychodrama to bring stories to life, guiding clients and lawyers alike to uncover truths that change the course of their cases—and their lives.

Psychodrama as a Catalyst for Discovery

Psychodrama doesn't just make your story better—it makes you a better storyteller. By stepping into the roles of different characters, you gain new perspectives and uncover hidden emotions that enrich the narrative. You feel the stakes, the struggles, and the triumphs, giving your story a depth that connects with audiences on a whole new level.

Imagine reenacting a pivotal moment in a courtroom case. You're not just describing a defendant's hardship—you *are* them, standing in their shoes, experiencing their emotions. Or picture stepping into the role of a juror, understanding firsthand what might persuade or alienate them. This isn't just storytelling; it's transformation.

For lawyers, psychodrama can uncover the human truth at the heart of a case, making arguments more compelling and relatable. For personal storytellers, it reveals layers of growth and resilience that might otherwise stay hidden. In either case, psychodrama isn't just a tool—it's a revelation.

Psychodrama brings the Story Spine to life, creating stories that don't just tell but *show,* don't just explain but *immerse.* It turns "Until one day" into a moment you can feel in your bones and "Because of that" into a ripple of emotions you can see unfold.

Here's how they work together:

1. **Start with the Spine:** Lay out your narrative arc—who, what, when, and where.
2. **Step Into the Scene:** Use psychodrama to embody the characters, actions, and conflicts.
3. **Discover Hidden Layers:** Let the enactment reveal emotions, insights, and angles you might have missed.
4. **Refine and Elevate:** Integrate what you've learned back into your Story Spine, turning a good story into a great one.

The beauty of psychodrama is that it's not just about the story; it's about what the story *does.* It connects people to their own emotions, fosters empathy, and inspires action. Psychodrama gives you the tools to make your narrative not just heard but deeply *felt.*

Psychodrama and Collective Storytelling

One of the most exciting aspects of psychodrama is how it turns storytelling into a team sport. In a group setting, participants step into different roles, bringing fresh viewpoints and unexpected emotions to the surface. This collective effort creates a richer, more nuanced narrative, one that leaves a lasting impact on everyone involved.

Picture this: a legal team gearing up for trial gathers to reenact the case using psychodrama. One person becomes the defendant, embodying their fears and frustrations. Another steps into the shoes of the jury, exploring what might sway their perspective. Someone else takes on the role of the opposing counsel, sharpening the arguments they'll face. Together, they uncover blind spots, deepen their understanding, and craft a story that feels authentic from every angle.

By blending individual insights with collective creativity, psychodrama helps build stories that aren't just compelling but profoundly empathetic. It's a way of saying, "Let's see this through *every* lens," ensuring the final narrative is as informed and as human as possible.

A Personal Story Spine

Once upon a time, I was a lawyer doing my best to connect with clients and their stories, but something always felt out of reach. I believed in the power of storytelling—of weaving facts into a narrative that could move hearts and minds—but there was a spark missing. My stories were clear, logical, and polished, but they lacked that emotional authenticity that could truly resonate with juries and judges.

Every day, I poured over facts, honed strategies, and polished arguments, presenting cases that were solid and professional. But deep down, I knew something wasn't clicking. The stories weren't landing the way I wanted them to. It felt like the heart of the matter—the raw, human truth—kept slipping through my fingers.

Until one day, everything changed. I attended a workshop on psychodrama, and they asked me to do something I'd never even considered before: act out a pivotal moment from a case I was working on. I stepped into the shoes of my client, a father fighting to hold on to visitation rights with his daughter. At first, it felt awkward and a little silly. But as I allowed myself to *become* him, his emotions hit me like a wave—his guilt, his fear, his desperation, and above all, his fierce love for his daughter. For the first time, I wasn't just hearing his story—I was living it.

Because of that, I discovered the transformative power of stepping into someone else's experience. It wasn't about understanding from a distance—it was about feeling their reality as if it were my own. I began incorporating psychodrama into my work, asking clients to act out pivotal moments in their lives. The results were nothing short of astounding. Clients who struggled to put their emotions into words found their voices. Painful moments became stepping-stones to clarity. Stories I had only skimmed the surface of suddenly became rich, layered, and profoundly human.

Until finally, I saw how these enacted stories transformed the courtroom. My clients weren't just names on a docket—they became real people to the jurors. Stories that once felt clinical or detached now had the depth to make jurors lean in, *feel* what my clients felt, and connect to the heart of the case. The difference wasn't just noticeable—it was undeniable.

And ever since then, psychodrama has been a cornerstone of my storytelling. It's not just a tool; it's a way to honor the humanity in every story and to ensure that it's told with heart and authenticity. Psychodrama taught me that the most powerful stories aren't just told—they're lived. And when stories are lived, they have the power to change everything: minds, decisions, and lives.

Now, every time I walk into a courtroom, I carry that lesson with me. Stories have to be more than compelling—they have to be *experienced.* And psychodrama has given me the way to make that happen.

The Future of Storytelling with Psychodrama

As storytelling evolves, psychodrama and the Story Spine stand ready to take it to new heights. In courtrooms, this dynamic duo offers endless possibilities for crafting stories that persuade and inspire. Imagine a courtroom argument that doesn't just present facts but immerses the jury in the defendant's experience.

This is the future of storytelling: blending structure with action, logic with emotion, and thought with movement. Psychodrama transforms storytelling from something static and dead on the page into something alive—a living, breathing experience that leaves a mark.

Psychodrama Core Elements

- **The Stage:** A physical or imagined space where the action takes place. This could be a courtroom, a home, or even a metaphorical location like "justice" or "forgiveness."
- **The Protagonist:** The central figure whose story is being explored. In a legal context, this might be the client, a witness, or even a concept like a legal rule.
- **The Director:** The facilitator guiding the action. The director helps shape the scene, encouraging spontaneity while maintaining focus on the story's goals.
- **The Auxiliary Ego:** Supporting players who represent other people, concepts, or forces in the protagonist's story. They might play roles like opposing counsel, a witness, or the protagonist's inner doubts.
- **The Audience:** Observers who witness the enactment. Their role is to provide feedback and offer new perspectives.

Psychodrama Techniques to Enhance Story Spines

Role Reversal:

- Step into the shoes of key players (e.g., opposing counsel, witnesses, jury) to understand their motivations and reactions.

Doubling:

- A participant mirrors the protagonist, voicing their unspoken thoughts or emotions to uncover hidden layers of the story.

Hot Seating:

- A participant embodies a single character (or entity) and answers questions or responds to prompts while staying fully in that role. The focus is on exploring the character's internal world, motivations, and emotional state.

Timeline Exploration:

- Enact each line in the Story Spine sequentially, from "Once upon a time" to "And ever since then," to refine the narrative's flow.

Future Projection:

- Looking to the future, enact the "And ever since then" moment to explore the long-term impact of the resolution and test its authenticity.

Benefits of Combining Psychodrama and Story Spine

- **Authenticity:** Psychodrama ensures that narratives feel real, grounded, and emotionally resonant.
- **Empathy:** Role reversals foster understanding of opposing perspectives, enriching the story's complexity.
- **Emotional Resonance:** Acting out pivotal moments reveals the emotional stakes, helping to connect with audiences on a deeper level.
- **Clarity and Insight:** Exploring the Story Spine through Psychodrama uncovers details and perspectives that static storytelling might miss.

A War Story: Uncovering Hidden Truths Through Role-Playing

I'll never forget the moment I first used psychodrama to prepare for a case. It was a complex personal injury case involving a mother who had lost her son. I invited the mother to step into her son's shoes and show me who he was. Initially, she was hesitant, but as she began speaking from her son's perspective, the room became electric.

Details she hadn't shared before started pouring out—small moments of joy, fear, and connection that painted a fuller picture of her son's life and the depth of her loss. That session not only transformed our case strategy, it also deepened my understanding of how psychodrama can reveal truths hidden beneath the surface. The process wasn't just about crafting a stronger narrative; it was about honoring the emotional core of a mother's story.

Conclusion

"When Story Spine meets psychodrama, storytelling isn't just something you hear—it's something you feel, live, and carry with you."

Psychodrama and the Story Spine are like peanut butter and jelly—a natural pairing that brings out the best in each other. The Story Spine gives your narrative a solid backbone, while psychodrama breathes life into it, turning abstract ideas into vivid, emotional experiences. Together, they create stories that aren't just told but lived, offering layers of complexity, depth, and authenticity that stay with your audience for a long time.

Bringing psychodrama to the party adds a creative touch that ensures your story hits a home run. It moves beyond facts and figures, straight to the heart of the matter, creating connections that inspire and transform. So, go ahead—pair your Story Spine with a little psychodrama. Step into the story, let it breathe, and watch, as your narratives come alive in ways you never imagined.

Fig 23: Steps in Psychodrama-Based Story Development

PRACTICE SPINES

Role Reversal Exercise

- **Objective:** Develop empathy and uncover hidden perspectives by stepping into different roles within a story.
- **Instructions:**
  1. Choose a story you're working on, such as a case narrative or a personal anecdote.
  2. Identify key roles in the story (e.g., Hero, Villain, Mentor, Ally).
  3. Act out a scene from the perspective of each role. For instance, if you're working on a courtroom story, become the client, the opposing counsel, and the judge.
  4. Pay attention to how each role views the conflict, their motivations, and their emotions.
- **Reflection:** How did this exercise change your understanding of the story? Did new emotions or insights emerge? Discuss how these perspectives can add depth to your narrative.

2. Scene Reconstruction with Emotional Layers

- **Objective:** Use psychodrama to recreate pivotal moments and uncover the emotional depth of the story.
- **Instructions:**
  1. Select a critical moment from your story, such as the "Until one day" or "Because of that" phase in the Story Spine.
  2. Act out the scene, focusing on the physical actions, dialogue, and emotional undercurrents of the moment.

3. After the initial reenactment, replay the scene while amplifying specific emotions (e.g., fear, anger, hope). Experiment with different interpretations of the same event.

4. Explore how the emotional tone shifts the meaning of the scene and its impact on the overall story.

- **Reflection:** Write down or discuss how the emotional variations influence the audience's connection to the story and its central characters.

3. The Inner Monologue Exercise

- **Objective:** Reveal internal conflicts and deepen the psychological complexity of a character or story.

- **Instructions:**

  1. Choose a character from your story, such as the Hero or Villain.

  2. Act out a pivotal scene, but instead of verbal dialogue, focus on the character's inner monologue. Speak aloud their thoughts, fears, and motivations as the scene unfolds.

  3. Replay the scene with another character's inner monologue to compare perspectives.

  4. Use this insight to refine how these roles interact within the story.

- **Reflection:** How does revealing the internal monologue change the way you view the character's actions? Incorporate this depth into the final narrative to create a more compelling story.

Chapter 12
Combining Story Spine and Dramatic Construction Game

"What happens when two storytelling giants team up? You get narratives that aren't just told—they explode with life."

Merging Frameworks for Maximum Impact

Imagine taking your favorite recipe and adding an unexpected but perfect ingredient—like a pinch of cinnamon to a savory dish. That's what happens when you combine the **Story Spine** and the **Dramatic Construction Game**. These two narrative frameworks, each a masterclass in storytelling on its own, come together to create stories packed with tension, emotion, and resolutions that nail the landing.

Here's the breakdown:

The **Dramatic Construction Game** is all about ratcheting up conflict and exploring complications before delivering a resolution. It's like the daredevil cousin of the Story Spine, nudging you to dig deeper into the messiness before cleaning it all up.

Here's how it works:

1. **Once upon a time there was a... who...**
2. **Then one day it happened that...**
3. **The problem was, however, that...**
4. **And the complication was that...**

5. **The consequence was that...**
6. **And so it came to the point that...**
7. **Then at last... And, forever** after...

Meanwhile, the **Story Spine** is your trusty roadmap:

1. Once upon **a time...**
2. **Every day...**
3. **But one day...**
4. **Because of that... (as many times as needed)**
5. **Until finally...**
6. **And ever since then...**
7. **And the moral** of the story is...

The Power of a Partnership

Picture this: the **Story Spine** sets the stage, establishes the norm, and guides your narrative to its destination. But along the way, the **Dramatic Construction Game** steps in like an instigator, whispering, "Sure, but what *really* went wrong?" It's the push your story needs to face its darkest moments before emerging into the light.

Example: A Legal Case in Action

- **Story Spine Opening:**

  "Once upon a time, a small-town doctor served her patients with care and kindness. Every day, she worked tirelessly to provide the best treatments. But one day, a series of supply-chain failures left her clinic unable to access crucial medications..."

- **Dramatic Construction Layer:**

"The problem was, however, that these failures weren't just bad luck—they were due to the negligence of a supplier. And the complication was that the supplier blamed the issue on unrelated circumstances, creating a tangled web of accountability."

- **Back to the Story Spine:**

  "Because of that, the doctor's patients suffered, and their community began to lose trust in the clinic. Until finally, the case reached the courtroom, where justice could be served."

By weaving these two frameworks together, you get a narrative that is as structured as it is emotionally gripping, leaving no stone—or complication—unturned. Merging the **Story Spine** and **Dramatic Construction Game** will elevate your storytelling game to new heights.

A Dynamic Duo for Deep, Engaging Stories

The Story Spine asks, "What happens next?" The Dramatic Construction Game counters with, "But what went wrong first?" It's the perfect storytelling partnership—one keeps you grounded, and the other keeps you on your toes.

The Dramatic Construction Game excels at teasing out conflict. Where the Story Spine introduces a single pivotal moment with its "Until one day" step, the Dramatic Construction Game insists on digging deeper:

- "The problem was, however, that…"
- "And the complication was that…"

In practice, these prompts add layers that ramp up the emotional stakes.

Example: A Courtroom Drama

- **Story Spine:** *"Until one day, a key witness refused to testify."*

- **Dramatic Construction Layer:** *"The problem was, however, that this witness held the evidence to exonerate the defendant. And* the complication was that new evidence emerged, further casting doubt on the defendant's alibi."

By piling on these hurdles, you craft a story that keeps the audience on the edge of their seats, wondering how the resolution will unfold.

Resolutions That Land with Impact

Both frameworks shine when it's time to wrap things up. The Story Spine's **"Until finally"** pairs seamlessly with the Dramatic Construction Game's **"And so it came to the point that..."** to connect every twist and turn to the ultimate resolution.

Example: From Challenge to Triumph

In a personal injury case:

- **Dramatic Construction Game:** *"The complication was that physical therapy was grueling, and the plaintiff faced mounting financial struggles."*
- **Story Spine:** *"Until finally, the jury delivered a verdict that acknowledged the plaintiff's perseverance, awarding them the means to rebuild their life. And ever since then, they've been an advocate for others facing similar challenges."*

This layered approach ensures that the resolution isn't just satisfying—it feels earned.

Balancing Structure and Complexity

Merging the Story Spine and Dramatic Construction Game is like pairing a sturdy skeleton with rich, textured skin. The Story Spine ensures logical progression, while the Dramatic Construction Game provides the emotional and narrative meat.

Example: A Family Law Case

- **Story Spine:** *"Once upon a time, a parent fought to maintain custody of their child."*
- **Dramatic Construction Game:** *"The complication was that their past addiction had strained their relationship. The consequence was that they entered recovery and began rebuilding trust."*

The result? A narrative that flows seamlessly while also delving into the emotional depths that make the story unforgettable.

A War Story: Building Layers with Collaborative Tools

In one challenging trial, I struggled to convey the complexity of my client's experience. Their story had so many moving parts that I feared the jury would lose focus. That's when I combined the Story Spine with the Dramatic Construction Game. I invited my team to participate, assigning roles and brainstorming scenes to clarify the story's pivotal moments.

Using the Story Spine, we outlined the core narrative, and with the Dramatic Construction Game, we layered in emotional beats and turning points. The result was a multidimensional story that captured both the factual timeline and the emotional undercurrent of my client's journey. This exercise not only strengthened our case but also taught me the power of blending frameworks to create narratives that resonate on every level.

Conclusion

"With the Story Spine and Dramatic Construction Game as your allies, no case is just a case—it's a story worth telling."

By integrating the Story Spine's clarity and flow with the Dramatic Construction Game's focus on conflict and consequences, lawyers can create narratives that are timeless. Together, these frameworks turn complex cases into compelling stories that engage both the emotions and the logic of judges, juries, and clients.

INTEGRATING TWO FRAMEWORKS

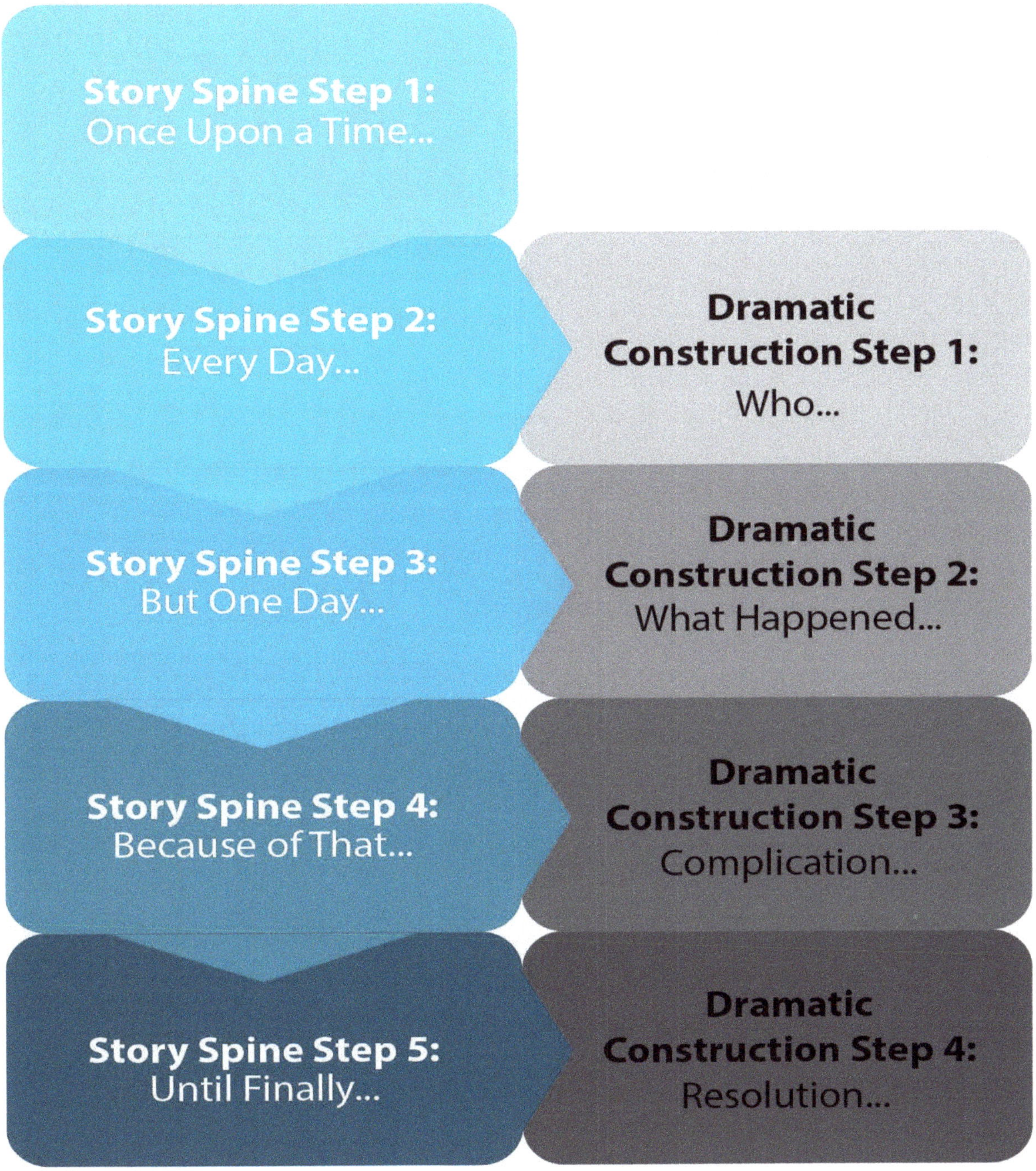

Figure 24: Integrating Two Frameworks – Story Spine and Dramatic Construction

Steps to Integrate the Frameworks

1. Start with Story Spine:

- Use the spine's straightforward prompts to outline the core narrative.
- Ensure the story is logical and causal, with each event naturally leading to the next.

2. Layer in Conflict and Complications:

- From the Dramatic Construction Game, add "The problem was..." and "The complication was..." to introduce deeper layers of conflict.

3. Balance Consequences and Turning Points:

- Use "Because of that" (from the Story Spine) to show the cascading effects of events, while "The consequence was..." (from the Dramatic Construction Game) adds emotional weight.

4. Conclude with Resolution and Reflection:

- Combine "Until finally..." and "Then at last..." for a climactic resolution and follow with "And ever since then..." and "Forever after..." to explore both immediate and long-term impacts.

5. Weave Emotional and Logical Elements:

- The Story Spine's logical structure supports factual arguments, while the Dramatic Construction Game's focus on complications ensures emotional engagement.

Examples of Integration in Different Areas of Law

1. Personal Injury Law: Maria's Fight for Justice

Context: A factory worker sues for negligence after a workplace accident caused by poor safety measures.

Integrated Narrative:

- **Once upon a time... (Story Spine)**

  "Once upon a time, Maria was a dedicated factory worker who relied on her job to support her family."

- **Every day... (Story Spine)**

  "Every day, she worked with heavy machinery, trusting her employer to maintain safe equipment."

- **But one day... (Story Spine)**

  "But one day, a poorly maintained machine malfunctioned, crushing her hand."

- **The problem was, however, that... (Dramatic Construction Game)**

  "The problem was, however, that Maria had reported the faulty machine months earlier, and nothing was done."

- **And the complication was that... (Dramatic Construction Game)**

  "And the complication was that the company tried to blame Maria, claiming she had operated the machine incorrectly."

- **Because of that... (Story Spine)**

  "Because of that, Maria was unable to work, faced mounting medical bills, and struggled to provide for her children."

- **The consequence was that... (Dramatic Construction Game)**

  "The consequence was that Maria fell into debt and faced eviction from her home."

- **Until finally... (Story Spine)**

  "Until finally, Maria filed a lawsuit, seeking justice and compensation for her losses."

- **Then at last... And forever after... (Dramatic Construction Game)**

  "Then at last, Maria won her case, and forever after, the company was required to implement strict safety protocols to prevent future accidents."

The Story Spine keeps the narrative laser-focused, while the Dramatic Construction Game piles on emotional tension, exposing the company's negligence with undeniable clarity.

2. Family Law: Lily's Journey to Stability

Context: A custody dispute where one parent claims the other is unfit to care for the child.

Integrated Narrative:

- **Once upon a time... (Story Spine)**

  "Once upon a time, Lily's parents shared custody and cooperated for her well-being."

- **Every day... (Story Spine)**

  "Every day, Lily thrived in a routine of love and stability, spending equal time with both parents."

- **But one day... (Story Spine)**

  "But one day, her father began missing scheduled visits without explanation."

- **The problem was, however, that... (Dramatic Construction Game)**

  "The problem was, however, that Lily's father had a history of substance abuse, which began to resurface."

- **And the complication was that... (Dramatic Construction Game)**

  "And the complication was that Lily's father refused to acknowledge his behavior, leaving her mother to pick up the pieces."

- **Because of that... (Story Spine)**

  "Because of that, Lily began to feel abandoned and anxious, struggling to trust her father."

- **The consequence was that... (Dramatic Construction Game)**

  "The consequence was that Lily's school performance suffered, and she began seeing a therapist for emotional distress."

- **Until finally... (Story Spine)**

  "Until finally, her mother petitioned the court for sole custody, supported by evidence of her father's relapse."

- **Then at last... And forever after... (Dramatic Construction Game)**

  "Then at last, the court granted custody to her mother, and forever after, Lily has lived in a stable, loving environment where she can heal."

The Story Spine lays out the foundation, while the Dramatic Construction Game hones in on emotional and psychological stakes, bringing Lily's struggle vividly to life.

3. Criminal Law: Michael's Redemption

Context: A defendant faces charges for theft, claiming they were falsely accused.

Integrated Narrative:

- **Once upon a time... (Story Spine)**

  "Once upon a time, Michael worked hard to support his family, earning an honest living as a store clerk."

- **Every day... (Story Spine)**

  "Every day, he followed the store's procedures and ensured every dollar was accounted for."

- **But one day... (Story Spine)**

  "But one day, Michael was accused of stealing cash after a discrepancy appeared in the register."

- **The problem was, however, that... (Dramatic Construction Game)**

  "The problem was, however, that another employee had manipulated the records to cover up their own theft."

- **And the complication was that... (Dramatic Construction Game)**

  "And the complication was that Michael's manager, eager to protect the store's reputation, refused to investigate further."

- **Because of that... (Story Spine)**

  "Because of that, Michael was fired, humiliated, and charged with theft."

- **The consequence was that... (Dramatic Construction Game)**

  "The consequence was that Michael's reputation was destroyed, and his family struggled financially."

- **Until finally... (Story Spine)**

  "Until finally, evidence surfaced proving Michael's innocence, implicating the real thief."

- **Then at last... And forever after... (Dramatic Construction Game)**

  "Then at last, the charges were dropped, and forever after, Michael fought to rebuild his life and clear his name."

The Story Spine provides the backbone, while the Dramatic Construction Game injects tension and drama, exposing the flaws in the system that led to Michael's ordeal.

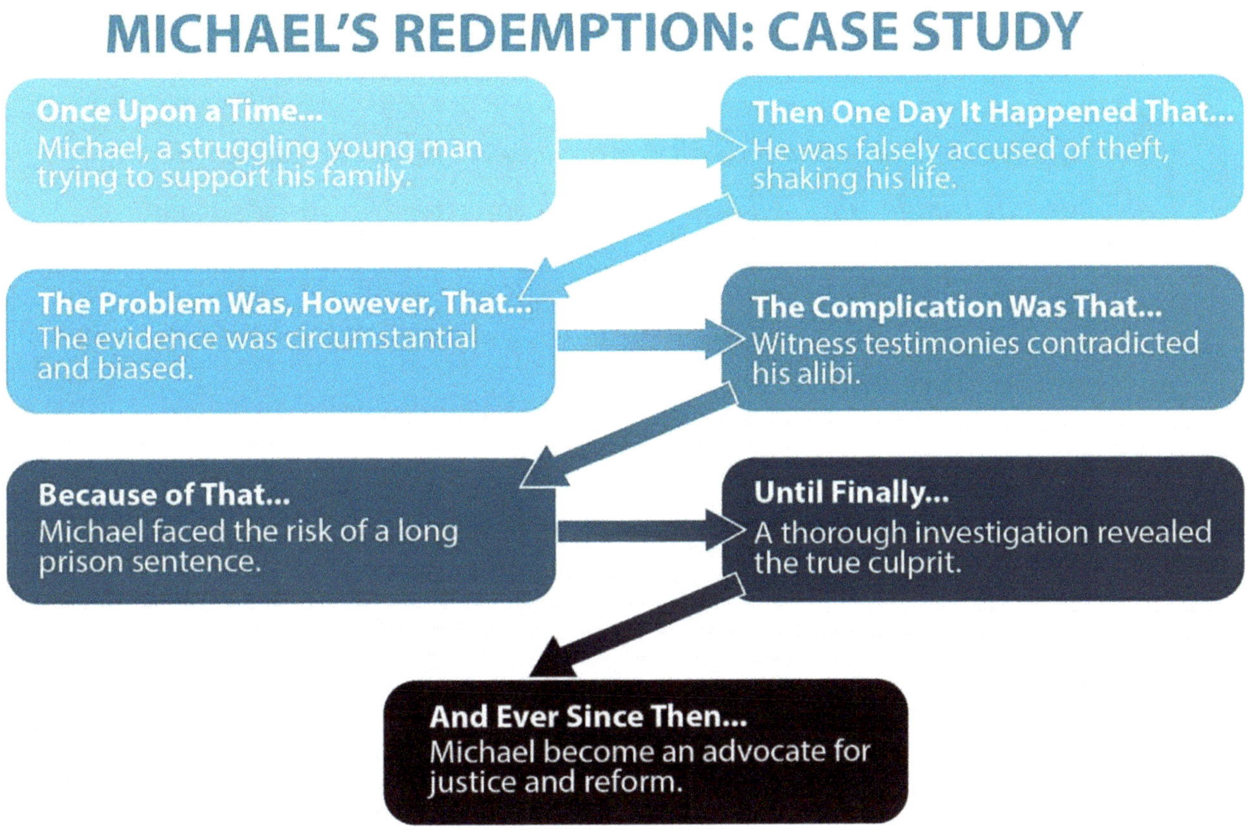

Figure 25: Michael's Redemption: Case Study

Chapter 13
Adding Another Line to the Story Spine

"The moral of the story isn't just the bow on the package—it's the gift inside that stays with you long after the story's been told."

The Moral of the Story: More Than a Line

The final flourish of the Story Spine—"And the moral of the story is..."—elevates a narrative from a series of events to a timeless lesson. It's the moment where your story stops being just *your* story and starts being *our* story. This line invites reflection, distilling the narrative into a clear, resonant takeaway that stays in the minds of your audience. For instance, in a courtroom, a lawyer might close with, "And the moral of the story is that justice isn't just about the law—it's about accountability for all." With one line, the narrative shifts from facts to values, leaving the jury with an idea that transcends the specifics of the case.

The moral of the story serves as a bridge between the storyteller and the audience, transforming a story from something heard to something felt. It's the key that unlocks the universal truths within a narrative, making them applicable to everyone. Imagine a manager recounting a challenging project, concluding with, "And the moral of the story is that obstacles are just opportunities in disguise." That single sentence ties the team's struggles to a broader truth, inspiring listeners to reframe their own challenges. The moral of the story doesn't just summarize—it empowers.

Finding Clarity in Complexity

Let's face it: life, like storytelling, can get messy. With twists, turns, and tangled emotions, a story can leave the audience feeling like they're caught in a whirlwind. That's where the moral steps in, offering clarity and focus. For example, in a narrative about perseverance, the storyteller might end with, "And the moral of the story is that every step forward counts, no matter how small." It's a neat little knot that ties the narrative together, ensuring the audience walks away with the essence of the story—even if they forget the details.

For the storyteller, this process is equally transformative. Crafting the moral forces you to reflect on what the story means to *you*. In doing so, you might uncover lessons you didn't realize were there, giving your narrative even greater depth.

Universal Truths and Shared Humanity

When you add the moral of the story, you're tapping into something bigger than the narrative itself: shared humanity. The moral is what connects your specific experience to universal themes like love, justice, resilience, or hope.

Imagine a lawyer wrapping up a closing argument with, "And the moral of the story is that everyone deserves a fair chance, no matter where they come from." That's not just a line—it's an invitation for the audience to reflect on their own values and beliefs.

The moral transforms a personal anecdote into a communal experience, bridging the gap between the storyteller's world and the audience's. It's the moment where your listeners see themselves in your story, forging a connection that's both emotional and intellectual.

The Moral as a Call to Action

A good moral doesn't just make you think—it makes you *do*. By distilling your narrative into a single, powerful idea, you can inspire your audience to act. For instance, a leader recounting a tough period for their company might say, "And the moral of the story is that resilience isn't built in the good times—it's forged in the fire." This isn't just a wrap-up; it's a challenge to the audience to see their own struggles as opportunities for growth. The moral becomes a catalyst for transformation, pushing the audience to think critically about their choices and possibilities. It turns the story from a passive experience into a spark for action.

When you add the moral to your Story Spine, you're doing more than closing the loop—you're opening the door to deeper connections and greater meaning. It's the line that elevates your story from memorable to transformative, ensuring that your audience doesn't just remember what happened but why it mattered. So, go ahead—tie that moral to your story. Make it resonant. Make it linger. Make it matter. Because the best stories don't end; they echo.

Transforming Stories into Legacy

When a story concludes with its moral, it shifts from being a fleeting moment to a lasting legacy. That single line encapsulates the wisdom gained, ensuring the story lives on as a beacon for others. Imagine a lawyer reflecting on a tough case: *"And the moral of the story is that justice isn't about winning—it's about standing up for what's right."*

With that one sentence, the narrative transforms. It's no longer just a recounting of events—it becomes a compass, guiding future decisions and inspiring those who hear it. By adding a moral, storytellers don't just entertain or inform; they create a ripple effect, shaping how others think, feel, and act long after the last word is spoken.

Where the Extra Line Fits in the Flow

Adding the moral to your Story Spine is like putting the cherry on top of an already delicious sundae. Here's how it fits:

1. **The first seven lines**—from "Once upon a time" to "Ever since then"—take the audience through the logical and emotional progression of the story.

2. **The eighth line, "And the moral of the story is…"** answers the deeper question: *"Why does this story matter?"*
3. By clearly articulating the moral, you leave a lasting imprint, ensuring the story stays with the audience well beyond its conclusion.

Why It Matters

A story without a moral is like a map with no destination—it might be an enjoyable ride, but it doesn't get you anywhere meaningful. The moral of the story is your chance to make a lasting impression, ensuring your audience doesn't just hear your story but *feels its significance.*

So, always ask yourself: *What do I want my audience to take away?* That's your moral. Deliver it with purpose, and you'll transform your stories into legacies that endure far beyond the moment. A great story doesn't just stay with people—it transforms them.

A War Story:
Deepening a Narrative Through Parallel Perspectives

During a trial involving a car accident, I realized that the Story Spine alone wasn't enough to convey the full depth of the story. While my client's perspective was clear, the other driver's actions seemed almost robotic—without motive or context. I decided to add another line to the narrative by exploring the perspective of the other driver.

Through research and deposition testimony, we uncovered their financial struggles, which contributed to their distracted state on the day of the accident. This parallel story didn't excuse their actions but added complexity that humanized both sides. By enriching the narrative with multiple dimensions, we built a case that felt authentic, compelling, and ultimately persuasive to the jury.

Practical Applications for the Additional Line

1. For Lawyers

- **Why It's Important:** Jurors, judges, and opposing counsel may process facts differently, but everyone responds to universal values like justice, accountability, and fairness. The moral ensures your case transcends its facts and connects with the audience on a human level.
- Example: In a case about unsafe working conditions: *"And the moral of the story is: When companies put profits above safety, they endanger the very people who make their success possible."* This ties the case to a universal value—protecting workers—while framing it as a cautionary tale.

2. For Professionals

- **Why It's Important:** Presenting data, proposals, or strategies often focuses too heavily on the "what" and "how." Adding a moral addresses the "why," giving your audience a reason to care and act.
- Example: In a pitch for a sustainability initiative: *"And the moral of the story is: Small changes today can create a healthier, more sustainable future for all of us."* This moral emphasizes collective responsibility and long-term impact, appealing to shared values.

3. For Everyday Storytelling

- **Why It's Important:** When you're recounting a personal anecdote or teaching a life lesson, the moral provides clarity and insight, ensuring your story is more than just entertaining—it's meaningful.
- **Example:** Telling a story about overcoming self-doubt: *And the moral of the story is: Believing in yourself is the first step to achieving what others say is impossible."* This moral leaves the listener with an uplifting, actionable takeaway.

Tips for Crafting Effective Morals

Here are six key strategies for developing effective morals in storytelling. Each strategy focuses on a specific aspect of moral communication:

1. **Inspire Action**: Suggestions on how to motivate audiences through actionable morals.
2. **Evoke Empathy**: Techniques for connecting emotionally with the audience using the moral.
3. **Provide Clarity**: Advice on making the moral clear and easily understandable.
4. **Highlight Shared Values**: Ways to resonate with universal truths and values.
5. **Leave a Lasting Impression**: Tips for making the moral memorable and impactful.
6. **Tailor to Your Audience**: Guidelines for customizing the moral to fit the specific needs and context of the audience.

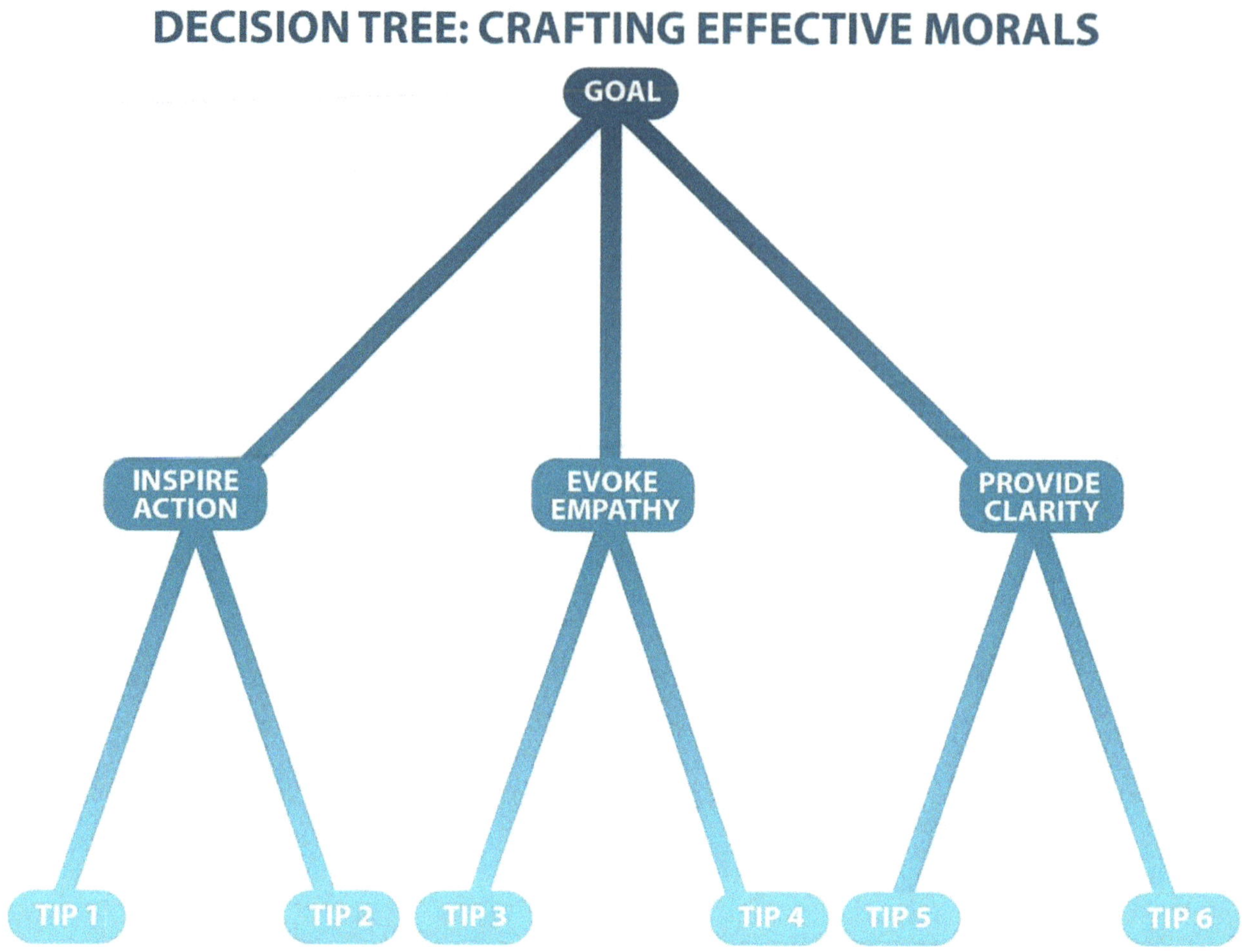

Figure 26: Decision Tree for Crafting Effective Morals

Refining the Moral for Maximum Impact

Crafting an effective moral requires careful thought. Here are some tips to ensure your Additional Line delivers maximum impact:

1. Keep It Simple

- Use clear, straightforward language. Avoid jargon or overly complex ideas.
- Example: Instead of *"Systemic negligence leads to widespread, unquantifiable harm,"* say *"Negligence affects us all."*

2. Make It Relatable

- Speak to universal values that appeal to a wide audience.
- Example: In a workplace discrimination case: And *the moral of the story is: Everyone deserves a fair chance to succeed."*

3. Tie It to the Audience's Role

- Frame the moral in a way that encourages action or reflection.
- Example: For jurors in a personal injury case: *"And the moral of the story is: Justice isn't just about laws—it's about protecting people and making things safe."*

4. Match the Tone of the Story

- Align the moral with the emotional arc of the narrative.
- Example: In a lighthearted anecdote, keep the moral playful. In a serious case, make it weighty and thought-provoking.

Conclusion

"The moral of the story doesn't just wrap things up—it sets the stage for transformation, leaving your audience forever changed."

Incorporating *"And the moral of the story is..."* elevates your storytelling into something bigger than just words. It's the bridge between the narrative and your audience's heart, ensuring your story isn't just heard but truly felt. The moral is the line that turns a tale into a takeaway. A great story doesn't end when the curtain closes—it lives on, sparking thought, action, and connection. The Additional Line is your chance to make sure your audience doesn't just remember your story but carries its meaning with them, ready to light their way when it matters most.

PRACTICE SPINES

Exercise 1: Summarize the Moral in One Sentence

- Write a full Story Spine for a specific case, project, or personal story.
- Identify the core theme or universal truth it conveys.
- Write a single sentence that encapsulates the moral, ensuring it connects the story to a larger meaning.

Exercise 2: Test the Moral's Universality

- Write the moral for a story you've crafted.
- Ask: *"Would this appeal to someone who has no connection to the specific details of the story?"*
- If the answer is no, refine the moral to make it more universal.

Exercise 3: Craft Multiple Morals

- Write three different morals for the same story, each targeting a different audience:
- **Jurors**: Emphasize justice and fairness.
- **Clients**: Highlight personal empowerment or hope.
- **Colleagues:** Focus on collaboration or shared responsibility.

Compare the morals and evaluate how each changes the story's impact.

Chapter 14
Exploring Key Storytelling Roles

"Every great story needs a cast of characters, each with a role to play in shaping the journey and tugging at the audience's heartstrings."

The Roles That Make Stories Unforgettable

Every great story has its cast: the hero we root for, the villain we love to hate, the friend who offers wisdom, and sometimes, the wild card who shakes things up. Without them, a story is just a collection of events. With them, it becomes a journey we can't look away from. Think about your favorite movie, book, or even a courtroom drama. What kept you connected?

It wasn't just the plot—it was the *people.* The ones who made you laugh, cry, and cheer. The ones who made you care. Understanding the roles that drive your story can transform a forgettable narrative into something that truly connects. So, grab your director's chair, and let's dive into the art of casting your story. Who are the players? What do they bring to the table? And how can you use their roles to create a story no one will forget?

Deepening the Narrative

Stories aren't just about what happens; they're about *who* it happens to, how they experience it, and *why it matters.* That's where storytelling roles come in. Think of them as the gears that keep your narrative machine running smoothly. The roles you assign in your story will shape its emotional punch and clarity.

In the Story Spine, these roles do the heavy lifting. They guide the audience through twists and turns, help unpack conflicts, and make the resolution feel satisfying. They're not just placeholders, they're the glue that ties your narrative together.

Meet the Cast: The Roles That Drive Your Story

Every great story has a cast of characters, and even in legal and professional storytelling, where the facts are fixed, roles are essential. They help your audience connect, care, and follow the journey you're taking them on. Let's meet the players that turn any narrative into a gripping tale.

1. The Hero: The Star of the Show

At the heart of every story is the Hero—the person whose journey forms the backbone of the narrative. In the Story Spine, the Hero experiences the "Until one day" moment that sets everything in motion. In a courtroom, the Hero might be your client, fighting for justice or redemption. In a jury trial, it's often the jurors themselves, as they navigate their role in shaping the story's outcome. The key is understanding what drives the Hero—fears, hopes, and transformation—and crafting a story that makes their journey compelling.

Example: In a personal injury case, your client's journey from victim to advocate becomes the emotional anchor that helps the jury connect and care.

2. The Mentor: The Wise Guide

Every Hero needs a Mentor—a figure who offers guidance, tools, or wisdom to help them overcome challenges. The Mentor often appears in the "Because of that" phase, empowering the Hero to face their obstacles. In a legal setting, the Mentor could be the attorney helping their client navigate the complexities of the case. In professional settings, it might be a supportive boss or mentor figure whose advice changes the Hero's path.

Example: As a lawyer, you might take on the Mentor role during trial, guiding the jury and your client through the emotional and intellectual terrain of the case.

3. The Villain: The Instigator of Conflict

Every good story needs a Villain—the source of the Hero's struggles. The Villain shapes the "Until one day" and "Because of that" phases by creating conflict and pushing the Hero to act. In a trial, the Villain might be an opposing party, corporate negligence, or even systemic injustice. In a business pitch, the Villain could be a problem your product solves. The most compelling villains are nuanced, with motivations that feel real and believable.

Example: In a wrongful death case, corporate greed might take center stage as the Villain, forcing the jury to confront its consequences.

4. The Trickster: Master of Surprise

The Trickster is here to keep things interesting! They inject unpredictability into the story, often complicating the Hero's journey with humor, mischief, or unexpected truths. In the Story Spine, the Trickster's presence is felt in the "And the complication was that" phase, shaking things up and forcing the Hero to adapt.

Example: In court, the Trickster might be a witness whose testimony takes a surprising turn, challenging everyone's assumptions.

5. The Victim: Evoking Empathy

The Victim represents vulnerability and loss, often serving as the emotional core of the story. Their experience raises the stakes and evokes an emotional response, giving the narrative a profound impact. In the Story Spine, the Victim's plight often drives the "Because of that" and "Until finally" phases.

Example: In a personal injury trial, the Victim could be a family struggling with the aftermath of an accident, reminding the jury why justice matters.

6. The Ally: The Hero's Backup

The Ally is the Hero's sidekick, offering support, encouragement, or practical help. They often appear during the "Because of that" phase, ensuring the Hero doesn't have to face their challenges alone.

Example: In a trial, the Ally might be an expert witness whose testimony strengthens the case or a trusted colleague who steps in when the Hero needs them most.

7. The Shadow: The Hero's Inner Struggle

The Shadow represents the Hero's internal conflicts or darker aspects of the journey. It's the doubt, fear, or regret that mirrors the external challenges and adds psychological depth to the story. In the Story Spine, the Shadow often surfaces in the "And the complication was that" phase, revealing the Hero's vulnerabilities.

Example: A lawyer preparing for trial might wrestle with imposter syndrome, their internal Shadow shaping the emotional undercurrent of the narrative.

8. The Catalyst: The Spark of Change

The Catalyst is the match that lights the story's fire. This role initiates the "Until one day" moment, disrupting the status quo and forcing the Hero to act.

Example: In a trial, the Catalyst might be a whistleblower's testimony or a key piece of evidence that changes the trajectory of the case.

9. The Observer: The Reflective Voice

The Observer doesn't actively participate but offers perspective, commentary, or context, often during the "And ever since then" phase. This role helps the audience understand the story's broader implications.

Example: In a trial, the Observer could be a community leader reflecting on the larger impact of the jury's decision.

Every story needs its cast of characters, whether they're literal people or symbolic roles. The Hero may be the star, but the supporting cast—the Villain, the Mentor, the Trickster—adds depth, tension, and richness to the tale.

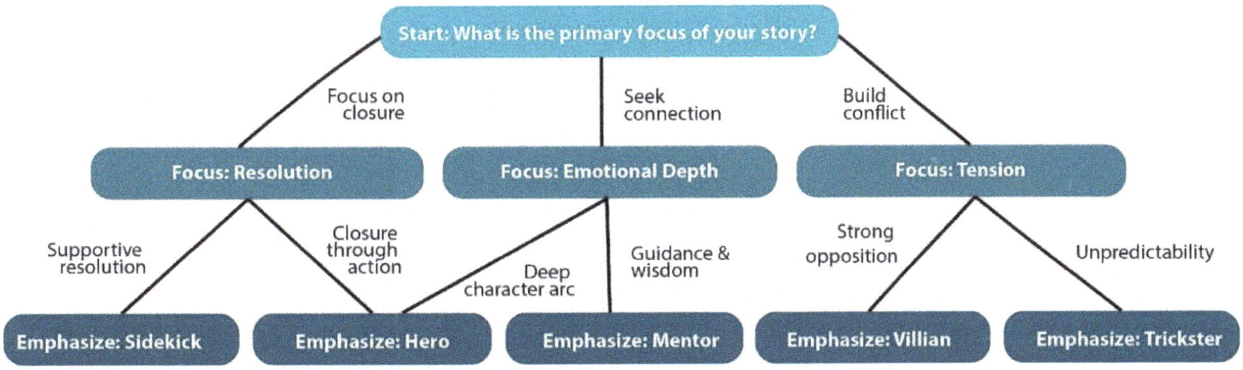

Figure 27: Decision Tree for Story Focus

Life Lessons: Exploring Key Storytelling Roles

Once upon a time...I was preparing for a trial where the dynamics were complex and the characters blurred. My client was clearly the protagonist, but the opposing party didn't fit neatly into the role of villain. The story felt incomplete, lacking the depth needed to resonate with a jury.

Every day...I had seen cases where the roles were too simplistic—good versus bad, right versus wrong. These narratives failed to reflect the complexities of real life, leaving juries disengaged and unsure of what to believe.

Until one day...I reframed the story, casting not just my client and their opponent but also the supporting figures—witnesses, experts, even the silent players like employers and policies—into meaningful roles. The narrative became rich and textured, with each role contributing to the unfolding drama.

Because of that... The jury connected deeply, not just with my client's plight but with the interplay of all the characters. They saw the antagonist's choices as misguided rather than malicious, creating space for empathy while still recognizing the injustice.

And ever since that day... I've taught lawyers to explore every role in their stories, ensuring that each character drives the narrative forward and connects with the audience on a human level.

Blending Roles for Richer Narratives

While storytelling roles have clear definitions, they're far from rigid. They're more like a dance—characters shifting, overlapping, and surprising us as the story unfolds. A Hero might take on the wisdom of a Mentor after learning hard-won lessons, or a Villain might unexpectedly become a Catalyst for transformation. These fluid roles help keep narratives dynamic and engaging.

Take a trial narrative, for example: A client's perceived flaws might initially frame them as a Victim. But as their story unfolds—showing their resilience, determination, and growth—they can emerge as a Hero, defying expectations and capturing the jurors hearts. Blending roles allow storytellers to craft multidimensional characters and narratives that feel authentic, layered, and anything but predictable.

Roles in storytelling are the building blocks of a narrative. They represent the forces—characters, dynamics, or even abstract ideas—that propel the plot and stir emotions. These roles help audiences connect with a story on a universal level. But here's the fun part: roles aren't static. They evolve as the story unfolds. A Victim might grow into a Hero. A Villain might reveal surprising layers of humanity. By understanding these roles and how they interact, you can create stories that feel rich, relatable, and deeply engaging.

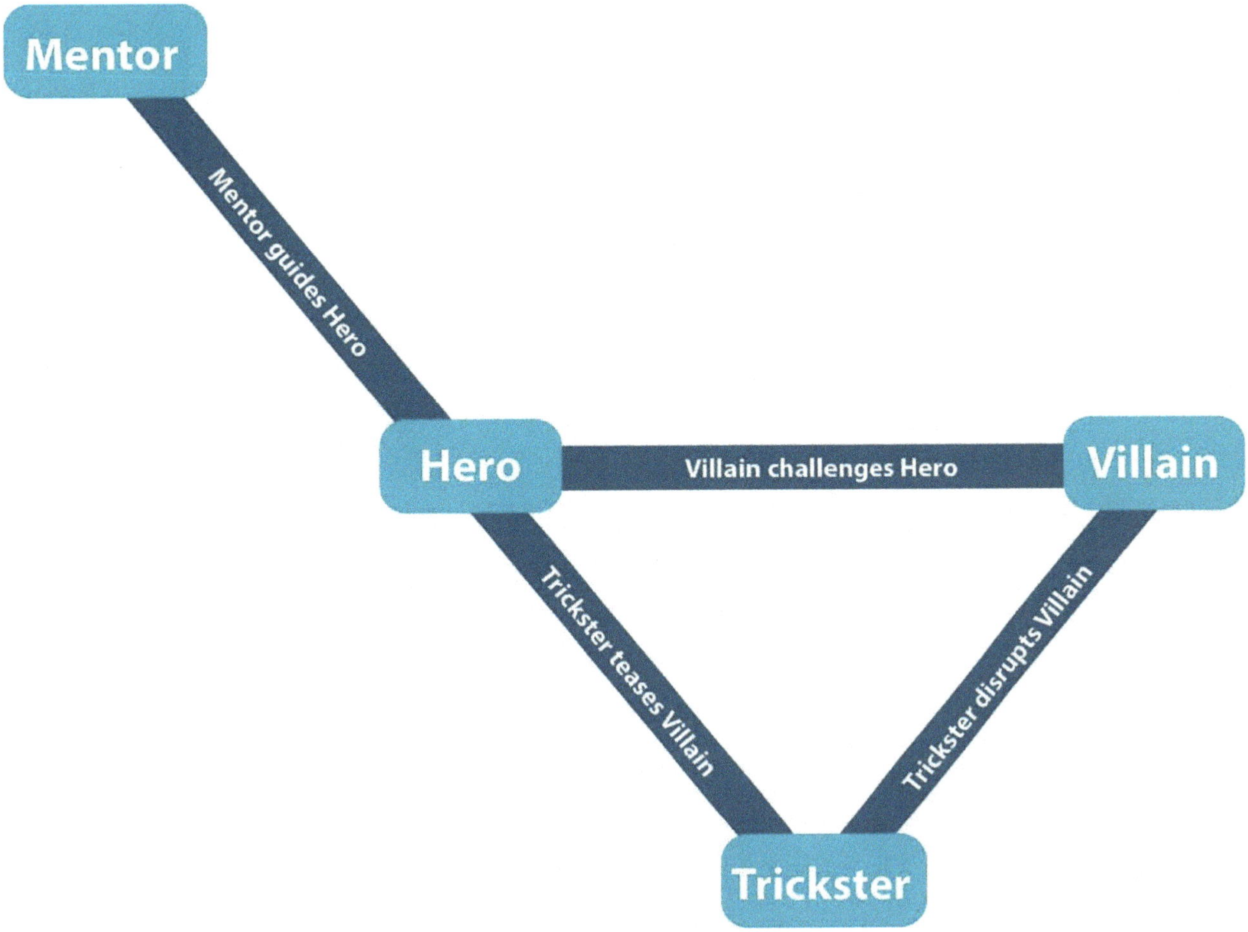

Figure 28: Character and Role Interaction Diagram

How Roles Take Shape

Roles are born from context, characters, and the themes you want to convey. The Hero rises from their journey of transformation. The Villain? Defined by their opposition to the Hero's goals. These roles don't exist in isolation; they're constantly shaped by the story's twists and turns, ups and downs, and rise and falls.

For example, let's say you're working on a workplace discrimination case. Your client might start as a Victim, overwhelmed by unfair treatment. But as the story unfolds, their resilience and courage emerge, and they step into the Hero's shoes, fighting for justice—not just for themselves, but for others, too.

By understanding how roles form and evolve, you can assign them intentionally to enrich your narrative and align it with the emotional heartbeat of your story.

Where Roles Enter the Story

Roles are the stars of your narrative, and their timing is everything. Each role steps into the spotlight at key moments, aligning beautifully with the phases of the Story Spine. Take the **Hero**, for example. They're your opening act, introduced in the "Once upon a time" or "Every day" phase. This is where we meet them, get a feel for their world, and start to care about their journey.

Then there's the **Villain** (or the conflict, if you prefer)—they often crash the party during the "Until one day" moment, throwing a wrench into the Hero's plans and setting the story into motion. And just when things seem insurmountable, the **Mentor** or **Ally** arrives in the "Because of that" phase, ready to offer guidance, support, or maybe just a pep talk. Of course, let's not forget the wildcard: the **Trickster** or **Shadow**, who might pop up during "And the complication was that," to keep the Hero (and your audience) on their toes.

Knowing when and where these roles enter ensures their presence feels natural and drives the story forward. A well-timed entrance isn't just about drama—it's about making the narrative flow effortlessly, drawing the audience deeper into the story.

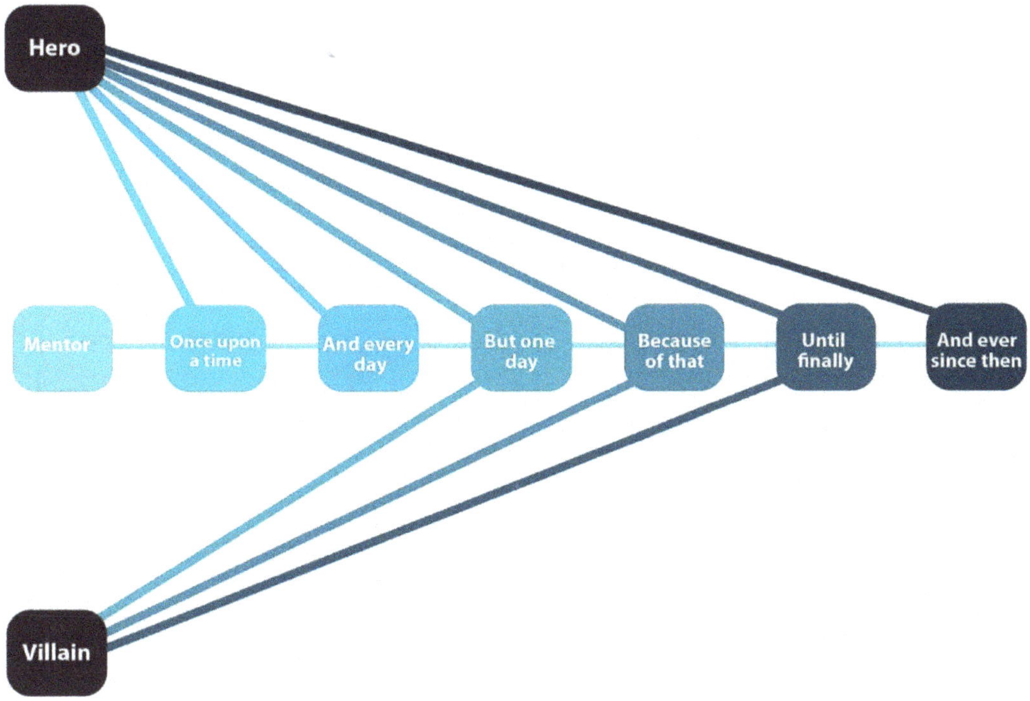

Figure 29: Where Roles Enter The Story Flowchart

The Must-Have Roles

Every story has unique needs, but some roles are non-negotiable. The **Hero** is your anchor, the person (or entity) whose journey carries the audience through the narrative. Without them, there's no one to root for, no emotional center. Then there's the **Villain** or conflict, the role that gives the story its stakes and makes the Hero's journey worth following.

Other roles, like the **Mentor**, **Ally**, or **Trickster**, are optional but powerful. A **Mentor** adds depth by offering wisdom that guides the Hero's transformation, while an **Ally** brings emotional warmth and camaraderie. And the **Trickster**? They keep things interesting with surprises, challenges, or a touch of levity. The key is knowing which roles your story needs and using them strategically. Too many roles can clutter a narrative, but just the right mix is storytelling gold.

Roles Reflect Story Themes

Think of roles as the embodiment of your story's themes. In a story about resilience, for instance, the **Hero's** battle with the **Villain** might symbolize an internal struggle against self-doubt. A **Mentor's** guidance could stand in for the importance of community, showing how shared wisdom lifts us when we stumble.

In a courtroom narrative, the roles take on even greater significance. Your client (the **Hero**) might represent hope or redemption, while the opposing party (the **Villain**) could symbolize systemic injustice. These thematic connections give your story emotional heft, transforming abstract ideas into tangible conflicts. When the roles align with the story's themes, they amplify its impact, leaving the audience with something to think about long after they leave the room. Roles are not there just for the storyteller. They're bridges, inviting the audience to step into the narrative and connect on a personal level.

In a trial setting, this dynamic becomes even more critical. Picture the jury as the **Hero**—their journey is deciding the case. Meanwhile, the attorney steps into the **Mentor** role, guiding them through the maze of evidence and arguments. This framing helps jurors connect to the story not just as passive listeners but as active participants, emotionally invested in reaching the right resolution.

Roles make a narrative tick. They bring depth, drama, and relatability to every phase of the story. By understanding when and where they enter, and how they interact with one another, you can craft narratives that don't just hold attention—they capture hearts. So, as you build your story, think about your cast of characters and their entrances. With the right roles at the right moments, your audience won't just listen—they'll feel, connect, and remember.

The Jurors: Heroes Armed with Common Sense

Jurors are the unsung heroes of the courtroom drama, handed the daunting task of weighing facts, applying the law, and delivering justice—all while navigating their own values, thoughts and instincts. Judges, in their role as the all-knowing Mentors, often instruct jurors to follow the law as explained by the court but also encourages them to rely on something equally important: good old-fashioned common sense.

Think of it this way: the judge hands jurors the rulebook (the law) and then says, "Now, use the supercomputer in your head—your everyday reasoning abilities—to figure out how this all fits together." It's like being given a recipe and told to tweak the spices to taste. They're not just there to process evidence robotically; they're bringing their life experience, intuition, and logic to the table.

Jurors are invited to step into their role as decision-makers, combining the structure of the law with the fluidity of human understanding. It's not just about following rules—it's about making sense of the story in a way that feels just and fair. In other words, they're doing what Heroes do best: finding meaning and making choices that have real-world impact.

A War Story: The Unexpected Antagonist

In one case, the antagonist wasn't the opposing party—it was a deeply ingrained system that had failed my client. This realization changed how I approached the story.

I positioned the insurance company's bureaucracy as the antagonist, detailing how it obstructed justice and denied my client's rightful compensation. The supporting characters—witnesses and experts—helped illuminate the antagonist's flaws, while my client emerged as a courageous protagonist fighting against the odds.

This shift in focus not only clarified the roles within the story but also empowered the jury to see themselves as agents of justice, working to correct a systemic wrong.

Conclusion

"Every great story is a team effort—even if you're the one up there telling it."

Roles give power, texture, dimension and life to your narratives. Each role carries a unique purpose, shaping how the audience experiences the journey. And don't forget the benefits of blending, evolving, and sometimes even omitting roles—it's these creative choices that turn a good story into a memorable one.

The next time you craft a story—ask yourself: Who's my Hero? Where's the tension? Who's complicating the journey? And most importantly, how can I use these roles to make my story linger long after it's told? Roles aren't just labels; they're the emotional glue that binds your audience to your story. Use them wisely, flexibly, and creatively, and you'll unlock the power to engage and move hearts in ways you never thought possible.

Practice Spines

Exercise 1: Role Assignment for a Real-Life Challenge

Think of a real challenge you've faced recently. Maybe it's a workplace disagreement, a personal decision, or even a DIY project gone hilariously wrong.

- **Once upon a time:** Who were you at the start of this story?
- **Every day:** What was the normal before the challenge?
- **Until one day:** What disrupted the status quo?
- **Because of that:** What roles emerged—were you the **Hero**? Was there a **Villain**, a **Mentor**, or a **Trickster** complicating things?
- **Until finally:** How did the resolution unfold?
- **Ever since:** What lasting lessons or changes came from this experience?

Example Prompt: "Once upon a time, I was a confident baker. Every day, I baked cakes for my friends. Until one day, my friend requested a wedding cake shaped like her dog. Because of that, I wrestled with fondant for hours and Googled 'how to fix lopsided cakes.' Until finally, I delivered a slightly crooked but adorable canine confection. Ever since then, I stick to cupcakes."

Exercise 2: Build a Trial Story Spine with Roles

Choose a mock legal scenario and assign roles to key players. Create a Story Spine narrative that integrates these roles.

Scenario: A tenant is suing their landlord for neglecting essential repairs, leading to a dangerous living situation.

- **Hero:** The tenant, struggling to provide a safe home for their family.
- **Villain:** The landlord, who ignored repeated repair requests.
- **Mentor:** The tenant's lawyer, guiding them through the legal process.

- **Catalyst:** A building inspector's damning report that shifts the case in the tenant's favor.

Sample Story Spine:

- **Once upon a time:** "Once upon a time, Mia was a single mom living in a cozy apartment she worked hard to afford."
- **Every day:** "Every day, she juggled work, parenting, and making a home for her son."
- **Until one day:** "Until one day, the ceiling in her son's bedroom began to leak, turning into a gaping hole."
- **Because of that:** "Because of that, Mia contacted her landlord repeatedly, but her pleas were ignored."
- **Until finally:** "Until finally, she found the courage to take legal action, armed with evidence of the neglect."
- **Ever since:** "And ever since, Mia has become an advocate for tenant rights, ensuring others don't face the same struggles."

Exercise 3: Reimagine a Famous Tale with Twisted Roles

Pick a well-known story and shuffle the roles around for fun. What if the **Villain** became the **Hero**, or the **Mentor** was also the **Trickster**?

Example Prompt: What if Cinderella was the **Villain**, the stepsisters were the **Heroes**, and the Fairy Godmother was a **Trickster** stirring the pot?

Chapter 15
Clarifying the Role of the Juror as Hero in the Story Spine

"A well-defined role isn't just a character—it's the beating heart of the story, driving its themes, conflicts, and ultimate resolution."

Juror as Hero in the Courtroom

In the Story Spine framework, the protagonist—the Hero—guides the audience through a journey of transformation. Typically, this role is filled by the client or a central character in the narrative. But what if the Hero isn't within the story being told, but in the audience hearing it? What if the juror is the Hero?

Positioning the juror as the Hero fundamentally shifts the narrative's focus. Instead of beginning with the case facts or the parties involved, the story starts with the juror's potential for impact. "Once upon a time, twelve people entered a courtroom, each carrying their own beliefs, experiences, and questions." This reframing transforms jurors from passive recipients of information into active participants in the pursuit of justice.

The Juror's Journey

The juror's story unfolds as they navigate the case, piece together evidence, and grapple with their own values and biases. Here's how the Story Spine adapts to center the juror:

- **Once upon a time:** Jurors arrive at court, uncertain of their role but willing to listen and decide.

- ❖ **Every day:** They hear arguments, evaluate evidence, and question their assumptions.
- ❖ **Until one day:** A pivotal moment—a witness's testimony, a revealing piece of evidence, or an emotional appeal—challenges their perspective.
- ❖ **Because of that:** They begin to see the human stakes and to feel the moral weight of their decision.
- ❖ **Until finally:** They reach a verdict, carrying the responsibility of their choice.
- ❖ **And ever since then:** The impact of their decision reverberates, influencing the lives involved and shaping their own understanding of justice.

Empowering Jurors Through the Story

When the juror becomes the Hero, the attorney's role shifts as well. The lawyer is no longer just an advocate for their client but a mentor guiding the jurors on their journey. The narrative must empower jurors to see their responsibility not as a burden but as an opportunity to make a meaningful difference.

For example, in a criminal case, you might describe the jurors as the ultimate decision-makers, entrusted with evaluating the evidence and ensuring the legal process reflects fairness and accountability. In a civil trial, they might be the voice of justice, and keepers of the Constitution, by serving to resolve disputes and restore balance.

By crafting a story that centers on the juror's transformation, you inspire them to rise to the occasion. The courtroom becomes not just a stage for legal arguments but a space where jurors step into their roles as decision-makers and heroes of the justice system.

Why the Juror-as-Hero Framework Works

This approach works because it taps into universal themes of empowerment, duty, and purpose. People want to feel that their actions matter, that their choices have weight. By positioning jurors as Heroes, you craft a narrative that engages them emotionally and ethically, giving them a reason to care deeply about the case.

In this version of the Story Spine, the juror isn't just watching a story unfold—they are living it, contributing to its resolution, and leaving the courtroom changed by their role in the process. So, the next time you step into the courtroom, remember: the most powerful Hero in the room might not be your client—it might be the twelve people sitting silently in the jury box, waiting for their story in the courtroom to begin.

Life Lessons: Clarifying the Role of Juror as Hero

Once upon a time... During a trial, I watched jurors sit quietly, their faces a mixture of boredom and detachment. Despite my best efforts, the story wasn't reaching them. They didn't see themselves as participants—only observers.

Every day... Jurors are treated as passive recipients of information, yet their decisions carry profound weight. Without feeling invested in their role, they struggle to see the importance of their contributions.

Until one day...I crafted a closing argument that reframed the jurors as heroes. I told them they held the power to right a wrong, to be the voice of justice in a story that desperately needed resolution. Their faces changed—they sat up and leaned forward, suddenly aware of their place in the narrative.

Because of that... The verdict wasn't just a win for my client; it was a triumph for the jurors. They left the courtroom knowing they had played a pivotal role, empowered by their ability to deliver justice.

And ever since that day...I've emphasized the juror-as-hero narrative, helping lawyers craft stories that make jurors feel seen, valued, and integral to the outcome.

Empowering Jurors Through the Hero's Arc

In the courtroom, jurors face challenges that closely mirror those of classic Heroes in storytelling. They must sift through conflicting evidence, wrestle with moral questions, and navigate the weight of their decision. During the "Because of that" phase, jurors confront the complexities of the case, grappling with their own biases and uncertainties. The closing argument becomes the mentor's guidance, equipping them with the tools they need to rise to the occasion and overcome these challenges. **Until finally,** they reach a verdict—an act that represents the culmination of their journey.

Positioning jurors as Heroes reframes their role, helping them see their task not just as deciding a case but as fulfilling a greater duty to justice. This perspective reinforces the gravity and importance of their decisions, inspiring jurors to embrace their part in shaping the narrative.

Jurors and the Moral of the Story

As Heroes, jurors don't just resolve the story, they define its moral. Their verdict determines the outcome of the conflict, setting a precedent and delivering justice that reflects the values of society. By the time they reach the "And the moral of the story is…" phase, jurors have moved from mere observers to active participants in the broader narrative of justice.

For instance, a lawyer might conclude with, **"And the moral of the story is that every voice deserves to be heard, no matter their circumstances."** This statement empowers jurors to view their verdict not as the conclusion of a single case, but as part of a larger legacy—one that upholds principles of fairness and accountability.

Jurors are more than factfinders; they are the moral compass of the courtroom narrative. As Heroes, their journey isn't just about determining what happened—it's about deciding what should happen, based on their collective values and sense of justice. Here, they face tough questions of fairness, intent, and the far-reaching consequences of their decision. By recognizing jurors as the story's Heroes, attorneys can appeal to their humanity, framing the trial as an opportunity to uphold principles that extend beyond the immediate case, influencing the fabric of society itself.

The Juror's Journey as a Personal Transformation

For jurors, serving on a trial isn't just a civic duty, it's a personal journey that leaves a lasting impact. Framing jurors as Heroes within the Story Spine framework highlights their potential for transformation. They begin as ordinary individuals but evolve through the trial, confronting moral and emotional challenges that deepen their understanding of justice and human complexity. During the **"Until finally"** phase, their verdict not only resolves the trial's conflict but represents a moment of personal growth, where they reconcile their beliefs with their responsibilities.

Crafting a narrative that honors this journey inspires jurors to approach their role with pride and accountability, ensuring they feel their participation is both meaningful and impactful. By positioning jurors as central figures in the story, you help them see their importance—not just to the trial at hand, but to the larger system of justice.

The Protagonist and Story Spine Roles

"A protagonist isn't just the hero in a cape—it's anyone driving the story forward, facing challenges, and evolving along the way. In the courtroom, that could be the juror, the client, or yes, even the villain." Every story needs a lead, but the concept of "hero" is wonderfully flexible. Depending on how you frame your narrative, the protagonist's role can shift, giving depth and direction to your story. Let's break it down:

- **Protagonist (Hero):** Faces challenges, makes decisions, and experiences transformation.
- **Villain (Antagonist):** Creates obstacles, adding tension and pushing the hero into action.

- **Supporting Characters:** Aid the hero in navigating conflict or achieving their goals.

But what if the juror is the hero?

When the Juror is the Hero

Casting jurors as the heroes of your story changes everything. Their journey doesn't begin with your case, it begins with their own lives, experiences, and values. By inviting jurors to see themselves as central figures in the trial's narrative, you give them a reason to care deeply about the process and its outcome.

Here's how the Story Spine evolves when the juror steps into the hero's role:

1. **"Once upon a time..."**

   Start with the juror's life before the trial. Set the stage by describing their everyday world.

   - *Example:* "Once upon a time, you were living your life—working hard, caring for your family, and making countless small decisions that reflect who you are."

2. **"Every day..."**

   Highlight their routine and values—fairness, integrity, and community. This grounds the story in what matters to them.

   - *Example:* "Every day, you made choices—big and small—that showed your belief in doing the right thing and standing up for fairness."

3. **"Until one day..."**

   The juror receives their summons, launching them into the story.

   - *Example:* "Until one day, you were called to serve as a juror, a role that asked you to weigh evidence, confront questions of justice, and make decisions with far-reaching consequences."

4. **"Because of that…"**

They face the challenges of the trial: conflicting evidence, moral dilemmas, and the gravity of their role.

   - *Example:* "Because of that, you stepped into the courtroom, ready to listen, reflect, and navigate the complexities of the case."

5. **"Until finally…"**

The juror reaches a verdict, overcoming challenges and fulfilling their duty.

   - *Example:* "Until finally, you made the decision that would impact lives and reaffirm your belief in justice."

6. **"And ever since…"**

Reflect on their transformation. They're not just jurors—they're champions of fairness.

   - *Example:* "And ever since, you've carried the knowledge that you played a vital role in protecting justice and fairness in the world."

Why This Approach Works

1. **Jurors as Decision-Makers:**

Framing jurors as heroes emphasizes their importance, engaging them emotionally and intellectually. They feel empowered to own their decisions.

2. **Connection to the Case:**

Starting with the juror's story bridges their values with the case, making the trial feel personal and relevant.

3. **Humanizing the Process:**

Positioning the trial as part of the juror's journey transforms their role from an abstract duty to a meaningful and memorable experience.

Comparing Juror as Hero vs. Client as Hero

Client as Hero:

- Begins with the client's story:
    - *"Once upon a time, Mr. Johnson was a hardworking father who never imagined his life would change so dramatically."*

Juror as Hero:

- Begins with the juror's story:
    - *"Once upon a time, you were living your life, unaware that you would soon be called to make a decision that could change everything for someone else."*

By focusing on the juror's perspective, you invite them to see the trial as a defining chapter in their own story. And when you step into their shoes using psychodramatic techniques, you can craft a narrative that speaks directly to their humanity and sense of purpose. After all, every hero needs a good guide—so why not make your storytelling the mentor they didn't know they needed?

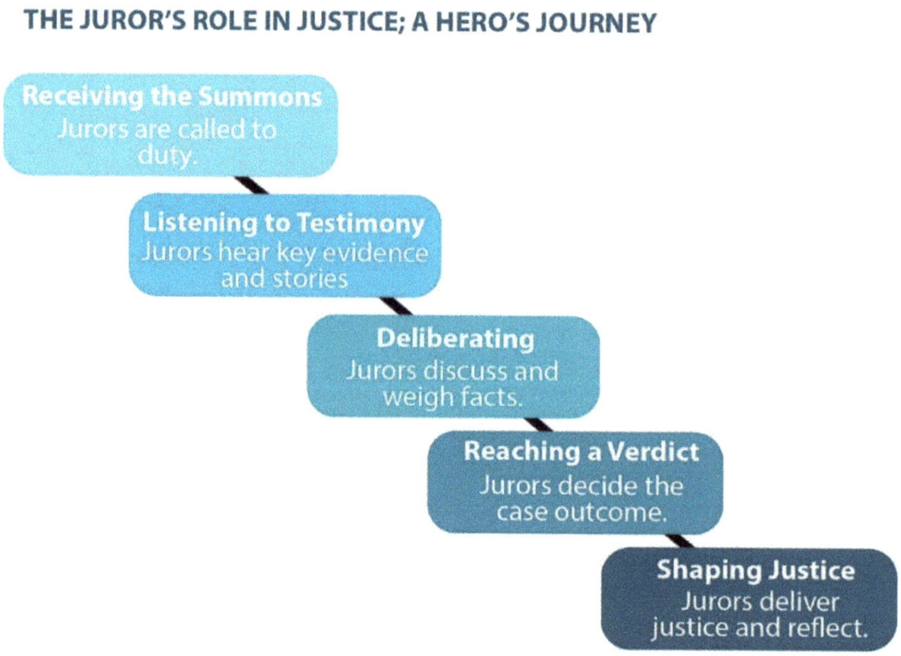

Figure 30: The Juror's Role in Justice: A Hero's Journey

How to Implement This in the Courtroom

Turning jurors into heroes isn't just a narrative trick—it's a way to invite them into a story that matters. By reframing the trial as their journey, you create a narrative arc that keeps them engaged, invested, and purposeful. Here's how you can bring this powerful storytelling into every stage of the courtroom experience:

1. Opening Statements: Setting the Stage for Their Journey

Start by acknowledging the jurors' vital role in the story. Make it clear that they're not passive observers but active participants with the power to shape the outcome.

- **Example:** "This isn't just my client's story—it's yours too. You hold the pen to write what happens next. Together, we'll uncover the truth, and you'll decide how this chapter ends."

  By framing the trial as their journey, you set a tone of empowerment and responsibility right from the start.

2. Voir Dire: Inviting Them into the Hero's Role

Use voir dire as a chance to connect jurors to their values and experiences. By framing your questions as part of their journey, you help them see how their own beliefs and insights shape the story.

- **Example:** "What does fairness look like in your daily life? How do you approach tough decisions when the stakes are high?"

These kinds of questions don't just inform jury selection; they create an early connection, making jurors feel seen and understood as individuals.

3. Closing Arguments: Delivering the Hero's Moment

Bring it all full circle by positioning the verdict as the climax of the jurors' journey. Highlight the significance of their decision, connecting it to their values and the legacy they'll leave.

- **Example:** "Your verdict is more than just a conclusion; it's the culmination of your journey in this courtroom. Today, you have the chance to write a chapter in the ongoing story of justice, one that reflects fairness, truth, and courage." This isn't just a conclusion—it's a call to action that places jurors at the heart of the story's resolution.

Why This Works

When you cast jurors as the heroes, the trial stops being a dry presentation of facts and becomes a story they're living. You're no longer just asking them to deliver a verdict; you're inviting them to embrace a role that reflects their values and contributes to something bigger. By starting with their "once upon a time," you shift the narrative from a chore to a calling. You inspire jurors to connect deeply, deliberate thoughtfully, and fulfill their role with purpose.

The best part? This approach doesn't just strengthen your case—it honors the profound responsibility and humanity of every juror, turning their duty into a defining moment in their own story. After all, who doesn't want to be the hero?

The Jury as the Hero – A Story Spine Trial Walkthrough

A Man Wrongfully Accused of Armed Robbery

Once upon a time... (Voir Dire – Setting the Stage & Engaging the Jury)

"Once upon a time, our justice system was built on a promise: that every person is presumed innocent until proven guilty. That cases should be judged based on evidence, not assumptions. That jurors—ordinary people like you—are the guardians of that promise."

- *The lawyer uses Voir Dire to introduce the core values of justice and to subtly ask jurors if they are willing to challenge their own biases.*
- *The goal is to set up the jury as the protagonist of this case—the ones who will uphold fairness when the system has already failed.*

And every day... (Opening Statement – Establishing the Routine & Defendant's Normal Life)

"Every day, Mark Reynolds went to work at the construction site, clocking in at 6:30 a.m. Every day, he worked a 12-hour shift, earning just enough to take care of his mother, who had recently been diagnosed with diabetes. Every day, he followed the same routine, like clockwork."

- *This step is crucial to humanizing Mark, making the jury see him as a hardworking, relatable individual—not just "the defendant."*
- *The lawyer reinforces the predictability of Mark's daily life, which will later be contrasted with the sudden accusation.*

But one day... (Opening & Witness Testimony – The Incident That Changed Everything)

"But one day, on October 15th, while Mark was eating dinner with his mother, a man in a ski mask robbed a liquor store five miles away. The clerk, in shock and fear, told police, 'It was a tall Black man in a gray hoodie.'"

- *The robbery is the moment of disruption—the event that throws Mark's life into chaos.*
- *This step also introduces how weak evidence and rushed police work led to Mark's wrongful arrest.*

Because of that... (Direct & Cross – Unraveling the Investigation's Failures)

"Because of that, police canvassed the area, and someone—who had never even seen the robbery—told them, 'I saw a tall Black guy in a gray hoodie at the bus stop earlier.' Because of that, the police arrested Mark two days later, even though he was nowhere near the liquor store that night."

- *Here, the lawyer highlights the* ***missteps and biases*** *in the investigation—how a vague description turned into an assumption, which turned into an arrest.*

- *This step builds tension, showing how small errors snowball into major injustices.*

Until finally... (Closing – The Turning Point & Jury's Power to Act)

"Until finally, after hearing the evidence, the truth became clear: No DNA. No fingerprints. No surveillance video of Mark at the scene. A shaky eyewitness statement made under stress. A single gray hoodie was all it took to turn an innocent man into a suspect. And now, the only thing standing between Mark and a wrongful conviction is you."

- *This is the moment the jury realizes their power—they are not just observers; they are the **only ones** who can stop this injustice.*

And ever since then... (Closing – The Jury's Role in Restoring Justice)

"And ever since then, juries like you have sent a message: That in this country, we convict based on evidence, not assumptions. That a hoodie is not a crime. That a man is innocent until proven guilty. And that justice only works when good people refuse to let an innocent man take the fall."

- *This step creates **a moral resolution**—the jury isn't just deciding Mark's fate; they are reaffirming the integrity of the justice system.*

The lawyer **mentally holds the story arc throughout the trial**—from Voir Dire to Closing—shaping how the jury sees the defendant, the case, and their role. By structuring the case as **a story where the jury has a heroic role**, they are more likely to feel invested and make the right decision.

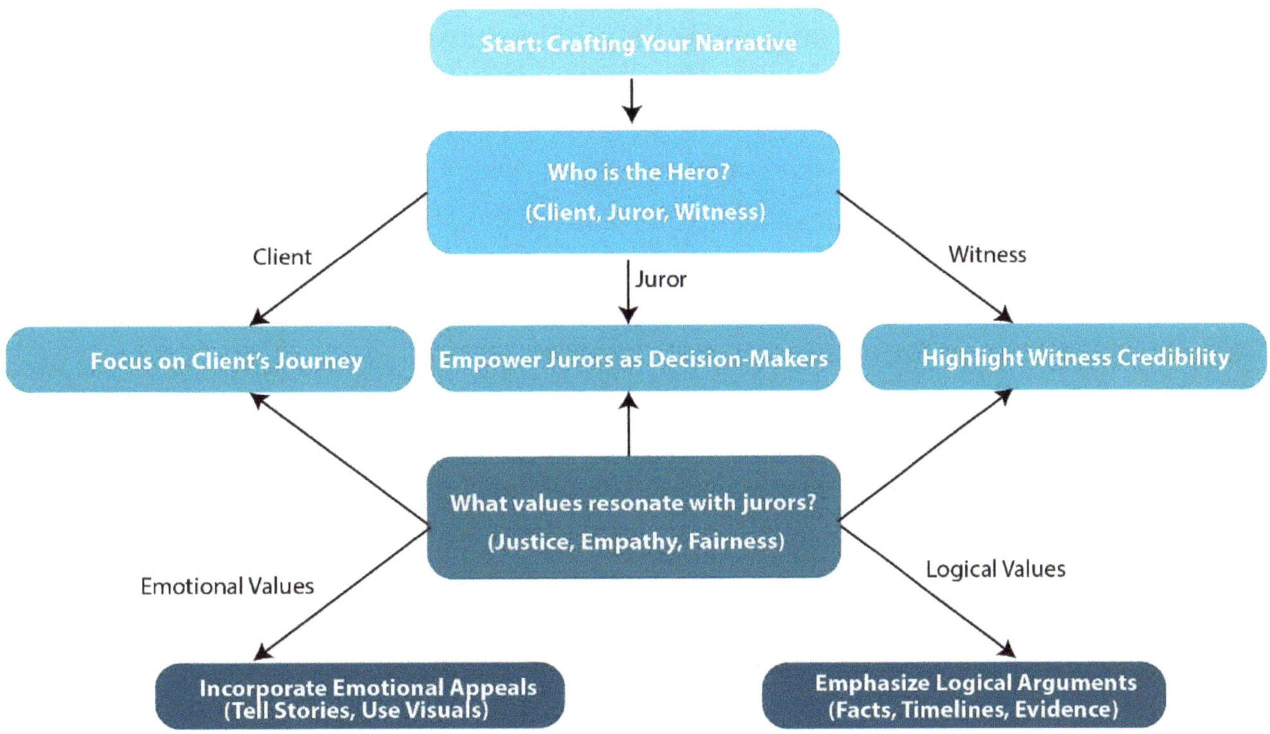

Figure 31: Crafting Your Narrative

A War Story: Inviting Jurors to Become Heroes

In one of my earlier trials, I realized how critical it was to engage jurors as active participants in the story. During closing arguments, I addressed them directly: "You are the only ones who can right this wrong. You have the power to restore dignity and ensure justice." In voir dire, I had shared a hypothetical about a person witnessing an act of kindness, where someone stepped in to help when no one else would. The jurors shared about what this meant to them and the times they had experienced this.

And then in closing, I brought it full circle, by saying, "That is what you're being asked to do here today, to step in and help." I said, "I am inviting you to be the heroes in this story—not just for my client, but for the principle of fairness we all believe in."

When the verdict came back in our favor, several jurors approached me afterward and said, "You made us feel like we mattered." That moment reinforced my belief that jurors, when empowered as the heroes of the narrative, can deliver outcomes that reflect their sense of justice and humanity.

Conclusion

"Roles aren't just characters on a page—they're mirrors, reflecting the audience's own fears, hopes, and humanity back to them."

When you understand and assign roles thoughtfully, you don't just tell a story; you build an experience. Roles give every plot twist purpose and every character a meaningful place. In redefining the role of the juror as the Hero within the Story Spine framework, this chapter underscores the transformative potential that narrative restructuring can bring to the courtroom.

By shifting the focus from the static details of the case to the dynamic journey of the jurors, the narrative empowers them, turning what is typically a passive role into one of profound influence and responsibility. This perspective not only enhances the engagement of the jurors but also elevates their role from mere decision-makers to pivotal heroes whose decisions resonate with deep moral and personal implications.

The journey mapped out in the Story Spine for jurors illustrates a narrative arc that mirrors classic heroic tales, where the protagonist overcomes obstacles, experiences personal growth, and ultimately impacts their world. In the courtroom, this translates to jurors navigating through evidence and testimony, challenging their preconceptions, and arriving at a verdict that they believe serves justice.

By concluding with the lasting impact of the jurors' decision, the narrative arc does not just end with the verdict, but extends into how this decision shapes the lives affected by it, including their own. This repositioning emphasizes that each juror's experience and decision are not merely procedural but are part of a larger, ongoing narrative of justice and societal values.

Through this reframing, jurors are seen not just as participants in a legal process, but as central figures whose decisions uphold the integrity of the justice system. This chapter compellingly argues that when jurors are viewed and treated as heroes within the story, they are more likely to act with a deeper sense of purpose and deliberation, truly embodying the "beating heart of the story" that drives toward a just resolution.

Figure 32: Juror As Hero Framework

PRACTICE SPINES

Exercise 1: Juror as Hero Story Spine

Objective: Help craft a trial narrative with the juror as the central figure.

Instructions:

1. Creates a Story Spine where the juror is the hero. They should include:
    - **Once upon a time:** Introduce the juror's life before the trial.
    - **Every day:** Establish their values and daily routines.
    - **Until one day:** The moment they receive the jury summons.
    - **Because of that:** The challenges they face during the trial, such as conflicting evidence or emotional testimony.
    - **Until finally:** The juror reaches a verdict that reflects their values and role in the justice system.
    - **And ever since:** Reflect on how this experience transforms them.

Exercise 2: Voir Dire Reimagined

Objective: Practice voir dire questions that cast jurors as heroes and connect them to their role in the trial's story.

Instructions:

1. Write three voir dire questions designed to uncover the juror's values and sense of responsibility.
2. Examples:
    - "When have you had to make a decision that impacted others?"
    - "What does justice mean to you?"
    - "How do you approach solving problems when you don't have all the information?"

Exercise 3: Heroic Closing Argument

Objective: Develop a closing argument that positions the juror as the hero resolving the story.

Instructions:

1. Write a closing argument, focusing on:
    - Reinforcing the juror's role as the one who ensures justice prevails.
    - Using Story Spine elements to emphasize how their verdict will bring resolution to the case.
    - Inspiring jurors to see their decision as a transformative moment.

Chapter 16
The Absence of Roles- A Narrative Gap

"Sometimes, what's missing in a story says more than what's present—absence can speak volumes."

What happens when a story leaves out a role? It might sound like a mistake, but it's often intentional, and when done right, it can make a story even more compelling. Imagine a **Hero** with no **Mentor**—suddenly, their journey is all about isolation, self-discovery, and finding strength within. Or consider a trial with no clear **Villain**—the story shifts inward, exploring the Hero's internal battle or moral gray areas instead.

Take, for example, a jury trial where no single person or entity is clearly at fault. The absence of a "bad guy" challenges jurors to wrestle with ambiguity and moral complexity. These gaps disrupt traditional expectations, offering a playground for creativity and innovation. The result? A narrative that stays with the audience long after the last word is spoken.

When the Mentor Is Missing

Picture a **Hero** embarking on a journey with no **Mentor** to guide them. Suddenly, the story becomes about self-reliance. Instead of wise advice or a magical map, the Hero must navigate uncharted waters using only their wits and courage. This absence intensifies their struggle, making their victories feel harder-earned and their growth more profound.

For example, in a courtroom drama, imagine a defendant representing themselves without the help of a seasoned attorney. The jury isn't just watching a trial; they're witnessing a David-and-Goliath battle of resilience, vulnerability, and raw determination. The lack of a Mentor transforms the narrative into one of personal grit, offering the audience a unique emotional connection to the protagonist's journey.

A Story Without a Villain

What happens when there's no clear **Villain**? Suddenly, the story turns inward, exploring internal struggles, moral dilemmas, or systemic issues. This absence forces the audience to reconsider their assumptions: who's really at fault, and is 'fault' even the right term to use?

Take a medical malpractice case where the central question isn't about negligence but about the inherent risks of a complicated surgery. Without a clear "bad guy," the jury's focus shifts to broader questions of accountability, trust, and the human limits of expertise. Such narratives challenge traditional storytelling conventions, inviting the audience to grapple with nuance instead of rooting for a clear winner or loser.

The Power of Ambiguity

Absence creates ambiguity, and ambiguity is a playground for storytelling creativity. Without every role neatly filled, the audience has to work a little harder—they start asking questions, filling in blanks, and engaging with the story in a more personal way. This active participation deepens their connection to the narrative, making it stay with them long after the story ends.

For instance, in a family law case, the absence of a **Villain** might reflect the complexity of human relationships. Maybe both parents love their child but have different, conflicting visions of what's best for them. This lack of a traditional antagonist forces the factfinder to focus on what's most important: the child's well-being. The absence of a clear bad guy creates an emotional and intellectual challenge, one that invites thoughtful deliberation rather than simple judgment.

Sometimes, the absence of a role allows for creative innovation by flipping the script entirely. In a corporate fraud case, what if the whistleblower is the **Hero**, but there's no obvious **Villain**? The narrative might focus on systemic issues, like corporate culture or flawed oversight processes, rather than pinning blame on one person. This shift turns the story into a broader exploration of accountability and reform, creating a more thought-provoking and memorable case.

Inviting the Audience to Fill the Gap

When a role is absent, the audience steps into it—whether they realize it or not. Without a Mentor, they might imagine themselves offering advice to the Hero. Without a Villain, they might question their own biases or internal conflicts. This gap becomes an invitation for the audience to become part of the story, making it deeply resonant and highly interactive. In a courtroom setting, this can be a powerful tool. If the jury doesn't see a traditional **Villain**, they might direct their energy toward solving the broader problem presented in the case. They stop looking for someone to blame and start looking for ways to create a fair outcome. That shift transforms passive listeners into active participants.

The absence of a role isn't a flaw—it's an opportunity. By leaving gaps in the narrative, you challenge the audience to engage more deeply, think more critically, and connect more personally. These narrative gaps create space for innovation and emotional resonance. In storytelling, what's left unsaid can be just as powerful as what's spoken. So, embrace the absence—it's where discoveries happen.

Life Lessons: The Absence of Roles – Narrative Gap

Once upon a time... In a focus group for a case, something felt off. The story was logical, the roles defined, yet the participants seemed confused, unable to connect with the narrative. A question lingered in the room: *What's missing?*

Every day... Stories falter when key roles are absent. Whether it's a missing perspective, an undefined antagonist, or an unexplored subplot, these gaps leave audiences adrift, unsure of how to engage with the story.

Until one day...I revisited the narrative, looking for what wasn't there. I realized we had overlooked the role of the system—the policies and practices that had contributed to my client's suffering. Once this gap was filled, the story transformed. It wasn't just about individuals; it was about a larger structure that needed change.

Because of that... The story gained clarity and momentum. The jury could see the broader implications, understanding how this case fit into a larger narrative of systemic failure and justice.

And ever since that day...I've made it a practice to identify and address narrative gaps, ensuring that every story I craft is complete, cohesive, and compelling. Because sometimes, it's not what's there—it's what's missing—that makes all the difference.

When Roles Overlap

In many stories, characters don't stick to a single role—they juggle multiple hats, adding complexity and depth. Picture a **Mentor** who's also a **Shadow**, their wisdom inadvertently revealing the Hero's greatest fears. Or a **Villain** who moonlights as a **Trickster**, creating chaos that pushes the Hero to adapt and grow. These layered roles make characters feel real and unpredictable, just like the complexities of real life.

In storytelling, overlapping roles keep the audience guessing and prevents one-dimensional portrayals. For instance, a witness in a legal case might start as a neutral **Observer** but evolve into a **Catalyst** with one unexpected revelation. When roles overlap, stories gain richness and texture, drawing the audience further into the narrative.

Roles as Mirrors for the Audience

The beauty of roles lies not only in their function within the story but also in the impression they leave on the audience. A **Hero's** struggles might mirror someone's personal challenges, while a **Mentor's** advice could echo the lessons we all learn from those who guide us. Even the **Villain** can hold a mirror to our fears, insecurities, or the obstacles we face in life.

When we as storytellers create roles that feel authentic and relatable, they invite the audience to see themselves in the story. When people recognize their own journeys within the narrative, they want to enter into it and become part of the story.

Adapting Roles to Fit Any Story

Roles are endlessly adaptable, bending and reshaping themselves to fit the needs of the story and the audience. In a personal anecdote, the **Shadow** might represent an internal struggle—a nagging self-doubt or a fear of failure. In a legal narrative, however, the **Villain** is often external: an opposing counsel, a flawed system, or an injustice looming over the case.

Sometimes, roles take on a symbolic flair. Imagine a survival story where a hurricane wreaks havoc—it's not just a **Villain** wreaking chaos but also a **Catalyst** for resilience and change. This kind of flexibility ensures that roles remain relevant and relatable, no matter the context. By understanding the principles behind these roles—who they are and how they interact—you can create narratives that feel both universal and deeply personal. After all, the beauty of storytelling lies in making each story uniquely your own.

Surprising the Audience with Role Evolution

There's nothing like a well-timed twist in a narrative. A **Villain** with a tragic backstory that makes us see their humanity. A **Trickster** who transforms into a **Mentor** at just the right moment. These shifts not only keep the story fresh but also reflect the multi-dimensional nature of real people and conflicts.

For example, in a story about overcoming systemic oppression, the **Villain** might also serve as a **Catalyst**—their unjust actions sparking the Hero's fight for change. These layered roles enrich the narrative, giving it depth and meaning that leave a lasting impression. Roles aren't just characters—they're your audience's way into the story. A relatable **Hero** invites empathy, while a well-crafted **Villain** creates intrigue. Supporting roles like the **Trickster** or **Ally** bring moments of connection, humor, or relief, ensuring the audience stays emotionally engaged.

In a courtroom, for example, you might frame the jury as the **Hero** of the story—placing them in the driver's seat of justice. Meanwhile, you step into the **Mentor** role, guiding them through the complexities of the case and empowering them to make the right decision. By crafting roles with your audience in mind, you turn spectators into participants, making the narrative not just compelling but also deeply personal.

Simplifying Complex Stories with Roles

When a story has layers upon layers—like a multi-defendant trial or an ensemble cast in a drama—roles become a vital part of the story. They help define who's who and what's what. Assigning roles such as **Hero**, **Ally**, or **Shadow** to different characters ensures clarity. Each role gets its spotlight, showing the audience exactly how each character contributes to the larger narrative.

For instance, in a courtroom case with multiple defendants, labeling one as the **Villain**, another as the reluctant **Ally**, and a third as the looming **Shadow** instantly clarifies their dynamics. This method keeps the story from turning into a chaotic mess and ensures that the central themes and conflicts stay crystal clear. Even the most sprawling narratives can feel manageable when roles anchor each character to the story's core purpose.

Roles don't exist in a vacuum. They interact, challenge, and shape one another. A Hero's growth often depends on the challenges posed by a Villain, the guidance of a Mentor, or the complications introduced by a Trickster. Sometimes a single character embodies multiple roles, and that's when things get really interesting.

This blending of roles reflects the complexity of real life, making characters feel more authentic and relatable. When storytelling roles overlap and evolve, they bring depth, tension, and unpredictability to your narrative. They turn one-dimensional characters into people your audience can see, feel, and root for.

A War Story: The Missing Voice That Changed Everything

Years ago, I took on a wrongful death case involving a young woman who had tragically died in a car accident caused by a reckless driver. The facts were strong: the defendant had been speeding through a residential neighborhood, ignoring every safety sign. Yet, as we prepared for trial, something about the story itself felt hollow.

The woman's parents and siblings had provided heartbreaking testimony, recounting their grief and loss, but it felt like we were still missing a strong connection to who she truly was. That's when my team and I used role reversals and psychodrama to find the missing crucial voice—that of her best friend.

We brought her friend to the stand, and what she shared transformed the narrative. With tears in her eyes, she described the moments before the crash: "We had just been planning her wedding. She wanted to have sunflowers everywhere because they reminded her of home and her late grandmother. She was so excited to start her new life with her fiancé."

This testimony didn't just fill a narrative gap—it gave the jury a vivid, emotional picture of the life that had been lost. It turned abstract grief into a concrete, human story. The jury's demeanor shifted, and for the first time, I saw them fully engaged with the heart of the case.

The missing role—the best friend and her story about wedding plans—became the bridge between the facts of the tragedy and the emotional resonance the story needed. It was a powerful reminder that every story has gaps, and finding the missing voice can mean the difference between a story that's heard and one that's deeply felt.

Conclusion: Embracing the Power of Absence

"Sometimes, the loudest story is told in the silence of what's missing—absence creates space for the audience to discover meaning on their own."

The absence of roles invites your audience to connect the dots on their own. It's a bold move—a creative dare that challenges traditional storytelling and taps into something deeper: the audience's imagination and empathy. These gaps can transform passive listeners into active participants. So, the next time you're crafting a narrative, don't be afraid to leave a space unfilled. You just might find that absence is the ingredient that makes your stories memorable.

Figure 33: Decision-Making Framework for Role Gaps in Storytelling

PRACTICE SPINES

Exercises: Exploring the Power of Absence

Exercise 1: A Story with a Missing Mentor

Craft a short story where the Hero must navigate their journey without a Mentor. How do they adapt, grow, or stumble without guidance?

Prompt: Imagine a young attorney preparing for their first trial after their seasoned mentor unexpectedly falls ill. Write a story spine where they confront the challenge, find strength within, and discover their own voice.

- **Reflection:** How does the absence of a Mentor shape the Hero's growth? What does it reveal about their character?

Exercise 2: The Trial Without a Villain

Create a narrative for a courtroom case where no one is clearly at fault.

- Describe how the absence of a traditional Villain shifts the focus.
- Who becomes the Hero, and what internal conflicts or systemic issues take center stage?

Prompt: A tenant and landlord are in dispute over a flooded apartment, but both are victims of an unexpected storm. Use the Story Spine to explore how the narrative evolves without a clear antagonist.

- **Reflection:** What challenges does the audience (or jury) face when no one is the "bad guy"? How does this ambiguity impact the resolution?

Exercise 3: Fill the Gap—Audience as the Missing Role

Write a story where the audience is invited to fill a missing role.

- Leave out a major perspective—like the Hero's resolution or the Villain's motivations—and challenge your audience to interpret what's unsaid.

Prompt: A case is presented where a factory worker is suing their employer for unsafe conditions. The lawyer deliberately avoids painting the employer as a Villain but instead highlights the systemic pressures both parties face.

- **Reflection:** What do you think the audience (jury) might assume or feel when a role is missing? How does this encourage deeper engagement or critical thinking?

Chapter 17
The Heart of the Story

"Facts might open the door, but emotions invite you inside and make you stay."

Make Me Feel Something

At their core, great stories explore what it means to be human. The best stories are not just a series of events—they're experiences that transport you into someone else's world and leaves an unforgettable impression. While the Story Spine provides a sturdy framework, it's the emotions that breathe life into the narrative.

Consider a courtroom example: The facts may tell us that a mother fought to regain custody of her children after a setback. But it's her fear of losing them, her hope for a second chance, and her determination to change that make her story unforgettable. Facts inform; emotions transform. When you let the audience feel the story, you turn them from passive listeners into active participants.

Complex Emotions: The Spice of the Story

Emotions are rarely simple. They're a blend of bittersweet, fiery, soothing, or sharp feelings, and embracing that complexity makes a story richer and more authentic. A protagonist might feel anger at a system that wronged them, but beneath that anger lies sadness, and alongside it, hope. Imagine a client suing after being denied a job due to discrimination. Their frustration might intertwine with gratitude for the community rallying around them. By layering these emotions, you show the complexity of the human experience, creating characters the audience can't help but root for.

Emotional Evolution: Shifting and Growing

Stories are journeys, and the emotional shifts along the way are what make them compelling. The "Until one day" and "Because of that" phases of the Story Spine are perfect places to explore these shifts. How often do we start a situation feeling one way and end it feeling another? A frightened underdog might evolve into a determined fighter, or a weary skeptic might grow into a hopeful believer.

These transitions don't just add tension—they keep the audience engaged, wondering where the story will lead next. For example, imagine a character who begins a lawsuit feeling powerless. By their "Until finally" moment, they've discovered a well of courage they didn't know existed. This arc of growth mirrors real life, making it all the more powerful.

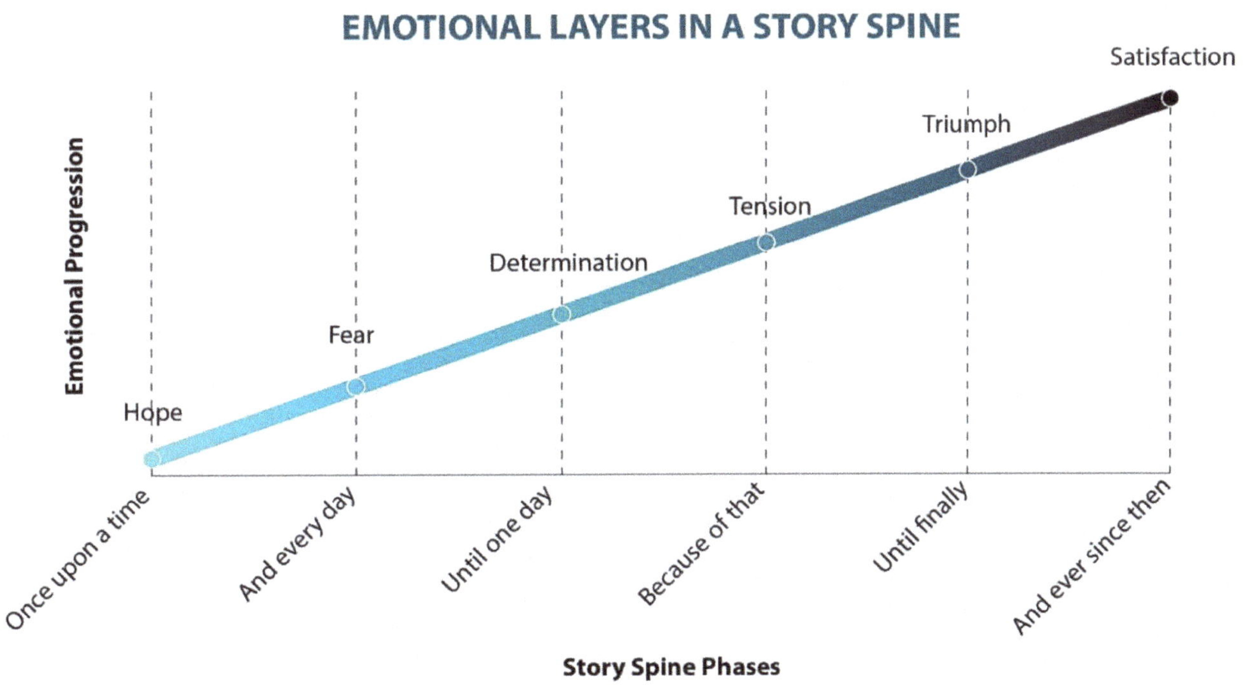

Figure 34: Emotional Layers in a Story Spine

A Story Spine About Redemption

Once upon a time, I was asked to consult on a case involving a young man facing a trial that could define his future.

Every day, his past mistakes seemed to overshadow the progress he was making.

Until one day, during a role-playing session, he stepped into his mother's shoes. Speaking with honesty and love, he revealed the version of himself she saw: flawed but full of hope and potential.

Because of that, we crafted a narrative not about excuses but redemption—showing how far he'd come and the man he was striving to be.

Because of that, the jury didn't just see his past; they saw his humanity and capacity to grow.

Until finally, their verdict reflected compassion and understanding, giving him a second chance to rewrite his story.

That experience reinforced for me the transformative power of storytelling to uncover truths and highlight humanity, even in the toughest of circumstances. The next time you sit down to tell a story, remember that it's not just the framework that matters—it's the heart you pour into it.

Crafting Emotional Highs and Lows

Human emotions are rarely simple—they're a swirling mix of contradictions: hope with fear, anger with love, despair with a flicker of possibility. When storytellers embrace this complexity, their narratives gain authenticity and depth.

Take a courtroom story about a parent fighting for custody. On the surface, it's about legal arguments, but beneath lies heartbreak, hope, and determination. By revealing these emotional layers, the story transforms from a legal case into a deeply felt human experience. It's not just about the outcome; it's about the meaning behind the fight.

These nuances allow audiences to see themselves in the characters, even in unfamiliar circumstances. Layering emotions into storytelling creates a multidimensional experience that resonates deeply. So, dive into the messy, complicated, and beautiful world of feelings—this is where great stories take shape.

The Transformative Power of Emotional Storytelling

Emotional storytelling challenges assumptions, sparks reflection, and inspires action. It reminds us what it means to be human: to struggle, grow, fail, and rise again. As storytellers, our job isn't just to inform but to connect. By embracing the heart of the story, with all its raw and beautiful emotions, we create narratives that transcend the moment and linger in the minds and hearts of our audience.

Consider a story of overcoming adversity. It doesn't just inspire applause—it encourages the audience to reframe their own challenges and embrace new possibilities. Emotional storytelling becomes a catalyst for transformation, turning simple narratives into sparks for growth or even societal change.

When storytellers reveal vulnerability—joy, sorrow, fear, or triumph—they invite their audience to do the same. This shared emotional journey creates intimacy, breaks down walls, and fosters understanding. Infusing the Story Spine with emotional complexity ensures the audience feels seen, heard, and valued.

Stories with emotional depth leave a lasting impression. Logic might win attention, but emotion earns trust and stays remembered. For example, a heartfelt story about a client's resilience doesn't just persuade jurors; it inspires them to carry its message forward. A great story doesn't just move the moment—it builds a legacy.

Emotions as the Unifying Thread

Emotions bridge a story's events, characters, and themes, turning a simple narrative into an immersive experience. But the act of infusing a story with emotion also transforms the storyteller. By diving into the emotional heart of a narrative, storytellers uncover deeper truths, gaining authenticity and confidence. A truly impactful story doesn't just evoke emotions—it fosters an emotional partnership between the storyteller and the audience. This shared experience creates a collective journey rather than a one-sided tale. It becomes a co-creation.

For instance, when a trial attorney uses the Story Spine to present a client's story of redemption, they invite the jury to feel the journey and reflect on their own values. Layered with emotion, the Story Spine evolves into a shared adventure that stays with the listener long after the story has ended.

A War Story: Finding the Emotional Core of a Tragic Loss

I once represented a family devastated by a preventable medical error that claimed the life of their son. The facts were clear, but the story's heart emerged when the father recounted a simple moment: teaching his son to ride a bike. His voice trembled as he described the boy's joy when he finally let go of the handlebars. "That's the memory I hold onto," he said, "because it's the last time I felt he was completely free."

That single moment became the emotional core of the case. It connected the jury to the family's pain in a way that transcended statistics and expert testimony. By anchoring the narrative in this heartfelt memory, we evoked empathy and meaning, which ultimately led to a verdict that honored the family's loss.

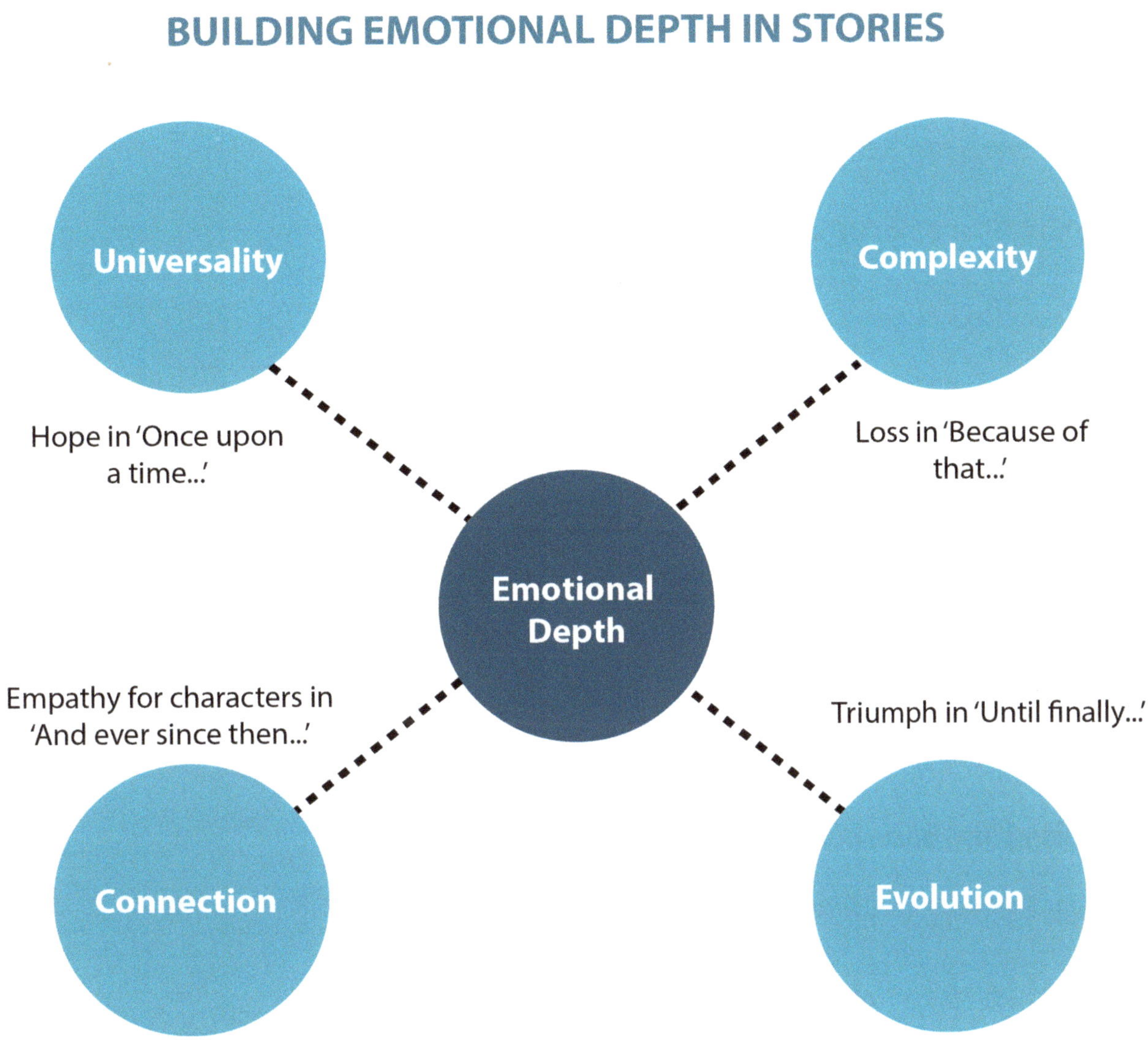

Figure 35: Building Emotional Depth in Stories

Conclusion

"When layered with emotion, the Story Spine stops being just a framework and becomes an adventure the audience takes with you."

Feelings are the essential ingredient that turns a sequence of events into a story that lingers in the heart and mind. By highlighting how characters experience and process events, storytellers create narratives that leave a lasting impression. When your story moves with feeling, it doesn't just inform—it transforms.

PRACICE SPINES

Practical Steps to Add Feeling and Complexity

1. Use the Story Spine as a Base

Start with the logical progression of the **Story Spine**:

- **Once upon a time...** (Set the scene)
- **Every day...** (Establish routine)
- **But one day...** (Introduce conflict)
- **Because of that...** (Escalate consequences)
- **Until finally...** (Resolve the story)
- **And ever since then...** (Show long-term impact)

2. Ask Feeling-Based Questions

For each section of the Story Spine, explore emotions:

- How does the protagonist feel in this moment?
- What fears, hopes, or doubts are they experiencing?
- How do other characters feel about this event?

3. Highlight Internal and External Worlds

Balance external events with internal experiences:

- External: What happened? (e.g., a contract was breached)
- Internal: How did it feel? (e.g., the character felt betrayed after years of trust.)

4. Layer Sensory Details

Bring feelings to life with sensory details:

- Instead of saying, "He was nervous," describe the feeling: "His hands trembled as he gripped the edge of the table, his pulse racing with every glance toward the jury."

5. Use Role Reversal (Psychodrama Technique)

Step into another character's shoes to uncover hidden emotions. How does the antagonist feel about their actions? How does a neutral party perceive the events?

Example: Enriching a Legal Narrative

Scenario: A client sues after being denied life-saving medication by their insurance provider.

Basic Story Spine:

- *"Once upon a time, Lisa was a schoolteacher battling a chronic illness."*
- *"Every day, she relied on her insurance to cover the medication that kept her condition stable."*
- *"But one day, her insurance provider denied her claim, citing a new policy."*
- *"Because of that, Lisa's health deteriorated rapidly, forcing her to take unpaid leave."*
- *"Until finally, she sought legal help and fought for the coverage she deserved."*
- *"And ever since then, Lisa has been a vocal advocate for patient rights."*

With Layers of Feeling:

- *"Once upon a time, Lisa found purpose in her work as a schoolteacher, delighting in her students' curiosity and growth."*
- *"Every day, she felt gratitude for the medication that gave her the strength to live fully, even with her chronic illness."*

- *"But one day, a cold, impersonal letter arrived from her insurance provider, denying her claim with no explanation."*

Chapter 18
Universal Truths and Themes

"Universal truths are the heartbeat of storytelling, connecting personal experiences to the shared human journey."

Developing Resonance

The most unforgettable stories touch on universal truths—those big, human ideas that make us all nod and say, "Yep, I get that." Love, loss, hope, justice, resilience—these truths weave through our lives, making them the perfect threads for storytelling. They're not just concepts; they're the glue that binds individual stories to the collective human experience.

In the Story Spine, universal truths can live in every phase. They're the unspoken yet deeply felt elements that make a story timeless. For instance, a courtroom story about a client's fight for justice isn't just about depositions and cross-examinations—it's about the universal yearning for fairness and dignity.

Using Themes to Sharpen Focus

While universal truths set the stage, themes zoom in, giving your story a clear perspective. Think of themes as the lens through which you explore a universal truth. Let's take resilience—it's a vast, sprawling concept. But by narrowing it to a theme like redemption or sacrifice, you can shape a narrative that feels sharp and intentional.

The Story Spine is your storytelling compass, and the theme is the map detail showing the twists and turns. For example, if you're telling a story about redemption, every phase of the spine—"Once upon a time," "Until one day," and

"Because of that"—should reflect growth and transformation. A well-woven theme ensures that your audience doesn't just hear the story; they feel its purpose.

In narratives with multiple layers or subplots, themes act as an anchor, ensuring the story stays cohesive. The Story Spine's structure provides clarity, while themes guide the storyteller's focus, ensuring each element aligns with the central message. For example, in a courtroom narrative involving complex legal arguments, the theme of fairness might run through every phase of the spine, tying the facts and emotions together. By keeping the theme central, storytellers can navigate even the most intricate narratives without losing sight of the universal truth they aim to convey.

A War Story: The Fight for Truth

It was a case involving a whistleblower who had uncovered a web of deceit within a powerful corporation. My client, a young employee, had risked everything—his career, his reputation, even his safety—to expose the truth about toxic workplace conditions that were causing severe harm to employees.

As I prepared for the trial, I realized that this wasn't just about facts and evidence; it was about courage and integrity. I decided to tell the story not just from my client's perspective, but through the lens of the system he was up against—a system designed to silence dissent and protect the powerful at all costs.

"Once upon a time," I began in my opening arguments, "there was a workplace built on promises of safety and fairness. Every day, employees showed up, trusting that they were protected. Until one day, the cracks began to show—unpaid medical bills, ignored complaints, workers falling ill. Because of that, my client took the extraordinary step of speaking out, knowing full well the consequences he would face. And the complication was that the company tried to bury the truth, silencing voices and spinning lies."

As I spoke, the jury listened intently. They weren't just hearing about policy violations and ignored regulations; they were seeing the human cost of those failures. They could feel the weight of my client's decision to stand up, alone, against a giant.

"Until finally," I concluded, "the truth came to light. And now, it is up to us to decide whether courage will be rewarded or silenced, whether integrity will triumph over greed."

By the end of the trial, the jury wasn't just deliberating over evidence—they were deciding on the values they wanted to see reflected in their community. The verdict was a victory not just for my client, but for everyone who believes in the power of truth. That case reminded me that storytelling isn't just a tool for persuasion; it's a way to bring humanity to the heart of justice.

The Emotional Arc of Universal Truths

Universal truths stick with us because they make us feel something. The Story Spine's structure naturally lends itself to building these emotional arcs. As the story progresses, the emotions deepen: anger at injustice, hope in adversity, joy in resolution.

Let's say you're crafting a story about courage in the face of fear. The turning point ("Until one day") might be the moment fear threatens to consume the protagonist. The "Because of that" phase explores how they confront their fear step by step, building tension. By the time you reach "Until finally," their victory feels earned, leaving your audience feeling triumphant right alongside them.

The beauty of universal truths lies in their ability to cross boundaries. Stories centered on resilience, love, or justice feel relevant whether you're speaking to a jury, writing a novel, or telling a bedtime tale. The Story Spine helps you root these truths in specifics, creating stories that feel immediate yet timeless.

Take a narrative about overcoming adversity. While resilience is the universal truth, you can explore it through themes like community, perseverance, or family sacrifice. This interplay ensures your story reaches a wide audience, appealing to people from all walks of life. So, next time you sit down to craft a story, remember: the truths we share are the ones that make stories unforgettable.

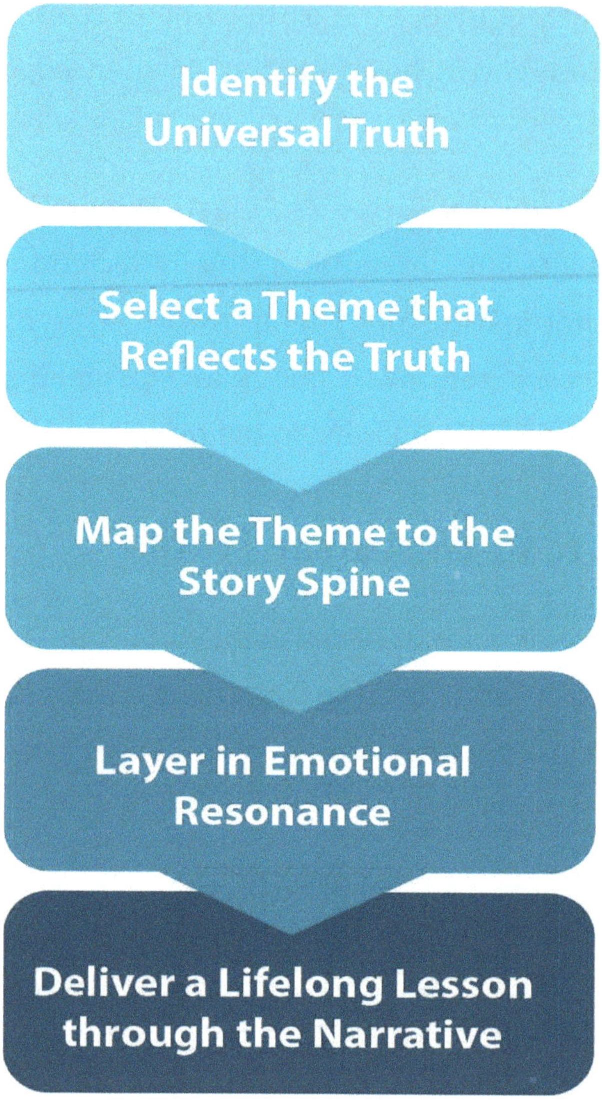

Figure 36: Steps for Creating Resonant Narratives

A Personal Spine: The Power of Courage

Once upon a time, I was just a young person trying to navigate a world that often felt too big and too broken to change. Every day, I saw injustice around me—people silenced, overlooked, or treated unfairly—and I wondered if speaking up could ever make a difference. Until one day, I found myself in a position where I couldn't stay silent anymore.

Because of that, I chose to take a stand, even though it meant risking comfort and security. And because of that, I learned that the power of one voice, when paired with unwavering determination, can inspire change in ways I never imagined.

Until finally, I realized that standing up for what's right isn't just about changing the world—it's about staying true to yourself. And ever since then, I've carried that lesson with me, using my voice and my actions to make an impact wherever I can.

The lesson? Sometimes, the greatest battles are the ones we fight with conviction, even when we're the only one standing.

Universality Without Losing Specificity

One of the challenges in integrating universal truths is ensuring they don't overshadow the specific details that make a story unique. Universal truths, like justice or love, hold power because they are deeply human, but their true impact comes from how they unfold in individual lives. The Story Spine allows storytellers to strike this balance by focusing on specific moments that reflect broader truths. For instance, a lawyer telling a story about redemption might describe a single decision their client made that symbolized transformation. This specificity gives the universal truth texture, making it understandable and tangible rather than abstract.

The beauty of storytelling happens where universal truths meet personal, specific moments. Take the truth that "love conquers all." Sure, it sounds poetic, but it comes alive when you show it through the journey of a single mother sacrificing everything for her child's future. In "Once upon a time," you introduce her humble beginnings.

In "Because of that," you highlight her struggles to make ends meet. By the resolution, her triumph becomes a mirror for the audience, reflecting their own capacity for love and resilience. This mixture of specific and universal makes the story both personal and relatable. It's the recipe for resonance—one-part raw humanity, one-part shared truth.

Universal truths transcend time, culture, and context, reminding us of the emotions and experiences that bind us together. Themes sharpen those truths, giving them focus and purpose, while the Story Spine provides the structure to bring them to life.

Whether you're crafting a trial argument or sharing a personal anecdote, stories grounded in universal truths and explored through thoughtful themes do more than captivate—they invite reflection, build connection, and spark transformation. So, the next time you tell a story, ask yourself: *What truth am I inviting my audience to discover?*

And lastly, contrast is a powerful tool for emphasizing universal truths. By presenting opposing ideas or emotions, storytellers can underscore the significance of the truth they're exploring. For example, a story about resilience might juxtapose moments of despair with those of hope, making the triumphs feel more profound.

Within the Story Spine, this contrast can be built into the "Because of that" or "And the complication was that" phases, where conflicts and challenges arise. This interplay between opposites enriches the narrative, allowing the universal truth to emerge more clearly and powerfully.

A War Story: The Power of Forgiveness

Several years ago, I represented a young man named Marcus in a civil case against a local school district. Marcus, once a promising athlete, had been injured due to gross negligence during a poorly supervised practice. The injury ended his dreams of playing professional sports, leaving him angry, bitter, and hopeless. His story was heartbreaking, but it was also filled with raw, unresolved emotion.

As we prepared for trial, I realized that Marcus's anger, while understandable, wasn't the story that would resonate most with the jury. Instead, I encouraged him to explore the deeper, universal theme running through his experience: the power of forgiveness and personal growth.

During his testimony, Marcus spoke not just about the pain of losing his dreams but about the unexpected lessons he'd gained. "At first, all I wanted was revenge," he admitted. "But over time, I realized that holding onto that anger was holding me back. I've learned to forgive, not just for their sake, but for mine. And now, I'm working to inspire other kids who feel like their lives are over because of a setback."

The courtroom was silent, the jury captivated by his words. Marcus's story wasn't just about loss—it was about resilience, growth, and the universal truth that forgiveness can set us free. In the end, the jury awarded him the compensation he deserved, but more importantly, they saw him as a symbol of strength and redemption. His story reminded me that universal truths—like the power of forgiveness—transcend the specifics of any one case and touch something deeply human in all of us.

Conclusion

"A story steeped in universal truth doesn't just inform—it transforms, turning a mirror on the audience and inviting them to see their own journey within it."

Universal truths and themes are the heartbeat of every unforgettable story. They're the key ingredient that elevates a narrative from ordinary to extraordinary, by capturing what it means to be human. By weaving your story with the shared threads of love, loss, hope, or justice—and focusing on the unique angles offered by your themes—you create something that is magnetic.

Examples of Universal Truths and Themes in Legal Contexts

1. Universal Truth: We all seek justice.

- **Case:** A whistleblower case where an employee exposes corporate fraud.
- **Theme:** Courage in the face of adversity.

Story Spine:

- *"Once upon a time, a young accountant took pride in their work, believing they were part of an ethical company."*
- *"Every day, they diligently balanced the books and ensured compliance with the law."*
- *"But one day, they discovered evidence of fraudulent activity that could harm thousands of people."*
- *"Because of that, they reported the issue, even though they knew it might cost them their job."*
- *"Until finally, their actions led to the company being held accountable and significant reforms being implemented."*
- *"And ever since then, they've been seen as a symbol of integrity, proving that doing the right thing matters."*

2. Universal Truth: We all experience loss.

- **Case:** A personal injury case involving a child's injury due to negligence.
- **Theme:** The resilience of families.

Story Spine:

- *"Once upon a time, a close-knit family lived in a quiet neighborhood, cherishing every moment together."*
- *"Every day, the parents worked hard to provide their children with a safe and happy life."*
- *"But one day, a preventable accident at the playground left their youngest child with life-altering injuries."*
- *"Because of that, the family faced months of medical treatments, financial strain, and emotional hardship."*

- *"Until finally, they stood together in court and won the compensation needed to rebuild their lives."*
- *"And ever since then, they've become advocates for safer playgrounds, ensuring no other family endures what they have."*

3. Universal Truth: We all want to belong.

- **Case:** A discrimination lawsuit involving workplace inequality.
- **Theme:** Fighting for equality.

Story Spine:

- *"Once upon a time, a talented professional joined a prestigious company, eager to contribute their skills and grow."*
- *"Every day, they worked harder than their peers, hoping their efforts would be recognized."*
- *"But one day, they realized that their achievements were being overlooked because of their race and gender."*
- *"Because of that, they felt isolated, undervalued, and determined to challenge the status quo."*
- *"Until finally, they filed a lawsuit that not only brought justice to their case but also inspired change within the company."*
- *"And ever since then, they've been a voice for inclusion, reminding everyone that belonging should never be conditional."*

PRACTICE SPINES

Exercises for Identifying Universal Truths and Themes

Exercise 1: Identify the Universal Truth

- Think of a story you want to tell personal, legal, or creative.
- Ask yourself: *What shared human experience does this story reflect?*
- Write down a single universal truth that underpins your story.
- Example: *We all experience loss.*

Exercise 2: Explore the Theme

- Once you've identified the universal truth, consider the specific angle your story takes on it.
- Write down a theme that aligns with your truth.
- Example: Universal truth: *We all experience loss.* Theme: *Healing from grief.*

Exercise 3: Map Truths and Themes to the Story Spine

- Use the Story Spine framework to map out your story, ensuring that each section reflects your chosen universal truth and theme.
- Review to ensure consistency and emotional resonance.

Chapter 19
Perspectives of Inanimate Objects

"When we give voice to silent witnesses, we reveal new dimensions of empathy, clarity, and persuasion."

Expanding Storytelling Horizons

The most compelling stories often come from unexpected narrators. By adopting the perspective of inanimate objects, you can transform a case or concept into a narrative that's fresh, memorable, and deeply resonant. Giving objects a voice offers an innovative way to underscore emotional stakes and key details. This approach not only captures attention but also strengthens your ability to connect with your audience on a human level.

This technique works across storytelling contexts—courtroom presentations, negotiation strategies, or even personal storytelling exercises. It allows you to shed new light on the familiar, framing the narrative in ways that emphasize overlooked details and create a stronger emotional connection.

Example: The House Speaks

In a property dispute, instead of recounting dry legal facts, imagine the house narrating its story:

"Once upon a time, I was filled with laughter and warmth. Every day, I provided a safe haven, echoing the memories of birthdays, holidays, and quiet evenings. Until one day, I became the center of a conflict over who owned me. Because of that, I saw families divided and walls grow cold under the weight of legal battles. Until finally, someone listened to my story and understood what I represent—more than a house, I am a home. And ever since, I've hoped to shelter love and unity once again."

This approach reframes the case, transforming the house into a poignant symbol of emotional and practical stakes, encouraging the audience to see beyond the legal arguments.

Example: The Toy's Perspective

In a product liability case, narrated from the viewpoint of the defective toy:

"Once upon a time, I was designed to bring joy. Every day, I dreamed of tiny hands unwrapping me, laughter filling the air. Until one day, a flaw in my design caused harm instead of happiness. Because of that, I became a source of heartbreak for a family and a reminder of what can go wrong when safety is overlooked. Finally, my story was told, and those responsible were held accountable. And ever since, I've stood as a lesson for making sure every child's joy comes without risk."

This narrative draws attention to the human cost of negligence, turning a product into a symbol of trust and accountability.

Using the voice of inanimate objects is a powerful storytelling tool that can deepen understanding and amplify emotional resonance. By reframing the narrative, you encourage your audience to see the case or concept from a fresh angle, making your message more impactful and memorable. The next time you craft a story, consider who—or what—might be the best narrator.

Life Lessons: Perspectives of Inanimate Objects

Once upon a time... During a storytelling workshop, I challenged participants to tell a story from an unexpected perspective. One woman chose the role of a courtroom bench. Her narrative revealed decades of silent observation—witnessing heartbreak, triumph, and the passage of countless lives.

Every day...I've watched stories fall into predictable patterns, missing opportunities for novelty and depth. Changing the perspective can unlock layers of insight that might otherwise go untold.

Until one day... In a trial prep session, I encouraged a lawyer to narrate their case from the perspective of a piece of evidence—a single photograph. The lawyer's storytelling shifted, capturing the emotional weight of the moment frozen in that image.

Because of that... The jury saw the case through new eyes, connecting with the story on a visceral level. The unconventional perspective brought fresh depth and originality to the narrative.

And ever since that day...I've embraced this creative technique, helping storytellers experiment with perspectives that surprise, engage, and reveal truths in unexpected ways.

Amplifying Key Details

Inanimate objects often offer a fresh perspective that can draw attention to overlooked details. Imagine a courtroom story about a car accident narrated by the car itself:
"And the complication was that my brakes began to fail, and I couldn't stop as the light turned red." This storytelling approach vividly illustrates critical evidence, helping jurors visualize the sequence of events. By adopting the voice of an object, storytellers can present key facts in a relatable and engaging way, maintaining narrative flow while reinforcing the case's core message.

Uncovering Emotional Stakes in Abstract Entities

Even abstract concepts like rules, laws, or principles can serve as narrators within the Story Spine framework. For example, a challenged law might tell its story:

"Once upon a time, I was written to protect the vulnerable. Every day, I ensured fairness and equality. Until one day, I was twisted to serve the powerful instead."

This unique perspective humanizes abstract ideas, making them tangible and emotionally impactful. It allows the audience to grasp the stakes of the story on a personal level, turning theoretical debates into compelling narratives.

Using objects as narrators pushes storytellers to explore unconventional viewpoints, fostering creativity and insight. This technique compels storytellers to consider how every element of a story—human or otherwise—plays a part in the larger narrative. In a theft case, for instance, the stolen object might narrate:

"Until finally, I was recovered, scratched and battered, but still holding the memories of the family I belonged to."

This method not only deepens the storyteller's understanding of the case but also captivates the audience, ensuring the narrative remains fresh and engaging.

Bridging Gaps in Understanding

Objects can simplify complex narratives, bridging gaps in understanding by presenting technical or intricate details in accessible terms. In a medical malpractice case, for example, a surgical tool might narrate its role:

"Once upon a time, I was chosen to save a life. Every day, I was carefully sterilized and prepared for precision. Until one day, I was left behind, unseen, causing harm instead of healing."

This approach clarifies technical aspects while emphasizing the emotional and practical consequences, ensuring audiences grasp the stakes without becoming overwhelmed.

Shifting Blame or Responsibility

Object narratives can also subtly redirect blame or highlight hidden accountability. In a workplace accident case, a malfunctioning machine might narrate:

"Because of that, I broke under pressure, injuring the worker who relied on me."

This perspective brings attention to systemic negligence, such as inadequate maintenance or faulty design, allowing the audience to infer responsibility without overt accusations. This indirect approach often makes the narrative more persuasive.

Building Tension and Suspense

Narratives from inanimate objects can inject a unique sense of suspense or dramatic irony. In a product recall case, the defective item might recount:

"Because of that, I ended up in a thousand homes, trusted to be safe. And the complication was that I wasn't."

This limited perspective creates tension, as the audience anticipates the consequences while the object remains unaware of the full picture. This dynamic keeps the narrative engaging and emotionally charged.

Highlighting Value and Loss

Objects often carry sentimental or symbolic weight, and their perspective can underscore what's truly at stake. For example, in a family heirloom dispute, the object might narrate:

"And the complication was that I became the center of a battle between siblings, my meaning forgotten in the fight for ownership."

This approach highlights not only the physical value of the object but also the emotional and relational stakes, adding depth and poignancy to the story.

Encouraging Audience Engagement

Giving voice to objects sparks curiosity and invites the audience to explore the story from an unexpected angle. In a trial about a stolen artifact, the artifact might recount its journey:

"Until finally, I was returned to my rightful place, my significance restored not just as an object, but as a symbol of cultural identity."

This creative approach not only captures the audience's imagination but also ensures they remain engaged and emotionally invested in the story's resolution. By adopting the perspective of inanimate objects, we unlock new ways to illuminate key details, evoke emotion, and engage the audience. This technique transforms storytelling into a dynamic, multidimensional experience that highlights the human and emotional stakes in any narrative.

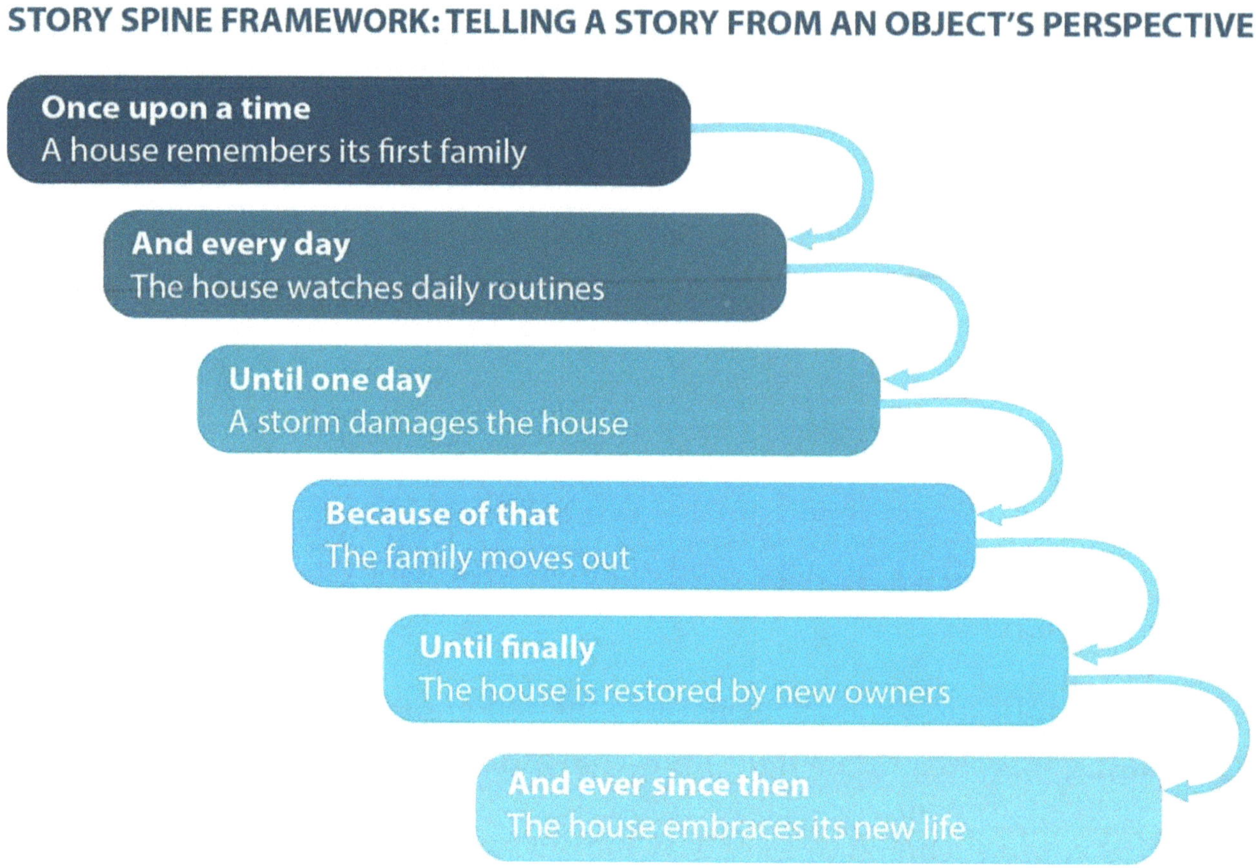

Figure 37: Story Spine Framework from an Object's Perspective

A War Story: The Voice of a Silent Witness

During a property damage trial, I experimented with telling part of the story from the perspective of the damaged building itself. "If these walls could talk," I said during opening arguments, "they'd tell you about the families they sheltered, the laughter that echoed through their halls, and the storm that tore them apart."

Using this perspective, I painted the building as a silent witness to negligence and loss. The jury listened intently, captivated by the novelty of hearing the story from the point of view of an inanimate object. By the end of the trial, the building wasn't just a structure—it was a symbol of resilience and injustice. This creative approach added emotional resonance and helped secure a just resolution.

Reimagining Storytelling Through Inanimate Perspectives

Using inanimate objects or abstract concepts as narrators enriches storytelling by uncovering layers of meaning often hidden in plain sight. Objects become vessels for human experience, transforming the mundane into extraordinary. For example, a house in a property dispute might recount the laughter it sheltered or the tears it absorbed, deepening the audience's connection to the stakes.

The Story Spine's adaptability allows storytellers to reimagine narratives in innovative ways. A defective product might narrate its journey, exposing design flaws or production oversights. This perspective challenges assumptions and reframes narratives to captivate and persuade on intellectual and emotional levels. By inhabiting the voices of objects, storytellers deepen their understanding of the material, fostering creativity and insight.

Using Inanimate Objects as Narrators in Trial

"In a courtroom, the most honest witness is often the one that cannot speak—an object that saw everything, remembers everything, and has no reason to lie."

The Broken Safety Valve That No One Fixed

Once upon a time... (Voir Dire – The Valve as a Silent Witness to Negligence)

"Once upon a time, this factory was a place where workers trusted their safety gear, their supervisors, and their equipment. And every day, workers like Joe Martinez showed up, trusting that if something went wrong, the company would fix it. But I want to ask you: Have you ever seen something broken and been told, 'It's fine, we called it in, just keep using it'?"

- *Voir Dire establishes the jury's connection to the theme of ignored warnings—something many have experienced in their own workplaces.*
- *The* ***broken safety valve*** *is introduced as a witness—an object that saw everything but couldn't speak up.*

The following questions are designed to explore jurors' attitudes toward workplace safety, responsibility, and accountability, which are central to the narrative of negligence in this case:

1. **Question about Personal Experience with Safety Issues:**
   - "Can you share an experience where you or someone you know felt that a safety issue at work was overlooked or not taken seriously by those in charge? How was that situation handled?"
2. **Question about Perceptions of Corporate Responsibility:**
   - "In your opinion, what should an employer's priority be when they are made aware of potential safety hazards in the workplace? How do you think such situations should be addressed?"
3. **Question about Trust and Authority:**
   - "Have you ever been in a situation where you had to decide whether to trust authority figures despite having concerns about safety or protocol? What influenced your decision in that situation?"

And every day... (Opening – The Valve's History of Being Ignored)

"And every day, the pressure in the pipes built up. Every day, the safety valve released just enough to keep the system from failing. Every day, it clicked, hissed, and did its job—until the company stopped maintaining it. Until one day, the warning signs were ignored."

- *The lawyer personifies the* ***safety valve*** *as something that had worked tirelessly, just like Joe Martinez. This builds the tension—foreshadowing the moment when it fails.*
- *The jury is forced to see the valve as more than metal—it is a* ***symbol of corporate neglect****.*

When preparing to use an inanimate object in an opening statement, it's crucial to ensure that the object's story focuses on how the object illustrates broader themes or legal principles. Here are some guiding questions lawyers can ask themselves when incorporating an inanimate object into their opening, along with three pro tips for effective usage:

Guiding Questions for Preparation:

1. **What is the symbolic significance of the object?**
    - Consider what the object represents within the context of the case. Does it symbolize negligence, responsibility, or loss? How does it connect to the key legal issues or the emotional underpinnings of your argument?
2. **How does the object's story advance the narrative of the case?**
    - Evaluate how the object's function or malfunction can be used to illustrate the defendant's actions or inaction. How does this object's history support the claims or defenses being made?
3. **What factual evidence can be linked to the object to support your case?**
    - Identify and prepare to present any maintenance records, expert testimonies, or historical data that relate to the object. How do these pieces of evidence correlate with the legal arguments you plan to make?

By thoughtfully integrating an inanimate object into your opening statement and considering these aspects, you can enhance your narrative, provide clear and compelling evidence, and effectively frame the legal issues at stake.

But one day... (Direct Examination – The Day the Valve Failed)

"But one day, the safety valve didn't hiss. It didn't release pressure. It stayed silent, because it was clogged with rust and debris. The company had ignored its last scheduled maintenance check. And Joe Martinez was working just feet away when the pipe exploded."

- *Through expert testimony, the lawyer walks the jury through **what the valve "saw"**—the gradual failure, the ignored maintenance logs, the emails requesting repairs.*
- *Instead of just **stating** negligence, the lawyer **lets the broken valve tell the story**.*

To effectively integrate the example of the safety valve's failure into direct examination, the strategy centers on utilizing the valve as an inanimate witness whose 'story' speaks volumes about the broader context of corporate responsibility and negligence. This approach requires a careful blending of factual testimony with the conceptual personification of the valve to illustrate its crucial role in the events leading to the accident. Here's how this can be achieved:

Strategies for Incorporating the Safety Valve in Direct Examination:

Contextualizing the Valve's Role:

- Begin by setting the stage for the valve as more than just a piece of machinery; treat it as a critical component whose failure was symptomatic of larger systemic issues within the company. This frames the valve not just as an object, but as a witness to the company's practices.

Detailing the Valve's Operational History:

- Use expert testimony to detail how the valve was supposed to operate under normal conditions and the standard practices for its maintenance. This establishes a baseline of expected safety measures and functionality.

Narrating the Failure:

- Proceed to describe the sequence of events leading up to the valve's failure. This includes the missed maintenance checks, the visible deterioration, and the ignored warnings from employees about its condition. Each detail serves to personify the valve, giving it a 'voice' to testify to the neglect it 'witnessed.'

Illustrating the Consequences of Negligence:

- Highlight the moment of failure—not just the technical aspects, but also the human and operational impact. Discuss the immediate effects of the explosion, the response of the company, and the repercussions on safety standards and trust within the workplace.

Techniques for Effectiveness:

1. **Use Visual Aids:**
    - Employ diagrams or animations to show the valve in its operational state versus its state at the time of the failure. Visuals can help jurors understand complex mechanical processes and see the valve as an active participant in the narrative.
2. **Incorporate Real Artifacts:**
    - If possible, bring the actual valve or parts of it into the courtroom. Allowing the jury to see the corroded valve can powerfully augment the narrative of neglect and the resulting failure.
3. **Expert Witnesses:**
    - Have mechanical engineers or safety inspectors testify about the valve's condition and the standard industry practices for equipment maintenance. Their insights will give credibility to the valve's story, framing it within expert knowledge of what should have been done to prevent its failure.

By treating the valve as a silent witness whose story is told through expert testimony, visual aids, and factual narratives, the direct examination can effectively communicate the themes of neglect and responsibility. This approach not only makes the testimony more engaging but also grounds it in tangible evidence that supports the legal arguments being made.

Because of that... (Cross-Examination – Exposing the Company's Pattern of Neglect)

"Because of that, hot steam shot through the factory floor, burning through Joe's protective gear. Because of that, he suffered third-degree burns over 60% of his body. Because of that, he spent the last 12 hours of his life in unimaginable pain. And because of that, this company—despite knowing about this valve for months—calls this a 'tragic accident.'"

- Cross-examining the company's maintenance supervisor, the lawyer forces the jury to see that **this was not an accident—it was preventable.**
- *By using the **valve as the narrator**, the case moves beyond dry expert testimony and becomes a **narrative of ignored warnings and lost lives**.*

Tying the example of the safety valve's failure into the cross-examination strategy requires a focus on highlighting the company's ongoing neglect and framing their inaction as a direct contributor to the tragedy. Here are some example questions for lawyers to consider when preparing for cross-examination, along with pro tips for effectively conveying this narrative to the jury.

Example Questions for Cross-Examination:

1. **Question about Prior Knowledge:**
   - "Isn't it true that you were aware of the malfunctioning valve several months before the accident occurred? What specific steps did you take to address this issue once it was brought to your attention?"

2. **Question about Maintenance Protocols:**
   - "Can you describe the standard maintenance protocol for safety valves within your factory? How does this protocol compare to the actions actually taken with the valve in question?"
3. **Question about Safety Inspections**:
   - "Can you detail the last three safety inspections that were conducted on the equipment prior to the incident? Were any issues reported related to the safety valve during these inspections?"
4. **Question about Employee Training and Awareness:**
   - "What training do employees receive regarding the operation and maintenance of safety valves? How often is this training updated, and did Joe Martinez receive this training?"

Pro Tips for Effective Cross-Examination:

1. **Highlight Discrepancies:**
   - Focus on any discrepancies between the company's stated safety protocols and the actions they actually took. This contrast can be very effective in highlighting negligence. Use documentary evidence such as maintenance logs, emails, and safety reports to back up your points.
2. **Use the Valve as a Narrative Device:**
   - Personify the valve during your questioning to emphasize its role in the story. For example, ask the witness to explain how a 'fully functional' valve could fail so catastrophically if proper procedures were followed. This approach can help the jury visualize the sequence of neglect and its consequences.

3. **Engage with Expert Testimony:**
   - Coordinate the points of your cross-examination with the facts established by your expert witnesses. This can involve asking the company's maintenance supervisor to confirm or deny expert statements about what could have been done to prevent the valve failure, thus reinforcing the negligence demonstrated by the company.

By structuring your cross-examination around these questions and strategies, you effectively expose the company's pattern of neglect and frame the incident not as an isolated accident but as a preventable tragedy resulting from a series of ignored warnings. This approach not only strengthens your case but also engages the jury by providing a clear and compelling narrative of cause and effect.

Until finally... (Closing – The Valve's Story as the Ultimate Proof of Negligence)

"Until finally, the valve that had done its job for years, the valve that had tried to hold back disaster, failed. But it wasn't the valve that killed Joe Martinez—it was the people who ignored it. And now, the only thing standing between more tragedies like this is you."

- *The valve, an inanimate object, becomes the **key witness**—a storyteller that doesn't lie, doesn't exaggerate, and had **only one job to do.**
- *The jury is left with one thought: If they don't hold the company accountable, how many more safety valves will go ignored?*

And ever since then... (Closing – The Jury's Power to Prevent This from Happening Again)

"And ever since then, juries like you have sent a message: That safety isn't optional. That broken equipment isn't just 'an accident waiting to happen'—it's a choice a company makes when they put profits over people. The only way to ensure that the next safety valve isn't ignored is to hold them accountable today."

- *This resolution shifts the focus—this isn't just about* ***Joe Martinez****, it's about* ***every worker in the country*** *who trusts that their equipment won't fail.*
- The jury is positioned as **the only force that can stop this from happening again.**

To effectively tie the example of the safety valve's failure into the closing arguments, a lawyer can utilize the narrative of the valve as a powerful metaphor for the company's negligence. Here are three example questions for the lawyer to ponder while preparing the closing statement, along with professional tips to ensure the message resonates deeply with the jury:

Example Questions to Ponder:

1. **How can I personify the valve to emphasize its role in the incident and the company's neglect?**
    - Consider framing the valve not just as a piece of equipment but as a silent guardian whose failure was a direct result of being overlooked by those responsible.
2. **What evidence can be revisited to highlight that the tragedy was preventable and a result of clear negligence?**
    - Focus on summarizing key evidence such as maintenance records, employee testimonies, and expert opinions that directly link the accident to negligence.
3. **How can I empower the jury to see their verdict as a pivotal decision that extends beyond this courtroom?**
    - Emphasize the broader implications of their decision, framing their role as critical in enforcing safety standards and holding corporations accountable for their actions.

Pro Tips for Crafting the Closing Argument:

1. **Use the Valve as a Symbolic Witness:**

- Refer to the valve as a 'witness' to the company's ongoing disregard for safety protocols. Describe how its failure was a culmination of ignored warnings, making it clear that the valve's breakdown was a direct result of negligence, not an isolated incident.

2. **Highlight the Human Cost:**

    - Make the human cost of negligence palpable by reminding the jury of Joe Martinez's suffering and the ultimate price he paid. Use emotional language to detail the personal impact of the company's decisions, helping jurors feel the weight of the tragedy.

3. **Call to Action:**

    - Conclude with a strong call to action, urging the jury to deliver a verdict that communicates a clear message about the importance of safety and the consequences of negligence. Suggest that their decision has the power to prevent future tragedies by making an example of what happens when safety is sidelined.

By integrating these elements into your closing arguments, you can effectively summarize the case, underscore the evidence of negligence, and impress upon the jury the critical role they play in delivering justice and safeguarding future workers. This not only strengthens your case but also positions the jury as key actors in a larger narrative of safety and accountability.

Inanimate Objects as Narrators Can Be Used Throughout the Trial:

- **Voir Dire:** Using objects to introduce themes (e.g., **scales** symbolizing justice).
- **Opening:** Setting the stage through an object's experience.
- **Direct & Cross:** Reframing perspectives (e.g., a **knife, a car dashboard, a security camera**).
- **Closing:** Delivering the final emotional impact.

By integrating these techniques throughout the trial, the jury experiences not just arguments, but a compelling narrative—one that leads them to do the right thing.

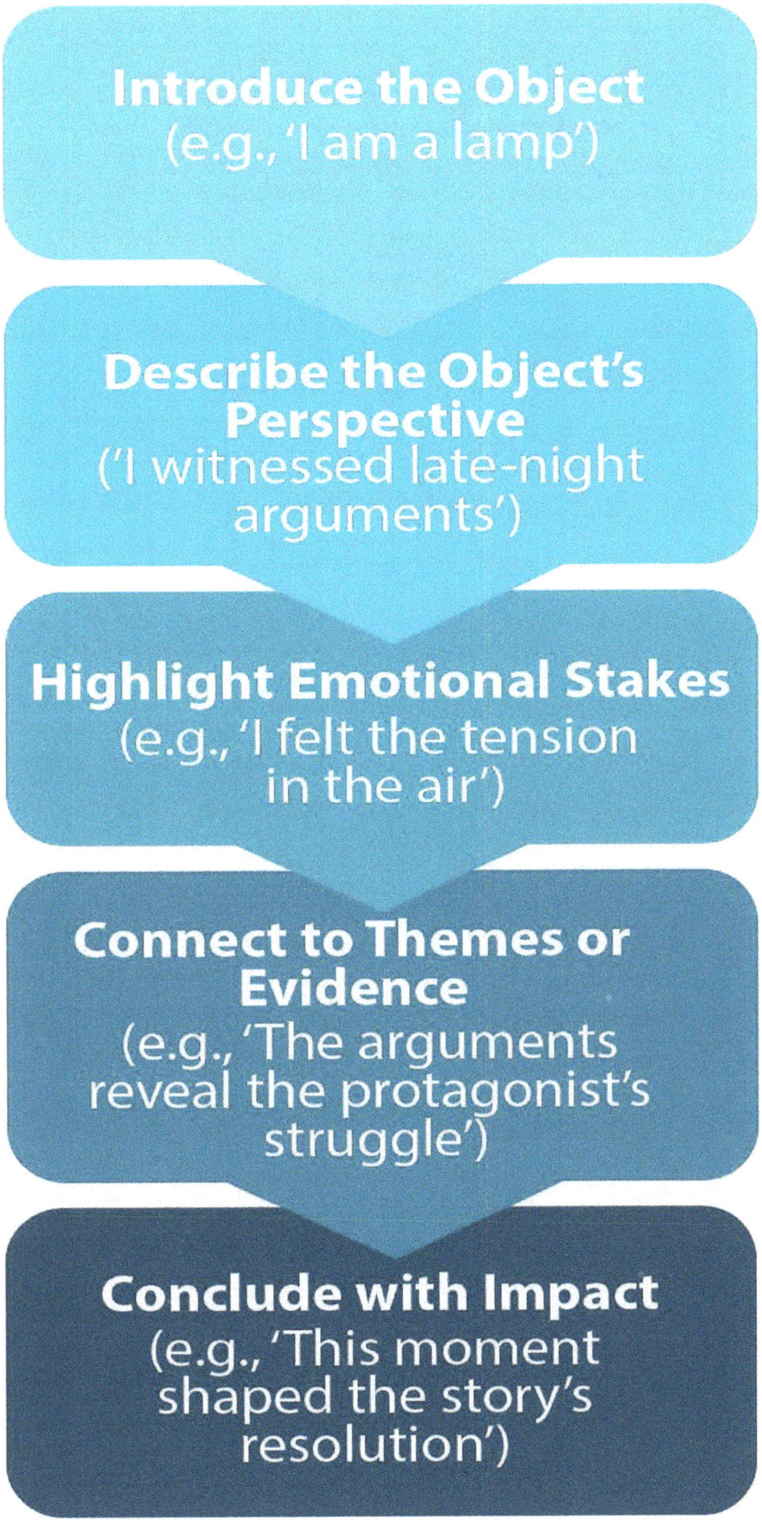

Figure 38: Narrative Flowchart for an Object's Perspective in Storytelling

A Personal Spine: From the Perspective of a Yellow Legal Pad

Once upon a time, I was a crisp yellow legal pad, blank and full of potential, waiting for someone to make use of my pages. **Every day**, I caught Leigh's notes, her arguments, and the threads of her ideas as she worked tirelessly on her cases. **Until one day**, she scribbled fiercely on my pages during a late-night session, frustrated by a case that refused to come together.

Because of that, I saw her cross-out lines, rework strategies, and finally, in a burst of clarity, sketch out a narrative that connected everything. **Because of that**, my pages carried her into court, the story she crafted flowing seamlessly from the notes I held. **Until finally**, I lay on the table as she celebrated a victory, my worn pages marked with the proof of her persistence. **Ever since then**, I've been her go-to legal pad, the trusted keeper of ideas that turn struggles into successes.

Conclusion

"Every object holds a story waiting to be told—let them speak, and you'll uncover truths that transform perspectives."

Using the Story Spine to narrate from inanimate perspectives is a powerful tool for crafting narratives that engage. These voices humanize abstract ideas and illuminate hidden dimensions of a story. In the courtroom, these fresh perspectives create memorable, impactful narratives that linger long after the story stops. By embracing the voices of inanimate objects, storytellers unlock a world of storytelling possibilities, reminding us that even the quietest elements of a story can have the loudest impact.

Adapting the Story Spine for Inanimate Perspectives

When writing from an object's point of view:

- Identify the **object's relationship** to the case or the people involved.
- Use the Story Spine framework to explore the object's "experience."

- Emphasize how the object "witnessed" or "experienced" key events.
- Conclude with how the object's perspective sheds light on fairness or justice in the case.

Examples of Inanimate Perspectives

1. The Rule (Civil Case)

Case Context: A company violated workplace safety rules, resulting in a worker's injury. The story is told from the perspective of the safety rule.

- **Once upon a time:** *"Once upon a time, I was created to protect workers from harm in dangerous industries. My creators studied accidents and wrote me with care, knowing lives depended on me."*
- ***Every day:*** *"Every day, I sat in the company handbook, a quiet reminder of what must be done to keep workers safe."*
- **But one day:** *"But one day, the company ignored me, cutting corners to save time and money."*
- **Because of that:** *"Because of that, proper training was skipped, equipment was left unchecked, and workers were put at risk."*
- **Until finally:** *"Until finally, an employee was seriously injured when faulty machinery failed, an injury I could have prevented if I'd been followed."*
- **And ever since then:** *"And ever since then, I've remained unused, while more workers face similar dangers."*
- **And the moral of the story is:** *"Rules exist to save lives, and ignoring them has consequences not just for businesses but for the people who trust them."*

2. The Toy (Custody Case)

Case Context: A custody battle centers on the emotional distress of a child. The story is told from the perspective of the child's favorite stuffed animal.

- **Once upon a time:** *"Once upon a time, I was given to Lily on her first birthday. I've been her constant companion, her comfort in the dark."*
- **Every day:** *"Every day, Lily hugged me tight as she told me stories, played pretend, and fell asleep beside me."*
- **But one day:** *"But one day, her parents began to fight, and Lily clutched me harder as tears rolled down her cheeks."*
- **Because of that:** *"Because of that, I sat with her on long car rides to her dad's new apartment, and I listened as she asked why her mom didn't come with us."*
- **Until finally:** *"Until finally, Lily began hiding me under her pillow at night, afraid I'd be left behind in the shuffle between homes."*
- **And ever since then:** *"And ever since then, I've become her only constant in a world that feels divided."*
- **And the moral of the story is:** *"Children need stability, love, and security during times of upheaval. Custody decisions must prioritize their emotional well-being."*

3. The Streetlight (Car Accident Case)

Case Context: A personal injury case involving a car accident is told from the perspective of a streetlight at the crash scene.

- **Once upon a time:** *"Once upon a time, I was installed at the corner of Main and Elm to brighten the intersection and keep drivers safe."*
- **Every day:** *"Every day, I lit up the night, watching cars pass by in orderly lines and slowing the rush of traffic."*
- **But one day:** *"But one day, I saw a car speed through a red light, its driver distracted by a glowing phone screen."*

- **Because of that:** *"Because of that, it collided with another car, spinning it into the crosswalk where pedestrians had just been standing."*
- **Until finally:** *"Until finally, the police arrived, piecing together what I had witnessed as the ambulance carried away the injured driver."*
- **And ever since then:** *"And ever since then, that intersection has become a place of mourning for those who remember the crash."*
- **And the moral of the story is:** *"Distracted driving endangers everyone on the road, and accountability is necessary to prevent future tragedies."*

4. The Bird (Criminal Case)

Case Context: A robbery case is told from the perspective of a bird perched on a power line near the scene.

- **Once upon a time:** *"Once upon a time, I built my nest in the big oak by the corner store, a perfect place to watch the comings and goings of the town."*
- **Every day:** *"Every day, I saw people stopping by for groceries, newspapers, and small-town chatter."*
- **But one day:** *"But one day, I saw a man in a hoodie dart into the store as if trying to hide, his hands stuffed in his pockets."*
- **Because of that:** *"Because of that, I heard shouts and saw the store clerk raise his hands, and the man ran out clutching a cash-filled bag."*
- **Until finally:** *"Until finally, the police arrived, questioning everyone nearby, but the man was already gone, vanishing into the alleys below."*
- **And ever since then:** *"And ever since then, the store has added cameras and stronger locks, a sign of how fear has changed this quiet town."*
- **And the moral of the story is:** *"Crime leaves more than financial losses—it leaves scars on the safety and trust of communities."*

PRACTICE SPINES

Steps to Craft an Object's Perspective

1. **Choose the Object or Entity:**

- Select something relevant to the case (e.g., a rule, a toy, a streetlight, or even a concept like "justice").

2. **Identify the Object's Role:**

- Determine how the object is connected to the case or key events.

3. **Use the Story Spine:**

- Write the narrative from the object's "point of view," focusing on what it "witnessed" or "felt."

4. **Emphasize the Lesson:**

- Use the moral line to connect the object's perspective to broader themes of justice, safety, or fairness.

Chapter 20
Mastering Scenes

"A great scene doesn't just tell you what happened—it invites you inside to live it, with all its heart pounding and adrenaline-fueled intensity."

The Building Blocks of Memorable Scenes

A scene isn't just a snapshot; it's a fully immersive experience that captures a moment in time. Packed with characters, actions, emotions, and stakes, each scene acts as a mini-story that propels the larger narrative forward. Mastering scenes is about breaking your story into vivid, impactful moments that stick with your audience.

A scene typically includes:

- **Setting:** Where and when does this moment happen?
- **Characters:** Who's in the room, and what are they up to?
- **Conflict or Action:** What's going down, and why should we care?
- **Change or Outcome:** How does this scene move the needle on the larger story?

When you focus on crafting scenes, your narrative becomes a series of emotionally charged moments that leave your audience eager for what's next.

Life Lessons: Leveraging Scenes with the Story Spine

Once upon a time...I was preparing a trial narrative for a case that hinged on one critical moment—a heated exchange between my client and their employer. The facts were straightforward, but the emotional gravity of the interaction was being lost in translation.

Every day...I struggled to align pivotal moments within a structured narrative. The stories often felt fragmented, with powerful scenes disconnected from the larger arc of the case.

Until one day...I used the Story Spine to frame a critical exchange as a climactic scene. We carefully crafted every detail—the setting, the dialogue, the rising tension—ensuring it aligned with the narrative's flow. The scene didn't just stand out; it propelled the story forward.

Because of that... The jury sat up and was paying attention. They could feel the weight of the moment and how it fit into the larger story. It wasn't just a scene—it was a turning point that made everything else click.

And ever since that day...I've taught storytellers to integrate dynamic scenes into the Story Spine, creating narratives that flow seamlessly and resonate deeply with their audience.

The Power of the Scene

Scenes take abstract concepts and ground them in visceral, tangible moments. Imagine a courtroom narrative where, instead of saying, "The client felt betrayed," you describe the exact moment they realized they'd been wronged: the sinking feeling, the tightening grip on a chair's edge, the tremor in their voice. Suddenly, the audience isn't just hearing the story, they're right there, living it.

Scenes are filled with emotional depth and impact that makes stories unforgettable. A well-crafted scene creates a connection and makes an impact. For example, instead of listing numbers in a business presentation, walk the audience through the moment an entrepreneur realized their innovation could change lives. Feelings anchor attention, and attention drives action.

Building Momentum, One Scene at a Time

Every scene should add something new: fresh details, bigger stakes, or unexpected twists. Think of a trial. First, there's the scene where the plaintiff recounts their struggle. Next comes the gripping cross-examination. Then, the aha moment when new evidence flips the narrative. By sequencing your scenes carefully, you create a story that's impossible to look away from. Each one builds on the last, pulling the audience deeper into your narrative until they're fully invested in the outcome.

Here's the golden rule: **a scene isn't just a "moment"—it's a *moment that matters.*** Something should shift, a character's mindset, the stakes of the story, or the audience's understanding. Take a courtroom scene where a witness falters under pressure. That hesitation? It's not just an action—it's a revelation. Suddenly, the jury sees doubt where there was confidence, and the narrative takes a turn. These moments of change are what make a scene dynamic, ensuring it drives the story forward instead of simply filling time.

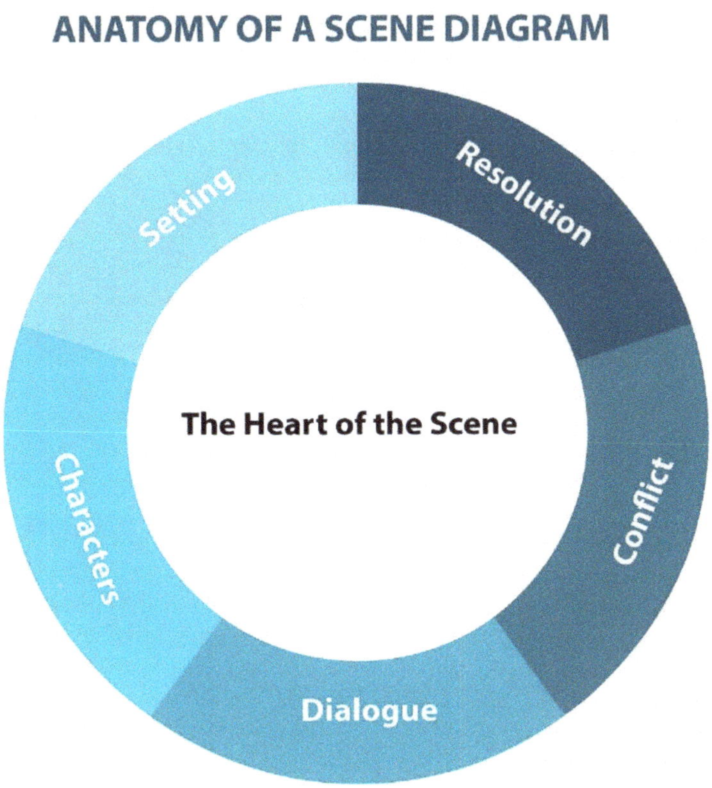

Figure 39: Anatomy of a Scene Diagram

The Devil's in the Details

What separates a scene that's fine from one that's unforgettable? **Details.** A courtroom isn't just a space—it's the shuffle of papers, the judge's measured stare, the nervous tap-tap-tap of a foot under the table. These tiny specifics don't just paint the picture; they bring it to life. When a character's trembling hand accidentally knocks over a glass of water, it says more about their nerves than any long-winded description ever could.

Specificity makes scenes sing. It transforms abstract moments into vivid realities your audience can see, hear, and feel. The more real the moment, the more powerful the impact. Scenes are the basic building blocks of any story. Master them, and you'll craft narratives that ignite.

Using Scenes Effectively

Crafting a great story is about choosing and building scenes that make your narrative shine. Here's how to wield the power of scenes like a pro:

1. Give Every Scene a Job

Scenes need purpose, not just pizazz. Each one should pull its weight in your narrative. Ask yourself:

- **Does it move the story forward?** Every scene should push the plot, reveal key information, or show a turning point.
- **Does it highlight important themes?** Use scenes to underscore ideas like a client's innocence, a breakthrough moment, or a personal lesson.
- **Does it captivate the audience?** The best scenes draw people in with vivid details, emotional depth, or good old-fashioned tension.

2. Keep It Relevant

Context is everything. Your scene needs to fit the story like a pair of warm winter gloves.

- **In courtrooms,** spotlight moments like the scene of an accident, a dramatic cross-examination, or the discovery of a smoking gun.
- **In the business world,** focus on a game-changing meeting, the lightbulb moment of innovation, or a customer's success story.
- **In everyday storytelling,** choose relatable turning points: a hilarious mishap, a personal triumph, or a tough-but-true lesson learned.

3. Pack It with Details and Emotion

Make it real. Bring your scenes to life with sensory details (what's seen, heard, smelled) and emotional undercurrents (what's felt, feared, or hoped).

- Highlight what's at stake. What's on the line? Why should your audience care?
- Use moments that reveal vulnerability or transformation—they're the emotional glue that binds your story to your audience.

Choosing the Right Scenes

Before you commit to a scene, put it through this quick litmus test:

Does this scene add value?

- **Does it matter?** If it doesn't reveal something critical, build tension, or pack an emotional punch, it's just filler. Let it go.

Does it fit my narrative goals?

- **Trial lawyers:** Focus on scenes that illuminate key facts or make your argument unshakable.

- **Business storytellers:** Highlight moments of breakthrough, resilience, or big wins.

Does it connect with my audience?

- **Choose relatable moments.** Think about your audience's values and experiences, then use scenes that relate on a personal level.

A Personal Spine on Scenes

Once upon a time, I struggled to make my stories pop. My narratives felt flat, like they were missing the spark that truly connects with people. Every day, I focused on the big picture, skipping over the small, vivid moments that bring stories to life. *Until one day,* I realized that stories aren't told in sweeping arcs but in carefully crafted scenes—snapshots full of action, emotion, and transformation.

Because of that, I started breaking my stories into scenes, anchoring each one with rich details and characters who felt real. *Until finally,* my stories transformed into immersive experiences that left my audiences captivated. *And ever since then,* I've embraced the power of scenes, knowing that every great story is built one moment at a time.

The Trial Lawyer's Scene Checklist

Let's say you're a trial lawyer (or just want to think like one). Here's what to look for:

- **Critical Events:** Nail those defining moments—like the instant an accident happened or the exact wording of an incriminating email.
- **Turning Points:** What changed the game? Was it a damning piece of evidence or a revealing admission?
- **Emotional Impact:** Pick moments that stir the jury's emotions—think struggle, triumph, or heartbreak.

When in doubt, trim the fat. A lean, purposeful story is better than one bogged down with extras. If a scene doesn't work hard enough, it's probably time to show it the door.

Entering and Exiting Scenes

Crafting compelling scenes isn't just about what happens in the middle, it's also about how you start and end. Nail these transitions, and your story will flow seamlessly, keeping your audience connected from one moment to the next.

1. Entering a Scene

"First impressions count—even in storytelling."

When you open a scene, think of it as jumping on a moving train: you want to start with momentum, intrigue, and just enough context to get the audience on board.

- **Start with Action or Decision:** Dive right into the heart of the moment. Avoid long-winded setups.
    - Example: Don't say, "It was a sunny day when the client entered the office." Instead, try:

      "The client stormed in, a stack of overdue invoices trembling in her grip, eyes blazing with panic."

- **Set the Tone:** Use sensory details, pacing, and dialogue to create an emotional backdrop for what's about to unfold.
    - Is it tense? Hopeful? Heartbreaking? Let your language show it.
- **Provide Just Enough Context:** Orient your audience with the essentials—but don't drown them in backstory.

2. Exiting a Scene

"Leave them wanting more—or at least something to think about."

How you end a scene determines if your audience is eager to follow you to the next one or mentally checking their to-do list.

- **End with Purpose:** With a revelation, a question, or a cliffhanger, make sure the audience knows why this scene mattered.
    - Example: Don't say, "The meeting ended amicably." Try:

      "As the door clicked shut, I realized this wasn't just a misstep—it was the pivot everything hinged on."

- **Create a Smooth Transition:** Drop breadcrumbs to hint at what's next or tie the scene neatly to what just happened.
- **Leave a Lasting Image:** Conclude with a powerful detail or line that stays in the audience's mind.

Sequencing Scenes

The order in which you present your scenes shapes how your audience experiences your story. Play with structure to maximize impact:

1. Chronological Order

- Perfect for clear, linear storytelling.
    - Example: Walk your audience through the day of the accident, what led to it, and its aftermath.

2. Thematic Order

- Group scenes by theme, rather than time, to emphasize patterns or points.

- Example: A lawyer could bundle moments that highlight the defendant's negligence, regardless of when they happened.

3. Intercutting

- Alternate between threads to build suspense or draw parallels.
  - Example: In a pitch, jump between customer struggles and how your product solves them.

4. Nonlinear Order

- Start with a bang, then rewind to show how it all unfolded.
  - Example: Open with the trial's climactic moment, then reveal the steps leading there.

Think Like a Director

Every scene is a chance to grab the spotlight. Enter with flair, exit with purpose, and sequence with intention. Your audience will be on the edge of their seats, ready for what's next.

Writing Descriptive and Moving Scenes

In storytelling, scenes are the snapshots that transform facts into vivid, living moments. Want to captivate your audience? Focus on these four elements:

1. Sensory Details

"If your audience can see, hear, or even smell your scene, they'll be connected."

Bring your story to life by engaging all five senses. Don't just tell them what happened—let them experience it.

- **Example:** Instead of saying, "The factory was unsafe," try:

  "The air smelled of burnt plastic, and the hum of faulty machinery echoed across the dimly lit floor, where oil pooled in every corner."

2. Show, Don't Tell

"Actions speak louder than adjectives."

Skip the summaries and let your audience feel the emotions through actions and dialogue.

- **Example:** Instead of saying, "The client was upset," try:

  "She slammed the report on the table, her voice trembling as she said, 'This is unacceptable!'"

3. Pacing

"The speed of your sentences is the heartbeat of your scene."

Vary the rhythm to match the mood. Short, punchy sentences build tension, while longer, descriptive ones create **reflection.**

- **Example:**
- **Action-packed moment:** *"He turned. The car was there. Brakes screamed. Metal collided."*
- **Reflective moment:** *"The room fell silent, except for the ticking of the clock. He stared at the empty chair, his thoughts swirling like leaves in a storm."*

4. Emotional Core

"If the characters don't feel it, neither will the audience."

Anchor your scene in emotions to show what's at stake.

- **Example:** *"As the jury's verdict echoed through the courtroom, he gripped the table's edge so tightly his knuckles turned white, bracing for the words that would change everything."*

A War Story: A Turning Point in the Courtroom

One of the most impactful moments of my career happened during a cross-examination. My client, a single mother, was testifying about how her landlord's neglect had left her family without heat during a brutal winter. I knew the scene needed to be unforgettable.

I asked her to describe a specific night. She paused, her voice breaking as she said, "My son was shivering so much I wrapped him in my coat and held him against me until morning." The courtroom was silent. The image was so vivid that no one needed further explanation.

That scene captured the stakes better than any argument or statistic ever could. Crafting such powerful moments taught me the importance of selecting the right details, emotions, and timing to engage an audience and drive a narrative forward.

Conclusion

"Details are the soul of a scene, transforming it from a description into an experience."

Scenes are the heart and soul of your narrative. They bring facts to life, connect audiences on an emotional level, and are the foundation for caring action. Mastering the art of creating, sequencing, and describing scenes will take your storytelling to new heights. Because in the end, great stories aren't remembered for what they say—they're remembered for how they make you feel.

Practice Spines

1. Personal Injury Case: The Moment Everything Changed

- **Once upon a time...** John was a truck driver who had never had an accident in 20 years on the road.
- **Every day...** He drove long hours, ensuring deliveries were on time to support his family.
- **But one day...** A defective brake line caused him to lose control on the highway.
    - **The scene:** Describe the moments as John fought to stop the truck. Was there the squeal of tires, the smell of burning rubber, or the desperate grip on the steering wheel?
- **Because of that...** He was seriously injured and unable to work.
- **Until finally...** He filed a lawsuit to hold the manufacturer accountable.

2. Family Law Case: A Child's Perspective

- **Once upon a time...** Lily's parents were divorced but shared custody peacefully.
- **Every day...** She packed her favorite stuffed bear to take between her two homes.
- **But one day...** A bitter argument left her waiting on the front steps for hours, unsure if her dad would pick her up.
    - **The scene:** Imagine Lily's perspective—how her legs dangled off the porch, how the evening grew colder, how she clutched her bear tighter with every passing minute.
- **Because of that...** Lily began to feel anxious and insecure.
- **Until finally...** Her mother petitioned for sole custody to give Lily stability.

3. Business Presentation: The Breakthrough Moment

- **Once upon a time...** The company struggled to meet deadlines and keep clients happy.
- **Every day...** The team worked late nights, trying to stay afloat.
- **But one day...** A brainstorming session led to a breakthrough idea that could revolutionize their workflow.
    - **The scene:** Paint a vivid picture of the meeting—half-empty coffee cups, a whiteboard crammed with ideas, the sudden silence as one suggestion captured everyone's attention.
- **Because of that...** The team implemented the new system, and productivity soared.
- **Until finally...** They landed their biggest client yet, securing the company's future.

Practice Exercise: Scene Lab

Your Challenge: Take one of the following prompts and craft a vivid, emotional scene using the elements we discussed—sensory details, emotional weight, and change.

Prompts:

1. A doctor delivering life-changing news to a patient.
2. A key moment in a courtroom when a witness hesitates before answering.
3. A student standing up to a bully for the first time.

Questions to Guide You:

- What does the setting look, sound, or smell like?
- How does each character feel in this moment? How do they show it?
- What changes or shifts because of this scene?

Pro Tip: Don't overthink—imagine you're the director of a movie, and this scene is the emotional centerpiece. What do you want your audience to see, feel, and remember?

Example: Scene Building in Action

Let's take a legal case and bring it to life with a scene that is filled with emotion and vivid details:

Case Context: A landlord-tenant dispute over unsafe living conditions.

Scene in Action:

The client, a young mother, had been complaining about the leaking ceiling for months, but nothing was done. Then one night, during a rainstorm, her kitchen ceiling collapsed.

Descriptive Scene:

"The rain pounded against the windows as Sarah stood at the sink, scrubbing the last plate from dinner. Above her, the ceiling groaned—a sound she'd heard before, but louder this time. She looked up just as the crack split wide, and with a deafening crash, water and chunks of plaster rained down. Her toddler cried in the next room, the sound piercing the chaos. The air reeked of mildew and damp wood, and Sarah, soaked and shaking, grabbed her son and ran outside into the storm."

Why It Works:

- **Sensory Details:** You feel the rain, hear the crash, and smell the mildew.
- **Emotion:** Sarah's fear for her child anchors the scene emotionally.
- **Change:** The collapse transforms Sarah's frustration into resolve—she will take action.

Now go forth and explore the beauty of crafting exquisitely moving scenes. Harness the power of your creativity to weave narratives that not only captivate and inspire but also resonate deeply with your audience. Remember, each scene you create is an opportunity to touch hearts, provoke thought, and ignite change.

Embrace the journey of storytelling, refine your skills, and elevate your narratives to art that endures and impacts. Let your stories be the mirror in which the essence of human experiences is reflected beautifully and profoundly.

Chapter 21
Leveraging Scenes with the Story Spine

"A great story doesn't just follow a structure—it lives and breathes in its moments."

Where Structure Meets Soul

Imagine a skeleton without muscle—functional, but hardly captivating. That's what a story is without scenes: technically complete—but missing its heart. Now, imagine a vivid moment—a witness's trembling voice in the courtroom or the flicker of hope in a struggling entrepreneur's eyes. These are the muscles and tendons that bring a narrative to life.

The Dance Between Scenes and Story Spine

The Story Spine is your GPS, guiding you from "Once upon a time" to "And ever since then." It ensures your story flows logically and purposefully. But scenes? Scenes are the pit stops where the real transformation happens—where the audience sees, feels, and experiences the journey. For instance, instead of saying, "The client's life changed due to an accident," use a scene: "The blare of sirens drowned out her thoughts as she sat dazed on the pavement, shards of glass glinting like tiny daggers around her. The weight of the EMT's hand on her shoulder felt distant, unreal." See the difference? One conveys information; the other paints a picture the audience won't forget.

Scenes as Emotional Anchors

While the Story Spine gives you structure, scenes create connection. Think of each scene as a chance to build emotional stakes.

In a business pitch, the "Because of that" phase might look like this:

- **The Story Spine says:** "Because of that, the founder faced a major setback."
- **The scene shows:** "Sitting alone in the dimly lit office, she stared at the rejection email. The words 'unfortunately' and 'declined' felt like knives twisting in her chest. Her coffee sat cold on the desk, untouched since morning."

By grounding pivotal moments in emotional detail, you ensure the audience doesn't just follow the story—they care about its outcome. This approach not only informs but makes the audience *feel* the moment's gravity.

Seamlessly Stitching It All Together

Scenes aren't isolated snapshots; they're threads in a larger tapestry. Each scene should build on the last, creating a seamless flow through the Story Spine.

For example:

- **Scene 1:** A worker injured on the job lies in the hospital, grappling with pain and uncertainty ("Until one day").
- **Scene 2:** Their lawyer discovers company records showing ignored safety violations ("Because of that").
- **Scene 3:** The trial reveals a culture of negligence, forcing the jury to confront systemic failure ("Until finally").

This progression keeps the narrative coherent, escalating stakes while immersing the audience in the story's arc.

The Balance: Structure Meets Creativity

The beauty of combining the Story Spine and scenes lies in their balance. The Spine ensures you stay on track, while scenes let you explore the depths of emotions, conflicts, and settings. This blend is especially crucial in high-stakes storytelling—like in court. A courtroom story about a whistleblower isn't just about facts—it's about the moment they decided to speak out, the fear in their voice, and the courage in their eyes. Pairing the Story Spine's logic with a scene's humanity makes the narrative unforgettable.

Recap: The Story Spine in Action

Here's the trusty Story Spine framework, your map for creating a clear, engaging narrative:

1. **Once upon a time...** Introduces characters, setting, and context.
2. **And every day...** Establishes routine or normalcy.
3. **Until one day...** Brings in the inciting incident or disruption.
4. **Because of that...** Highlights consequences and escalating actions.
5. **Because of that...** (Yes, another one!) Builds tension and stakes.
6. **Until finally...** Reaches the climax or resolution.
7. **And ever since then...** Reflects on the lasting impact.

But here's the twist: each phase becomes richer when paired with a well-crafted scene.

Scene Spotlight: Bringing the Spine to Life

Let's take a quick tour of how scenes amplify each step of the Story Spine:

1. **Once upon a time...**

   Scene Example: Personal Injury Case

"The playground was alive with laughter as Mr. Smith chased his son across the monkey bars. His sneakers scuffed the pavement, and the warmth of the sun on his face was a reminder of how good life was."

Purpose: Contrast the client's life before the accident with what came after.

2. **And every day...**

Scene Example: Employment Discrimination Case

"Every day, Ms. Johnson sat at her desk, the hum of productivity around her. She led brainstorming sessions, her ideas lighting up the room. Her name was synonymous with success—until it wasn't."

Purpose: Show the baseline of success that will later be disrupted.

3. **Until one day...**

Scene Example: Contract Dispute

"In the cold conference room, Mr. Taylor's confidence drained as the opposing party slid altered documents across the table. The words on the page rewrote the deal he'd fought so hard for."

Purpose: Highlight the pivotal moment when everything changed.

4. **Because of that...**

Scene Example: Medical Malpractice Case

"The sterile smell of antiseptic filled the hospital room as Mr. Davis woke to a doctor's solemn face. The surgery hadn't gone as planned, and his life would never be the same."

Purpose: Show immediate consequences with emotional weight.

5. **Because of that...**

Scene Example: Business Litigation

"In the boardroom, chairs sat empty after layoffs were announced. Partnerships dissolved like sand through fingers, leaving the company adrift."

Purpose: Escalate stakes and show the ripple effects.

6. **Until finally...**

   Scene Example: Wrongful Termination Case

"Ms. Carter clutched the termination letter as her belongings were boxed up around her. The echo of her footsteps out of the office felt like the closing chapter of a 15-year career."

Purpose: Bring the story to its emotional and logical climax.

7. **And ever since then...**

   Scene Example: Family Law Case

"The child sat at the kitchen table, staring at unfinished homework. 'Why can't we all just be together again?' she whispered, the question hanging heavy in the air."

Purpose: Illustrate the enduring impact of the case.

The Perfect Blend of Logic and Emotion

The Story Spine and scenes are dance partners, each bringing out the best in the other. The Story Spine provides the choreography, ensuring your narrative is purposeful and logical, while scenes add the flair, sweeping your audience off their feet with vivid moments and emotional depth. Together, they create storytelling that's both grounded and captivating, turning a simple narrative into an unforgettable experience.

For example:

- **Logic (Story Spine):** "Because of that, the company faced a financial crisis."
- **Emotion (Scene):** "In the boardroom, the CEO stared at the empty chairs of her laid-off employees, her voice catching as she announced yet another partnership that had dissolved."

By using both, you create a story that is as clear as it is compelling.

Why This Fusion Works

When you combine the clarity of the Story Spine with the vibrancy of scenes, you're not just telling stories, you're inviting your audience to live them. This approach ensures:

1. **Clarity:** The Story Spine keeps your narrative clean and purposeful, so nothing feels out of place.
2. **Connection:** Scenes make your audience feel like they're right there, experiencing the emotions, decisions, and stakes alongside your characters.
3. **Memorability:** By pairing facts with feelings, you craft stories that stick—not just in their minds but in their hearts.

As you practice this approach, you'll notice your storytelling becoming more intuitive and impactful. You'll naturally find ways to blend structure and emotion, creating narratives that aren't just well-told—they're well-felt.

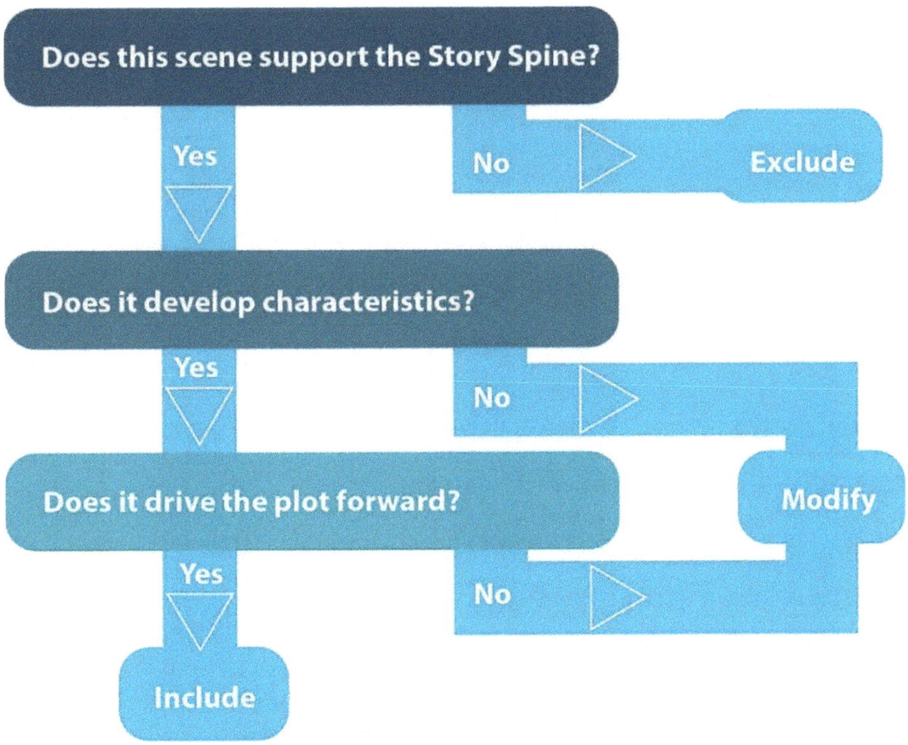

Figure 40: Scene Support Flowchart

A War Story: The Scene That Turned the Case

In a medical malpractice case I worked on, the turning point was a single, vivid scene we brought to life for the jury. My client was an elderly woman whose surgery had gone disastrously wrong, leaving her permanently disabled. As part of the case, we used the Story Spine framework to structure the narrative, but it was a specific scene from her recovery that captured the jury's empathy.

I asked my client to recount the moment she realized she could no longer hold her granddaughter's hand during their walks because she now needed both hands to steady her walker. Mrs. Parker paused and stared off into the distance before answering, "Leslie looked up at me and playfully asked, 'Grandma, why can't you hold my hand anymore?'" she recounted, her voice trembling. That scene illustrated the profound loss of independence and connection she felt. This poignant moment underscored the deep sense of loss she experienced, both in her independence and in her connection with her granddaughter.

Placing this emotionally charged moment within the Story Spine framework allowed us to tie it to the stakes, her resilience, and the ultimate demand for justice. It was a pivotal scene that transformed the jury's understanding of her suffering and secured a verdict in her favor.

Conclusion

"A well-crafted scene isn't just what happens; it's how it feels, why it matters, and what it changes for the characters—and the audience."

By combining the Story Spine's structure with the emotional depth of scenes, you don't just tell stories—you craft experiences. Whether persuading a jury, pitching an idea, or sharing a personal moment, this approach ensures your audience not only hears your story but lives it.

Practice Spines

These exercises will help you craft narratives that are both clear and captivating, turning facts into stories that resonate with your audience.

Practice Spine 1: The Stolen Backpack Mystery

Scenario: A student is accused of stealing a classmate's backpack, but they claim innocence.

- **Once upon a time...**
  Chris was the go-to helper in their class, always the one classmates relied on for borrowing supplies or study tips.
- **And every day...**
  Chris showed up early, stayed late, and even shared their lunch with classmates who forgot theirs.
- **Until one day...**
  The class's most expensive backpack went missing, and someone pointed the finger at Chris.
- **Because of that...**
  Chris faced angry accusations, lost friends, and even got called to the principal's office.
- **Because of that...**
  They were determined to prove their innocence but struggled to find anyone who would believe them.
- **Until finally...**
  Security footage revealed the real culprit: a stray dog that had wandered onto campus and dragged the backpack into the bushes.
- **And ever since then...**
  Chris regained their reputation, and the school implemented a new rule: no leaving expensive items unattended (or too tempting for curious canines).

Practice Spine 2: The Lemonade Stand Rescue

Scenario: A group of kids must save their lemonade stand from closing after a summer storm destroys their supplies.

- **Once upon a time...**
  There was a group of best friends who ran the neighborhood's most popular lemonade stand.
- **And every day...**
  They poured ice-cold cups for their neighbors, saving their earnings for a giant end-of-summer pool party.
- **Until one day...**
  A freak summer storm wiped out their supplies and damaged their stand.
- **Because of that...**
  They couldn't afford to buy new lemons, and their big summer plans were in jeopardy.
- **Because of that...**
  They decided to host a car wash fundraiser, enlisting help from family and neighbors to raise money.
- **Until finally...**
  They repaired their stand, bought fresh supplies, and re-launched their lemonade business bigger and better than ever.
- **And ever since then...**
  Their lemonade stand became a local legend, known not just for great lemonade but for the determination behind it.

Practice Spine 3: The Courtroom Twist

Scenario: A defendant on trial for a stolen heirloom proves their innocence in a dramatic courtroom reveal.

- **Once upon a time...**
  Jordan, a local jeweler, was known for their impeccable work and trustworthiness.
- **And every day...**
  Jordan's clients entrusted them with their most prized possessions, including restoring a priceless family heirloom: a diamond necklace.
- **Until one day...**
  The necklace was reported stolen, and Jordan was accused of the theft.
- **Because of that...**
  They faced public shame and a legal battle that threatened to destroy their career.
- **Because of that...**
  Jordan hired a lawyer who painstakingly pieced together evidence to prove their innocence.
- **Until finally...**
  During the trial, the necklace was found hidden in the accuser's own safe—a ploy to claim insurance money!
- **And ever since then...**
  Jordan's name was cleared, and they became a symbol of integrity in the community.

Your Turn! Create Your Own Practice Spines

Try crafting a Story Spine for these scenarios:

1. **The Lost Recipe:** A baker competes in a high-stakes contest after losing their family's secret recipe.
2. **The Office Mix-Up:** A worker is wrongly accused of deleting an important client file but uncovers the real culprit.
3. **The Accidental Hero:** A dog unintentionally saves a neighborhood during a power outage.

Challenge Yourself: Add vivid scenes that bring each step to life—sights, sounds, and emotions. Show the stakes, the transformation, and the resolution!

Chapter 22

Antagonists vs. Villains in the Story Spine

"Every hero needs a nemesis—with a stubborn rival or a full-blown evil mastermind, the story's heartbeat lies in the clash."

What's a story without a little (or a lot) of conflict? Antagonists and villains keep our protagonists on their toes, challenge their beliefs, and sometimes make us cheer when they get what's coming. But not all opposition is created equal. Antagonists create obstacles; villains turn up the drama. Knowing the difference—and when to use each—is what separates a flat story from one that leaves your audience on the edge of their seat. Every hero needs opposition. Whether it's a relentless rival or an outright malicious foe, the core of any story lies in its conflicts.

Every great story thrives on tension, and at the heart of that tension is someone—or something—standing in the protagonist's way. Sometimes it's a rival with valid goals (the antagonist), and sometimes it's a force of pure malevolence (the villain). Understanding the difference between these two is key to creating a story that's as layered as it is gripping.

Antagonists vs. Villains: What's the Difference?

Antagonists: Obstacles with a point. They might be strict, frustrating, or fiercely opposed to the protagonist's goals, but they aren't necessarily bad. They add realism and complexity to the story by representing real-world challenges.

Villains: Pure troublemakers. They're not just obstacles—they're the moral opposition, embodying injustices, selfishness, or outright cruelty. Villains don't just create conflict; they raise the stakes to high drama.

The Antagonist: An Obstacle to Overcome

Antagonists push the protagonist forward, forcing them to grow and adapt. Think of them as the well-meaning professor who assigns way too much homework or the competitor fighting for the same prize. They're not evil, they just make life harder.

Example in the Story Spine:

- **Until one day...** The antagonist steps in and blocks the protagonist's path.
- **Because of that...** Tensions rise, and the protagonist must confront this challenge head-on.

Legal Example:

An opposing counsel in court who isn't corrupt but is doggedly determined to prove their case. They represent the conflict, but they're also relatable, bringing a layer of realism to the narrative.

The Villain: A Force to Confront

Villains kick it up a notch (or ten). They don't just oppose the protagonist—they actively harm, deceive, or destroy. A villain transforms a simple conflict into a battle of good vs. evil, adding emotional weight and higher stakes.

Example in the Story Spine:

- **And the complication was that...** The villain's actions escalate the stakes, threatening not just the protagonist but their values or loved ones.

- **Until finally...** The ultimate showdown. Will the villain be defeated or win the day?

Legal Example:

A corrupt corporation hiding evidence to cover up negligence, endangering lives in the process. The villain's actions aren't just wrong—they're morally repugnant, making the audience root for justice.

When Antagonists Turn Into Villains

Sometimes, the line between antagonist and villain blurs. An antagonist might start out as a reasonable adversary but cross into villainy through unethical behavior.

Example:

- A rival lawyer begins as a capable and ethical opponent but fabricates evidence to win. Suddenly, they're not just an obstacle—they're a villain.

The Story Spine's **"Because of that"** and **"And the complication was that"** sections allow for this evolution, adding depth and intrigue to the story.

Personifying the Antagonist

The best antagonists are fully fleshed-out characters with their own motivations and struggles. They may even be sympathetic, forcing the audience to see the story's conflict from multiple angles.

Example:

An insurance adjuster denying a claim not out of malice but because they're constrained by company policy. This adds a layer of realism and makes the conflict more nuanced.

Pro Tip: Use scenes to explore the antagonist's perspective—just enough to create empathy without shifting focus from the protagonist.

Villains as Catalysts for High Stakes

Villains amplify the stakes. Their presence raises the tension to its breaking point, making the protagonist's triumph feel hard-won and satisfying.

Example:

A whistleblower case where the villain is a CEO silencing employees to hide a toxic workplace. The villain isn't just opposing the protagonist, they're threatening the values of fairness and accountability.

Internal vs. External Challenges

Sometimes, the antagonist or villain isn't a person but an internal struggle or abstract force.

- **Internal Antagonist:** A character fighting their own fear of failure.
- **Villainous Force:** A corrupt system or cultural bias.

The Story Spine lets you explore these conflicts in phases like **"Because of that"** or **"And the complication was that,"** layering the story with complexity and relatability.

Balancing the Power Dynamic

A strong antagonist or villain should be powerful enough to pose a real challenge, but not so overwhelming that the protagonist's victory feels implausible.

Example:

- **Too Weak:** A villain who is easily defeated robs the story of tension.
- **Too Strong:** An invincible antagonist makes the protagonist's success seem unrealistic.

The Story Spine helps map out this balance, showing the gradual shift in power dynamics through escalating conflicts and resolutions.

Why We Need Both

Antagonists Keep It Real:

A well-written antagonist grounds your story in reality. They might be misguided, overzealous, or just plain stubborn, but they reflect the everyday struggles and conflicts we all face. For example, a judge sticking to rigid rules might complicate a trial—but their actions come from a place of order, not evil. This relatability draws the audience into the story.

Villains Raise the Stakes:

Villains add that extra spice to the mix. They force the protagonist to dig deeper, fight harder, and confront bigger questions of morality and justice. They turn a typical story into a battle of right versus wrong. A greedy CEO exploiting employees for profit? That's a villain who'll have your audience ready to grab their pitchforks.

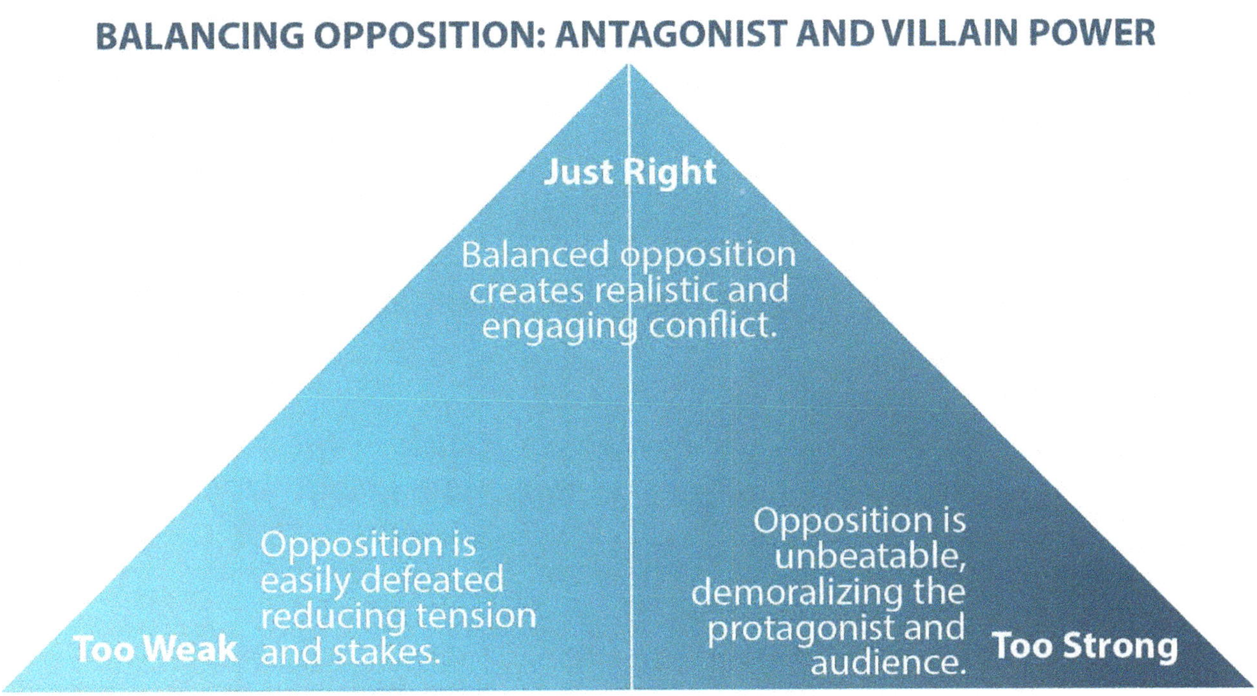

Figure 41: Balancing Opposition: Antagonist and Villain Power

Life Lessons: Antagonists vs. Villains in the Story Spine

Once upon a time...I handled a case involving a company's negligence, but the opposition wasn't a villainous entity—it was a group of well-meaning people who made a series of bad decisions. Casting them as evil felt dishonest, yet ignoring the conflict felt incomplete.

Every day...I saw stories falter because the antagonist's role was oversimplified. Not every antagonist is a villain, and failing to distinguish between the two can weaken the narrative's credibility and impact.

Until one day...I reframed the opposition as antagonists—people with conflicting goals rather than malicious intent. This nuanced approach created a richer story, one where the conflict was relatable and the resolution more satisfying.

Because of that... The jury didn't just hear a one-sided argument; they saw the humanity on both sides. This balance deepened their engagement and made the verdict feel just.

And ever since that day...I've encouraged storytellers to embrace complexity, crafting antagonists who challenge the protagonist in meaningful ways without resorting to clichés of villainy.

From Opposition to Transformation

The power of antagonists and villains lies in their ability to challenge the protagonist and push them to grow.

- **Antagonists**: A demanding boss might challenge the protagonist to refine their skills and prove their worth.
- **Villains**: A corrupt official could force the protagonist to take a stand against injustice, transforming them into a true hero.

By the time the story reaches "Until finally," the protagonist has evolved—not in spite of these challenges, but because of them.

Crafting Complexity: The Human Side of Opposition

While villains revel in their nefarious ways, antagonists are more complicated. Humanizing an antagonist adds depth and subtlety to your narrative.

For instance:

- An insurance adjuster denying a claim isn't evil—they're just following company policies.
- A rival lawyer might fiercely oppose your client, but they're fighting for their client with the same passion that you are fighting for yours.

Exploring these nuances creates a layered story that impacts emotionally while maintaining its tension.

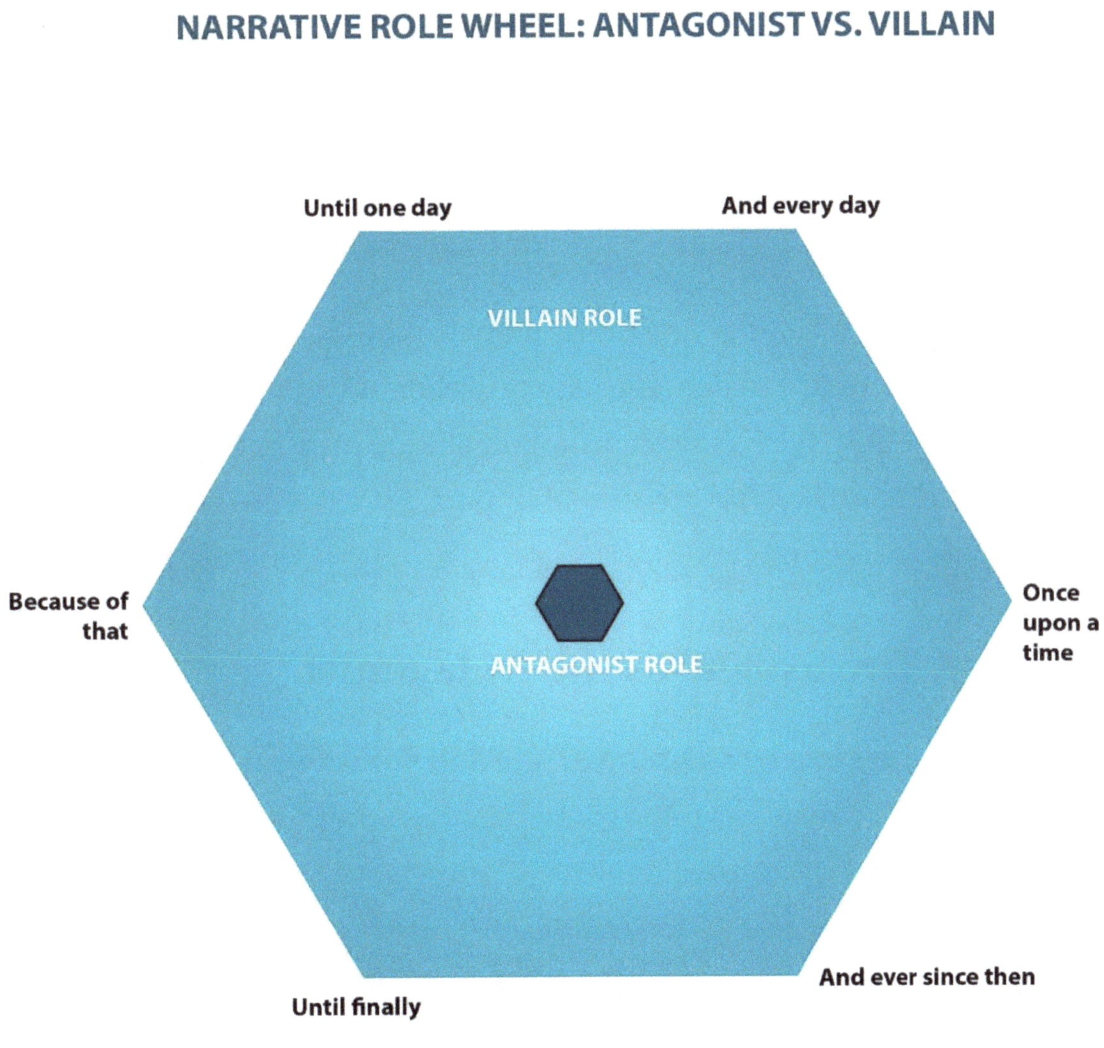

Figure 42: Narrative Role Wheel: Antagonist vs. Villain

The Story Spine in Action: Antagonists vs. Villains

Here's how these roles play out in the Story Spine framework:

- **Once upon a time...** Your protagonist's life is stable, but challenges are brewing.
- **Until one day...** The antagonist's actions disrupt the protagonist's path.
- **Because of that...** The conflict escalates, with the antagonist standing firm.
- **And the complication was that...** A villain ups the ante, revealing deeper stakes.
- **Until finally...** The protagonist rises to overcome both the opposition and the injustice.
- **And ever since then...** The resolution reflects growth, justice, or accountability.

The Verdict

Antagonists and villains are more than troublemakers; they're essential to storytelling. Antagonists make the story relatable, while villains make it unforgettable. Together, they shape a protagonist's journey, creating a narrative that overflows with authenticity and emotional impact. So, ask yourself: Who's blocking the path, and who's lighting it on fire?

A War Story: The System as the Antagonist

In a case involving a whistleblower, the antagonist wasn't a single person—it was the corporate bureaucracy that had silenced her. My client, a mid-level manager, had exposed dangerous safety violations, only to face retaliation. While the company's CEO seemed like an obvious villain, the real conflict came from the culture of fear and complicity within the organization.

I reframed the story to show that the antagonist was the system itself, a faceless machine that crushed anyone who dared challenge it. By focusing on the system rather than a single villain, we highlighted the moral courage of my client. The jury didn't see her as someone taking on a CEO—they saw her as a David battling an institutional Goliath.

This nuanced portrayal of the antagonist gave depth to the narrative, showing that not all conflicts stem from outright malice, but sometimes from systemic failures that need to be confronted.

Conclusion

"Antagonists make the protagonist sweat, but villains make them dig deep. Together, they turn stories into battles worth cheering for."

Highlight your adversary. Choosing an antagonist to challenge your protagonist or a villain to spark their fight for justice defines the core of your story. Antagonists create tension that tests determination, while villains spark moral battles that reveal character. By weaving these roles into your Story Spine, you can craft narratives that don't just capture attention but leave a lasting impression.

So, the next time you're building a case ask yourself: Do you need a sturdy obstacle or a flame-throwing nemesis? Or maybe a bit of both? With the right mix of opposition, your story becomes not just a recounting of events, but a journey of growth, truth, and purpose—one your audience won't soon forget.

Examples in Different Contexts: Antagonists and Villains in Action

"Not every obstacle is a villain, but every villain is a juicy plot twist waiting to happen."

1. Legal Stories

Antagonist:

- A corporate defendant opposing a lawsuit brought by the plaintiff.
- Their motivation? Protecting their business—even if their methods seem cold.

Villain:

- A corrupt corporation knowingly endangering public safety for profit.
- Their actions? Less "corporate strategy," more "movie villain in a boardroom."

Story Spine in Action:

Antagonist Example:

- *"Until one day, the defendant denied responsibility, arguing the injury was caused by a third party."*
- They're digging in their heels but aren't necessarily breaking the rules.

Villain Example:

- *"Until one day, evidence surfaced showing the defendant falsified safety reports to avoid liability."*
- They've crossed the moral event horizon—cue the jury's collective gasp.

2. Business Stories

Antagonist:

- A competing company launches a similar product, trying to win over your audience.
- It's business as usual, not a plot for corporate espionage.

Villain:

- A competitor spreading false claims about your product to sabotage your success.
- Oh, it's *personal* now.

Story Spine in Action:

Antagonist Example:

- *"Because of that, the rival company's aggressive marketing campaign captured a significant portion of our audience."*
- Competitive? Yes. Shady? Not so much.

Villain Example:

- *"Because of that, the competitor's false claims led to product recalls and damage to our reputation."*
- Ethical? Who's she? Not this villain.

3. Personal Stories

Antagonist:

- A boss who piles on work, unintentionally stressing you out.
- They're a challenge, sure, but they're not plotting your downfall.

Villain:

- A coworker spreading rumors to wreck your career.
- This one came straight out of the "office politics" horror anthology.

Story Spine in Action:

Antagonist Example:

- *"And every day, my manager pushed for more results, unaware of the strain it was causing."*
- Frustrating, but fixable with a conversation (or maybe some deep breaths).

Villain Example:

- *"And every day, my coworker planted doubts about my competence, undermining my standing in the office."*
- It's gloves off—this villain is playing dirty.

Why It Works

By distinguishing between antagonists and villains, you can fine-tune your narrative. Antagonists bring tension and realism; villains raise the stakes and fuel the drama.

PRACTICE SPINES

Using Antagonists and Villains in the Story Spine

1. Factual Perspective

- Clearly define the antagonist or villain's actions.
- Highlight their motivations and how they oppose the protagonist.

2. Emotional Perspective

- Show the impact of their actions on the protagonist.
- Use emotional language to create sympathy for the protagonist or outrage toward the villain.

3. Objective Perspective

- Provide a balanced view of the antagonist's motives, even if they are a villain.
- Acknowledge the antagonist's perspective to build credibility.

Crafting the Antagonist and Villain Roles in Your Story

Antagonist:

- **Complexity:** Give them a clear, understandable motivation.
- **Believability:** Their actions should feel realistic and proportionate to their goals.
- **Resolution:** Show how the protagonist overcomes their opposition.

Villain:

- **Evil Intent:** Highlight their malicious actions and unethical decisions.
- **Dramatic Contrast:** Make them a clear foil to the protagonist's values.
- **Resolution:** The climax should involve a decisive confrontation with the villain.

Chapter 23
Start With the Villain First

"Why wait to spill the tea? Start with the villain and let the drama unfold from there."

Engaging the Audience

Nothing grabs attention like a bad guy in action. Whether it's a shady corporation cutting corners, a reckless driver ignoring the rules, or a landlord refusing to fix dangerous conditions, starting with the villain creates an immediate interest in what happens next. Picture this: Instead of easing into your narrative, you dive right into the juicy bits.

"The defendant knowingly sold defective products, endangering lives just to boost their bottom line."

Now the stakes are clear, the tension is palpable, and your audience is already rooting for justice.

Setting the Stage for Accountability

Opening with the villain's actions immediately sets the tone. It establishes who's responsible and why this fight matters. This approach avoids common pitfalls, like contribution bias, which can sneakily shift blame onto the victim. For example:

"The defendant ran a red light at 50 miles per hour, putting every family in the intersection at risk."

By starting with the villain's choices, you guide your audience to focus on the harm caused and the justice needed, not on second-guessing the victim.

A story that kicks off with the villain sparks an instant emotional response—outrage, empathy, frustration—setting the audience up to care deeply about the outcome. Imagine opening with this:

"For months, the landlord ignored leaking pipes and rampant mold, forcing a single mother to live in unsafe conditions."

Suddenly, it's not just a legal issue—it's a personal injustice. Emotions like these turn passive listeners into active supporters.

Prime the Audience for Resolution

When you lead with the villain, you're building anticipation for the hero's journey. The audience already understands what's at stake and craves resolution. In a fraud case, for instance, you might start with:

"The company fabricated financial reports, misleading investors and costing families their life savings."

This framing primes the audience to cheer for the protagonist's eventual triumph, making the resolution that much more satisfying.

Highlighting the Hero's Struggle

Starting with the villain also makes your protagonist's journey shine. The contrast between the wrongdoing and the hero's resilience is striking. For example, in a whistleblower case:

"The corporation dumped toxic chemicals into local waterways, threatening an entire community."

This stark opening makes the whistleblower's courage and determination feel even more compelling and heroic.

Clearing Up Complexity

When a case is layered with technicalities, starting with the villain simplifies the narrative by providing a clear focal point. Consider this for a medical malpractice case:

"The surgeon left a sponge inside the patient, violating basic safety protocols."

Now, even the most complex case has an easy entry point, helping the audience understand and invest in the story.

Establishing What's Right

Starting with the villain's actions also sets a moral compass for the narrative. In an environmental case:

"The company knowingly dumped toxic waste into the community's drinking water supply."

This is a call for accountability and a reminder of why justice matters.

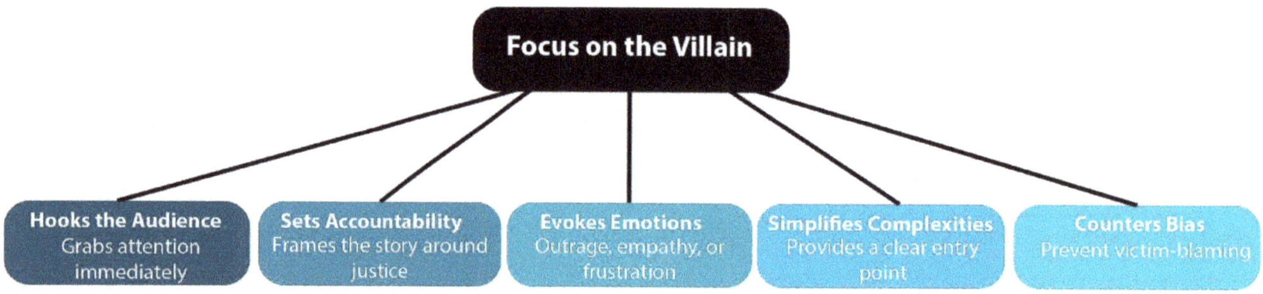

Figure 43: Focus on the Villain

A Personal 'Villain First' Story Spine

"A good story fights for justice, but a great story starts with injustice."

- **Once upon a time,** I was knee-deep in trial prep for a client wrongfully terminated by a corporation. **Every day,** I pored over evidence, knowing the other side would try to twist facts, shift blame, and bury us in discovery. **Until one day,** I stumbled upon emails revealing the company's calculated scheme to oust older employees under the guise of "restructuring."

- **Because of that,** I had the proof I needed to expose them as villains, not just opponents. **Because of that,** I flipped my strategy, leading with their deliberate injustice instead of starting with my client's plight. **Until finally,** the jury saw the truth—a company driven by greed, not fairness—and handed down a verdict for my client. **And ever since then,** I've framed my cases with villains front and center, knowing the fight for justice begins with unmasking the wrongdoers.

Remember, when you start with the bad guys, it makes the good guys shine brighter.

Starting With the Villain First in Trial

"Villain First" in Voir Dire

Set the stage for justice by making jurors feel the weight of wrongdoing from the get-go. Voir dire isn't just a jury selection—it's your chance to shape the narrative lens. Starting with the villain first ensures jurors frame the case through accountability and fairness. Without explicitly diving into the specifics, you can weave in themes of injustice that connect universally.

For example, in a corporate negligence case:

"Have you ever worked somewhere that seemed to value profits over people? How did that make you feel?"

This question taps into personal experiences while planting the seed: someone's actions caused harm. Instantly, you're steering jurors toward empathy for the victim and a critical view of the villain's choices.

"Villain First" in Opening Statements

An opening statement is your chance to hook the jury, and nothing reels them in like an unapologetic villain. By beginning with the villain's choices, you instantly establish stakes and guide the jury's emotions.

In a workplace discrimination case:

"This is a case about a manager who systematically ignored the contributions of women, denying promotions based on gender rather than merit."

Now the jury knows who to hold accountable, and they're already invested in uncovering the injustice.

Build the Moral Framework

Framing the villain first turns the case into a moral crusade. In a product liability trial:

"The defendant knowingly sold defective brakes, risking lives to save a buck. That choice led directly to the crash that changed this family's life forever."

This opening gives the jury a cause to rally behind, positioning your client as the hero seeking justice in a world of negligence.

"Villain First" in Direct Examination

During direct examination, starting with the villain ensures the jury's attention is where it belongs—on the wrongdoing. Lead with questions that emphasize the villain's choices and their impact.

In a landlord-tenant case:

"What did your landlord say when you reported mold growing in your child's bedroom?"

This not only sets the narrative tone but also anchors the jury emotionally.

Build Empathy Through Testimony

In a medical malpractice case, ask:

"When did you first realize that the surgeon had ignored established safety protocols?"

Follow it with:

"How has that decision affected your daily life?"

This sequence keeps the villain at the forefront while humanizing your client's struggles, creating an emotional connection for the jury.

"Villain First" in Cross-Examination

Cross-examination is your chance to make the villain squirm under the spotlight. Begin with their most damning actions to frame the narrative clearly.

In a corporate negligence case:

"You were aware of the safety violations in March, weren't you?"

By forcing them to acknowledge their role, you solidify the narrative of accountability for the jury.

Highlight Intent and Recklessness

In a medical malpractice case:

"You proceeded with the surgery despite staff warnings, didn't you?"

These precise, pointed questions keep the jury focused on the villain's culpability, painting a clear picture of their negligence.

"Villain First" in Closing Arguments

Your closing argument is the jury's final impression of the case. Grounding it in the villain's actions ensures the narrative remains focused on accountability.

In a discrimination case:

"This employer chose to sideline qualified employees based solely on their age. That's not just unfair—it's illegal."

This framing reinforces the stakes and aligns the jury with the moral imperative for justice.

Leave a Lasting Impression

In a product liability case:

"The defendant prioritized profits over people, ignoring the defect that led to this preventable tragedy. Your verdict is an opportunity to ensure this never happens again."

This final push leaves the jury with a clear call to action, ensuring the villain's actions linger in their minds as they deliberate.

Reducing Bias by Spotlighting the Villain

1. Contribution Bias

People love to blame victims—unfair, but true. When you lead with the villain, you cut off this tendency at the knees by making it crystal clear where the harm originated.

Example:

In a personal injury case, instead of starting with your client's injuries, begin with the company's negligent maintenance of faulty equipment.

"For years, this company ignored repeated warnings that their equipment was a ticking time bomb, until one day, that bomb went off—leaving my client unable to walk."

This approach ensures jurors see the harm as systemic and preventable, not just bad luck or user error.

2. Confirmation Bias

Audiences cling to their assumptions like kids clutching candy. If they're inclined to think your client shares blame, you need to shatter that illusion early. Start with the villain's actions to redirect their focus to hard, irrefutable facts.

Example:

If jurors assume your client played a part in their own misfortune, interrupt their preconceptions with this opener:

"This isn't a case about accidents—it's about choices. The defendant chose to ignore safety protocols, and that choice caused the harm you'll hear about today."

When you hit them with objective causation upfront, you leave little room for assumptions to cloud their judgment.

3. Fundamental Attribution Error

Audiences often chalk up actions to personality flaws rather than external circumstances. By starting with the villain, you contextualize their behavior, making the wrongdoing impossible to dismiss as "just who they are."

Example:

In a corporate negligence case:

"The defendant didn't just cut corners—they built an entire business model on ignoring safety standards. The harm wasn't an accident; it was inevitable."

Now the jury isn't just judging the villain—they're seeing the context that led to the harm, which keeps the blame squarely where it belongs.

4. Halo and Horn Effects

First impressions are powerful. If the jury already has warm fuzzies for the defendant or doubts about your client, starting with the villain resets the narrative.

Example:

In a landlord-tenant dispute:

"This case is about a landlord who prioritized profits over people, leaving families to live with mold, leaks, and crumbling ceilings."

Suddenly, it doesn't matter if the landlord looks respectable or your client once missed rent. The villain's actions take center stage, steering perceptions in the right direction.

Caution: Don't Lose the Jury by Starting Too Hot and Heavy

While starting with the villain can be a powerful way to grab attention, there's a risk: coming in too hot and heavy might overwhelm or alienate your audience. If you open with an all-out assault, diving straight into villainous details without context, you could leave the jury behind—confused, skeptical, or even unconvinced.

It's important to balance drama with clarity. Instead of unleashing every damning detail at once, set the stage with a clear and concise outline of the stakes. Guide your audience through the narrative, ensuring they understand not just *what* the villain did, but *why* it matters.

Think of it as setting the hook without snapping the line. Present just enough to pique interest and establish credibility before layering in the details. By pacing your delivery, you allow the jury to follow along, feel the stakes grow, and arrive at their own sense of outrage.

In storytelling—and especially in courtroom narratives—timing is everything. Draw the jury in, but don't rush them. Let the tension build naturally, so the impact lands harder when the full scope of the villain's actions is revealed.

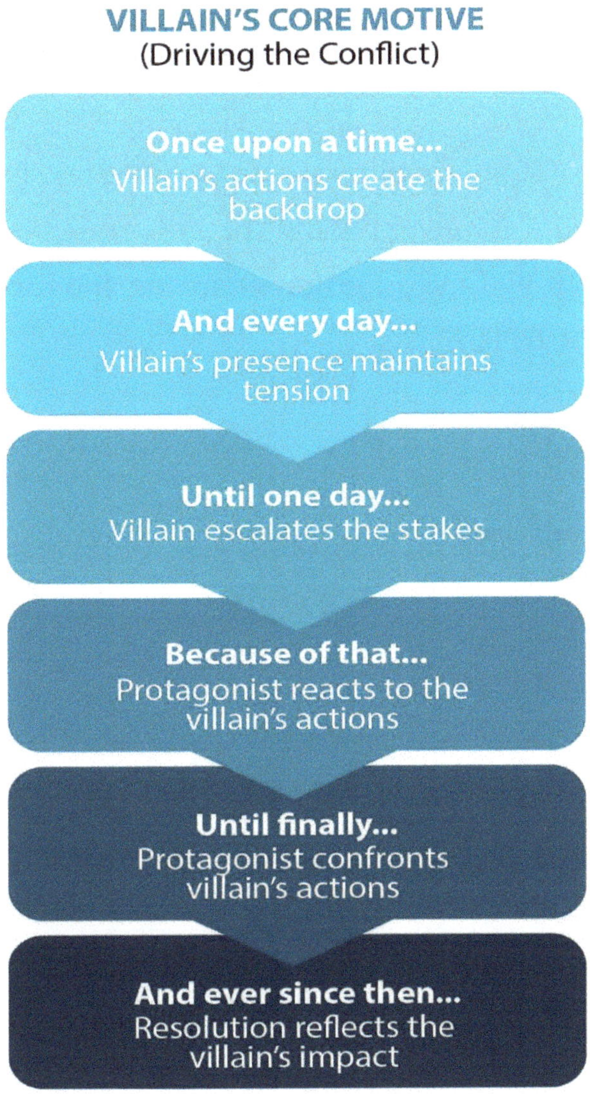

Figure 44: Villain's Core Motive in Storytelling

A War Story: The Villain's Actions Spark the Story

In a high-stakes fraud case, I decided to open the story with the villain, a charming yet manipulative investment advisor who had drained my client's life savings. From the outset, I painted a picture of his deceit: the polished office, the smooth-talking promises, and the carefully crafted façade of trust.

"Imagine walking into an office where every detail—from the leather chair to the perfectly framed degrees on the wall—whispers, 'You can trust me,'" I told the jury. "That's what my client thought—until the day her retirement fund disappeared."

Starting with the villain's actions created immediate tension and gave the jury a clear sense of the stakes. By establishing the antagonist first, we set the stage for my client's journey from victim to fighter, ensuring the jury was with us from the opening moments of the trial.

Conclusion

"When you start with the villain, the stakes rise, biases fall, and justice takes the lead."

Highlighting the villain is a strategic power play. By framing the harm through the villain's actions, you guide the audience's focus, dismantling biases before they take root. In voir dire, opening statements, or cross-examinations, this approach ensures the jury is both emotionally invested and logically aligned with your client's pursuit of justice. So, paint the villain's misdeeds with bold strokes, but remember: every great story is about how the light shines brighter because of the shadow.

PRACTICE SPINES

1. Identifying the Villain and Antagonists in Your Case

- **Objective:** Differentiate between villains and antagonists and determine how each contributes to the story.
- **Instructions:**
  1. Review the details of your case and list all parties, forces, or circumstances opposing your client.
  2. Identify which of these elements represent a **villain** (malicious intent, ethical or moral wrongdoing) and which are **antagonists** (neutral or systemic opposition, without moral malice).
  3. For each villain, write a brief paragraph detailing their actions and motivations. For antagonists, describe how their opposition creates conflict without intentional harm.
- **Application:** Use this exercise to sharpen your understanding of the players in your case and craft targeted narratives that highlight the villain's culpability while addressing the antagonist's role with nuance.

2. Crafting an Opening Statement with the Villain First

- **Objective:** Practice starting your opening statement by focusing on the villain's actions.
- **Instructions:**
  1. Identify a pivotal act of wrongdoing committed by the villain in your case.
  2. Write the first two paragraphs of your opening statement, starting with the villain's actions. For example: **"The defendant chose**

profit over safety, knowing the consequences of their negligence."

3. Ensure your opening introduces the conflict clearly, evokes an emotional response, and sets the stage for your client's story.

❖ **Reflection:** Share your draft with a colleague or mentor and discuss its impact. Adjust to ensure it engages the audience and frames the narrative effectively.

3. Framing Cross-Examination with the Villain's Actions

❖ **Objective:** Structure cross-examination questions to emphasize the villain's harmful actions.

❖ **Instructions:**

1. Identify the villain's key actions in the case and their consequences.
2. Draft five cross-examination questions that focus on these actions. For example:
    - **"You were aware of the safety violation before the incident, weren't you?"**
    - **"Is it correct that you chose not to act despite repeated warnings?"**
3. Arrange your questions to build a clear narrative of the villain's responsibility during cross-examination.

❖ **Reflection:** Practice delivering your questions with a partner playing the role of the witness to refine your tone and effectiveness.

4. Villain-First Narrative in Closing Arguments

❖ **Objective:** Practice closing arguments by emphasizing the villain's actions and their impact.

- **Instructions:**
    1. Write a draft of your closing argument that starts by recounting the villain's most egregious action: **"The defendant's refusal to fix the faulty product led directly to this tragedy."**
    2. Connect this action to the emotional and factual stakes of the case.
    3. Conclude by showing how addressing this wrongdoing is not just justice for your client but a stand against similar behavior in the future.
- **Reflection:** Record or deliver your closing argument to an audience and get feedback on the emotional impact and clarity of your message.

5. Role-Playing Villain and Antagonist Perspectives

- **Objective:** Deepen your understanding of the villain's and antagonist's motivations by stepping into their roles.
- **Instructions:**
    1. Role-play as the villain, narrating their side of the story using the Story Spine framework:
        - **"Once upon a time, I prioritized profit over safety..."**
        - Continue through each phase, exploring their perspective.
    2. Repeat the exercise as the antagonist, focusing on their opposition without malice.
    3. Reflect on how these perspectives inform your understanding of the case and refine your storytelling strategy.
- **Reflection:** Discuss insights with a partner or team, identifying new ways to frame your narrative effectively for jurors or judges.

Chapter 24
Beyond People I

"When the unseen becomes the victim and the intangible becomes the villain, your story leaps from the ordinary to the unforgettable."

Stretching the Boundaries of Victims and Villains

Who says victims and villains must always be people? Some of the most powerful stories emerge when these roles are assigned to ideas, places, or abstract concepts. What if your villain wasn't a person, but a corrupt system? What if your victim wasn't an individual, but a vanishing freedom or a struggling river?

This fresh approach expands the dimensions of your narrative, inviting audiences to think beyond personal conflicts and engage with larger, more universal stakes. It's the perfect strategy for tackling stories that address systemic injustice, environmental harm, or internal struggles.

When Systems Are the Villains

Systems can be the most chilling antagonists of all. Unlike a single person, they're faceless, pervasive, and harder to dismantle. In a wrongful imprisonment case, for example, the villain isn't just an overzealous prosecutor or an unreliable witness—it's the entire justice system's obsession with convictions:

"Once upon a time, the justice system promised fairness. But one day, it became more about numbers than truth, turning innocence into collateral damage."

By framing the villain as a system, you show the audience that this isn't just one person's story, it's everyone's problem.

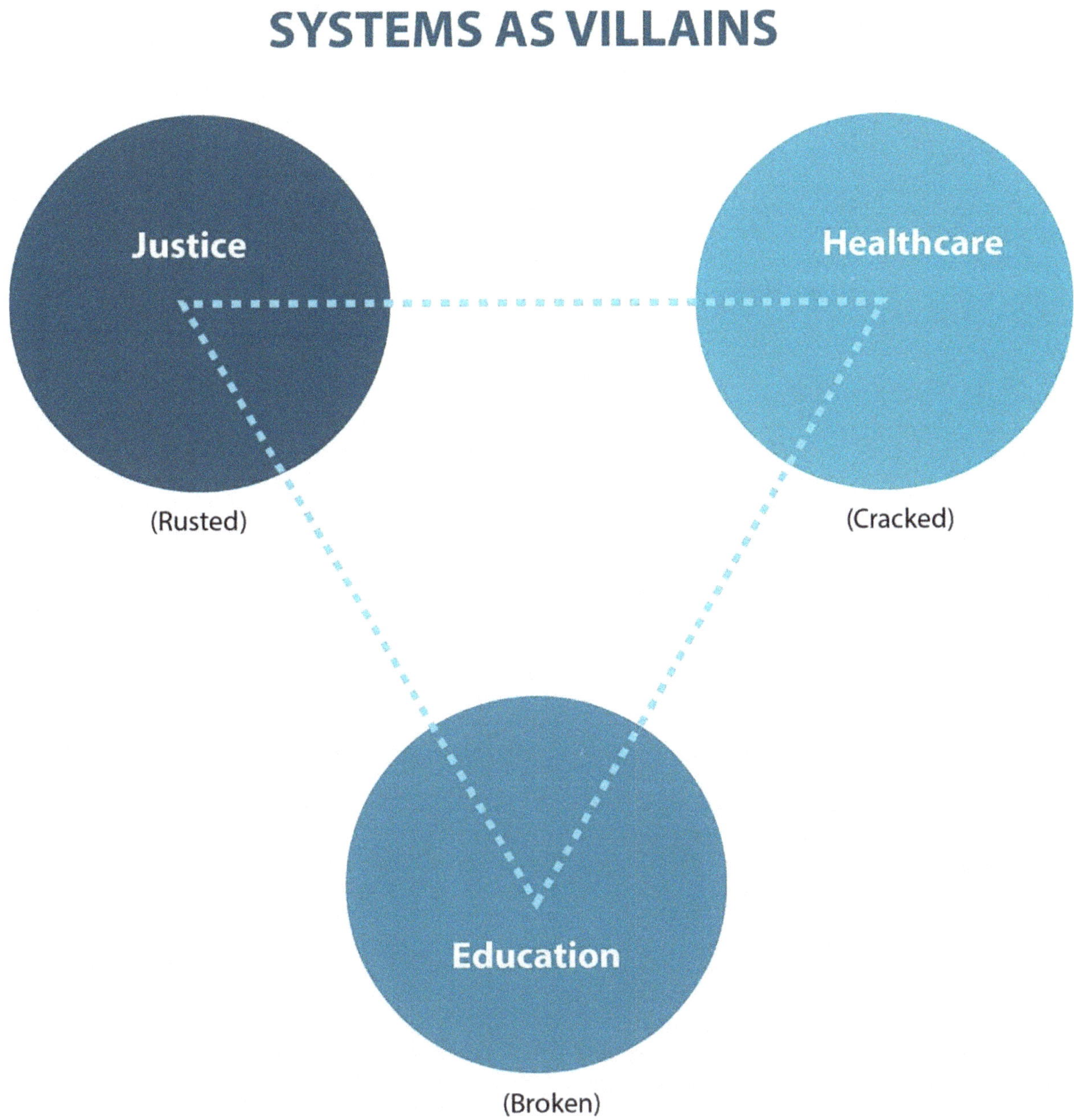

Figure 45: Systems as Villains

When Principles Become Victims

Victims aren't always individuals—they can be values we hold dear, like trust, fairness, or privacy. Imagine framing privacy as the victim in a case about government surveillance:

"Because of that, our most sacred right—the right to live free from intrusion—was eroded, one hidden camera at a time."

Abstract victims tap into universal ideals, making the audience care deeply about the stakes, even if they've never faced the exact situation.

When Nature Takes Center Stage

Environmental storytelling thrives when nature becomes the victim—or even the villain. A river poisoned by industrial waste isn't just a backdrop; it's a central character with its own tragic arc:

"Once upon a time, the river teemed with life, a sanctuary for countless species. But one day, toxic runoff turned it into a wasteland, silencing its song forever."

By giving the environment a voice, you help the audience see it as something to be protected, not just a setting.

Life Lessons: When Nature Takes Center Stage

Once upon a time... Growing up in Florida, hurricanes were a normal part of life. I remember one storm in particular, a massive force of nature that ripped through my neighborhood, leaving chaos in its wake. For weeks, we lived in the aftermath—debris-strewn streets, shattered homes, and the eerie quiet of a place trying to piece itself back together. The storm itself wasn't a person, but it was a character in our lives, shaping every decision, every moment.

Every day...I thought about how that storm represented something larger—a force that, while faceless, dictated our actions and challenged our resilience. Years later, in the courtroom, I realized abstract forces like this often play a similar role in cases. They aren't just background—they're drivers of the narrative.

Until one day...I began crafting stories where concepts like greed, corruption, or even hope were given narrative roles. These forces weren't just referenced; they were framed as active characters influencing the choices and struggles of the people in the story.

Because of that... Juries didn't just see isolated events; they saw the larger forces at play, the systems and contexts that shaped individual actions. The story gained depth and power.

And ever since that day...I've looked beyond people when crafting narratives, assigning roles to abstract forces that drive the story forward and resonate deeply with audiences.

Internal Struggles as Villains

Not all villains wear suits and ties. Sometimes, the battle is within. Fear, addiction, or trauma can become the central antagonists in deeply personal stories. In a personal injury case, for example, the villain might be the shadow of the client's past pain:

"Because of that, every creak of a floorboard sends her heart racing, a constant reminder of what was stolen from her."

Internal villains humanize the conflict, forging an emotional bridge between the protagonist and the audience.

Places That Tell a Story

Locations themselves can become characters in your narrative, playing the roles of either victim or villain. A neglected neighborhood might symbolize lost opportunity:

"Once upon a time, this block was full of promise. But one day, neglect turned it into a shadow of what it could have been, leaving families trapped in its decay."

Conversely, a treacherous road could embody the villain, a silent player in repeated tragedies:

"Because of that, another life was lost on a curve that's claimed too many already, while those responsible looked the other way."

By incorporating places into your narrative, you ground the story in a setting that feels real, tangible, and memorable.

A War Story: Life In The Trenches

Once upon a time...

It was late one night during my time in the military, working communications in a combat unit. The air around us was heavy with tension, not from a visible enemy but from the oppressive force of uncertainty. The battlefield was quiet, eerily so, but the silence carried its own weight, one that pressed down on every soldier like an invisible hand gripping their throats.

Every day...

Our job wasn't just about relaying orders—it was about navigating the chaos of a war where the enemy wasn't always flesh and blood. The desert didn't just hold combatants; it held whispers of danger that could strike anywhere, at any time. The unseen was always there: the heat, the isolation, deadly insects, the grinding uncertainty that ate away at our nerves.

Until one day...

During a mission briefing, we intercepted a fragment of communication. The message was garbled and vague, but its undertone carried a chilling menace that changed everything. It wasn't just the words that unsettled us—it was the gaps, the unspoken threats that hung heavily in the air.

The desert around us seemed to come alive, no longer just a backdrop but an active force. The relentless heat, the endless dunes, and the oppressive silence all felt like they were conspiring with the unknown threat, amplifying our vulnerability and making every moment feel more precarious.

Because of that...

We weren't fighting a conventional enemy. The villain wasn't just a person or a force—it was the desert itself, an intangible antagonist that tested our endurance and our trust in one another. The heat became an accomplice to fear, the wind an echo of every doubt we carried. Each decision felt heavier, every step more treacherous, not because of what we could see but because of what we couldn't see.

And because of that...

The story of that mission became one of survival against an invisible foe. It wasn't just the soldiers who were heroes; it was the team's resilience, the bond forged in the face of an enemy that couldn't be seen, only felt. The desert became a character in our narrative—hostile, relentless, and unforgettable.

Until finally...

We completed the mission, but we left the battlefield forever changed. The story wasn't just about what we did—it was about what we endured. It taught me that the most powerful narratives often stretch beyond the visible, assigning roles to forces and environments that shape the human experience in profound ways.

And ever since that day...

I've used this understanding in my storytelling, weaving intangible forces into the fabric of my narratives. Whether in courtrooms, focus groups, or personal reflections, I recognize that villains and victims aren't always people. Sometimes, it's the unseen—the environment, the systems, the fear—that drives the story forward, turning it from ordinary to unforgettable.

When the unseen becomes a victim or villain, your story transcends the personal to become something greater, something universal. By redefining these roles, you don't just tell a story; you create an experience that lingers, challenges, and transforms.

"So, who's the villain in your story? A system? A fear? A forgotten place? Let it speak—and watch your audience listen."

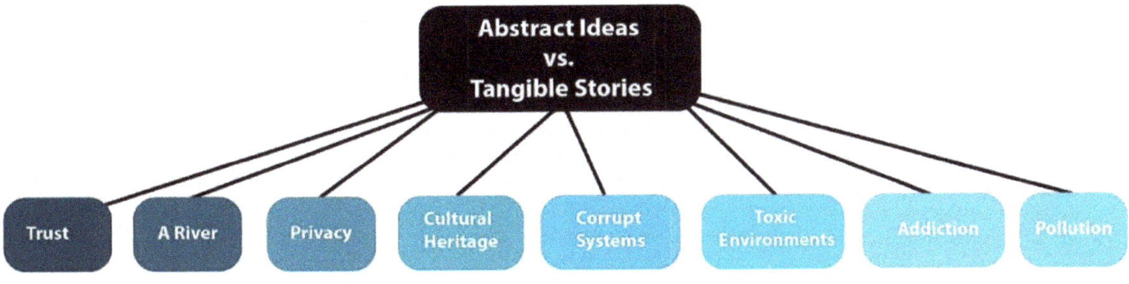

Figure 46: Abstract Ideas vs. Tangible Stories

Non-Human Victims in the Story Spine

Justice. Equality. Freedom. These lofty ideals may seem untouchable, but when violated, they become victims in their own right. Imagine a whistleblower case where the real casualty isn't just an employee's career but the principle of honesty itself:

"Once upon a time, transparency and truth were the lifeblood of this company. But one day, greed drowned integrity, silencing anyone brave enough to speak up."

Framing abstract concepts as victims shifts the narrative from individual harm to systemic impact. It widens the story's scope, appealing to shared values and creating a deeper connection with the audience.

Everyday Objects with Big Meanings

Victims don't always have to be grand or intangible—they can be as ordinary as a child's desk or a tattered teddy bear. In a school shooting case, for instance, a damaged desk can symbolize shattered innocence:

"This desk once cradled a child's dreams of becoming an astronaut. Today, its surface bears the scars of violence no child should endure."

These small, everyday items carry immense emotional weight, transforming the ordinary into poignant symbols of what's been lost.

Non-human victims are often the perfect mirror for human suffering. Take a land dispute, for example, where the sacred ground of an Indigenous community is the victim:

"Once upon a time, this land was a wellspring of spiritual strength. But one day, its sanctity was sold off for profit, leaving its people without a piece of their soul."

This interplay doesn't just layer the narrative—it deepens it. By connecting the harm done to the land with the cultural and personal losses of the people, you create a story that resonates both emotionally and intellectually.

Sometimes, an object's story can be the most heart-wrenching of all. Imagine a custody battle where a torn teddy bear takes center stage:

"Once upon a time, this bear was her protector, her confidant, her comfort. Until one day, it was left behind, a casualty of her parents' chaotic separation."

By giving the object a voice, you create a visual and emotional anchor that pulls your audience into the story. The bear's journey reflects the child's, making the stakes impossible to ignore.

Cultural and Historical Victims

What happens when progress bulldozes history? A historic neighborhood at risk of demolition can become a victim of development:

"Once upon a time, these streets echoed with stories of resilience and community. Until one day, the wrecking ball arrived, silencing generations of voices."

Using cultural or historical victims reminds audiences of the intangible losses that ripple through communities, grounding abstract harm in a tangible and relatable context.

Technology as a Modern-Day Victim

Even tech can take a hit. A breached firewall, for instance, can become the victim of a cyberattack:

"Once upon a time, this firewall stood as a digital fortress, protecting private lives. But one day, it was breached, leaving personal information exposed to prying eyes."

Framing technology as a victim helps humanize abstract problems like cybersecurity. It also sets the stage for broader discussions about trust and accountability in the digital world.

Internal Spaces as Victims

Sometimes, the harm isn't physical or tangible—it's a feeling or atmosphere that's been shattered. Take a workplace harassment case, for example:

"Once upon a time, this office buzzed with creativity and camaraderie. But one day, toxic behavior seeped in, turning it into a place of dread."

By making the workplace itself a victim, you show how harm can poison environments, relationships, and even the soul of a community.

Mirroring the Protagonist's Struggles

Non-human victims can act as emotional mirrors, reflecting the protagonist's journey. In a domestic abuse case, a neglected garden might symbolize the victim's lost sense of self:

"Once upon a time, this garden bloomed with life and color. Until one day, it withered under the weight of despair."

This metaphor deepens the emotional resonance, tying the protagonist's personal recovery to the restoration of something tangible and beautiful.

From Loss to Redemption

Non-human victims can also symbolize hope and renewal. In a bankruptcy case, a shuttered café could embody the potential for a fresh start:

"Once upon a time, this café was a hub of connection and joy. Until one day, economic challenges forced its closure. But today, it stands as a beacon of resilience, ready to thrive again."

Shifting the narrative from despair to recovery transforms the story into one of inspiration, engaging audiences with the possibility of change.

Challenging Perspectives with Intangible Loss

Non-human victims can challenge audiences to see harm in new ways. In an urban gentrification case, the victim might be a neighborhood's culture:

"Once upon a time, these streets were alive with history and tradition. Until one day, development erased its stories, leaving only empty facades."

By framing the loss as cultural and communal, the narrative broadens beyond individuals, urging the audience to reflect on shared values like identity and belonging.

The Silent Witness as a Victim

Sometimes, an object tells the story best. In a domestic violence case, a shattered table might stand in for the unspoken pain:

"Once upon a time, this table was the heart of family dinners and laughter. Until one day, it bore the weight of anger and fear."

This subtle storytelling technique lets the audience infer the depth of harm, making the narrative poignant without being overtly graphic.

Representing Absence as Loss

Nothing conveys the gravity of harm like something that can never return. In a conservation case, the victim might be a lost species:

"Once upon a time, this forest rang with the songs of creatures that thrived for generations. Until one day, their voices were silenced forever."

This approach emphasizes the permanence of loss, urging the audience to consider the consequences of inaction.

Non-Human Victims as Collective Voices

Sometimes, the victim represents more than itself—it embodies the collective experience of many. In a labor dispute, the factory itself might symbolize workers' shared struggles:

"Once upon a time, this factory was a place of dignity and opportunity. Until one day, its walls echoed only with the silence of lost jobs."

This technique connects individual stories to a larger communal identity, making the stakes feel both personal and systemic.

Illustrating Long-Term Impact

Non-human victims excel at showing how harm endures across generations. In a toxic waste case, the victim might be the land itself:

"Once upon a time, this soil nourished families and futures. Until one day, chemicals seeped into its heart, leaving it barren for decades."

This framing drives home the importance of accountability, making the long-term consequences impossible to ignore. By shifting focus from individuals to ideals, storytellers tap into universal values like fairness and innovation, resonating with audiences on a deeper level.

Non-human victims expand the story's scope, adding layers of meaning and emotional depth. They challenge assumptions, highlight ripple effects, and connect abstract harm to human experiences. Whether it's a principle, a river, or a teddy bear, giving these silent victims a voice ensures your narrative isn't just heard—it's felt.

Conclusion

"Stories come alive when they challenge us to see the world through unexpected lenses. By giving voice to non-human victims, we invite our audience to reflect not just on what was lost, but on why it matters to everyone."

Thinking beyond people as victims and villains isn't just an exercise in creativity, it's a strategy for deepening emotional resonance and expanding the impact of your narrative. Whether it's a river poisoned by neglect, an idea stolen by greed, or a neighborhood erased by development, non-human elements can carry weighty truths that connect your audience to larger societal values. When we widen the lens of storytelling, we uncover universal truths that transcend individual experiences, making our narratives richer, more engaging, and impossible to forget.

"After all, justice isn't just about people. Sometimes, it's about the things we hold dear, the values we fight for, and the places we call home."

PRACTICE SPINES

Let's flex those storytelling muscles! Use these prompts to create your own Story Spine featuring non-human victims and villains:

1. Environmental Destruction Spine

- *Once upon a time...* This forest was a sanctuary for countless creatures and a source of clean air and water for nearby communities.
- *Every day...* It provided shade, shelter, and beauty to everyone who knew it.
- *Until one day...* A corporation began illegal logging, cutting down acres without permits.
- *Because of that...* Wildlife was displaced, rivers became polluted, and families nearby started experiencing respiratory issues.
- *Because of that...* The community banded together, filing lawsuits and raising awareness of the environmental damage.
- *Until finally...* The court ordered the corporation to cease operations and fund restoration efforts.
- *And ever since then...* The forest has slowly started to recover, reminding everyone of the power of unity in protecting shared resources.

2. Intellectual Property Spine

- *Once upon a time...* This innovative app was designed to help underprivileged students access free learning tools.
- *Every day...* Students used it to learn, grow, and chase their dreams.
- *Until one day...* A tech giant stole the design, rebranding it and charging high subscription fees.
- *Because of that...* Many students lost access to vital educational resources.

- *Because of that...* The original creator struggled to regain control, facing mounting legal fees.
- *Until finally...* The court ruled in favor of the creator, restoring the app's mission of accessibility and education for all.
- *And ever since then...* The app has continued to empower students worldwide, a symbol of standing up for what's right.

3. Cultural Preservation Spine

- *Once upon a time...* This historic neighborhood thrived, its streets alive with traditions and stories passed down for generations.
- *Every day...* Families gathered in its community centers, festivals lit up its plazas, and small businesses flourished.
- *Until one day...* Developers arrived, planning to replace it with luxury apartments.
- *Because of that...* Longtime residents were displaced, and the neighborhood began losing its identity.
- *Because of that...* Activists fought tirelessly to preserve key landmarks and protect residents from eviction.
- *Until finally...* The city passed measures to preserve the neighborhood's cultural and historical significance.
- *And ever since then...* It stands as a testament to the resilience of community and the importance of honoring our past.

4. Workplace Toxicity Spine

- *Once upon a time...* This office was a place where employees felt valued and motivated.
- *Every day...* Teams collaborated, morale was high, and productivity flourished.

- *Until one day...* A new manager brought fear, favoritism, and micromanagement to the workplace.
- *Because of that...* Employees started dreading coming to work, and turnover skyrocketed.
- *Because of that...* The company's reputation and bottom line suffered as key talent left.
- *Until finally...* Leadership replaced the toxic manager and implemented policies to rebuild trust and foster collaboration.
- *And ever since then...* The office has regained its positive culture, proving that accountability can pave the way for renewal.

5. Data Security Breach Spine

- *Once upon a time...* This company was trusted to keep its customers' sensitive data safe.
- *Every day...* People relied on it to protect their financial information and personal privacy.
- *Until one day...* Hackers exploited a vulnerability, stealing data from millions of users.
- *Because of that...* Customers faced identity theft and financial ruin, losing faith in the company.
- *Because of that...* The company was forced to overhaul its security measures and rebuild trust.
- *Until finally...* They implemented state-of-the-art protections and made restitution to affected users.
- *And ever since then...* The company became a leader in cybersecurity, a cautionary tale turned success story.

It's Your Turn!

Try crafting your own Story Spine with a non-human victim or villain:

- Who or what represents the conflict?
- How can you show the impact on broader ideals or communities?
- What resolution would feel satisfying and just?

Chapter 25

Beyond People II

"What if your story's villain wasn't a person but an idea, a system, or even complacency itself? Non-human villains don't just wreak havoc—they provoke thought, drive reflection, and inspire action."

Non-Human Villains in the Story Spine

Sometimes, the most captivating stories don't feature a mustache-twirling villain. Instead, they reveal the subtle, insidious forces—like bureaucracy, tradition, or greed—that silently wreak havoc. By framing non-human villains, storytellers can tackle systemic issues, abstract conflicts, and societal flaws head-on, turning invisible forces into compelling antagonists.

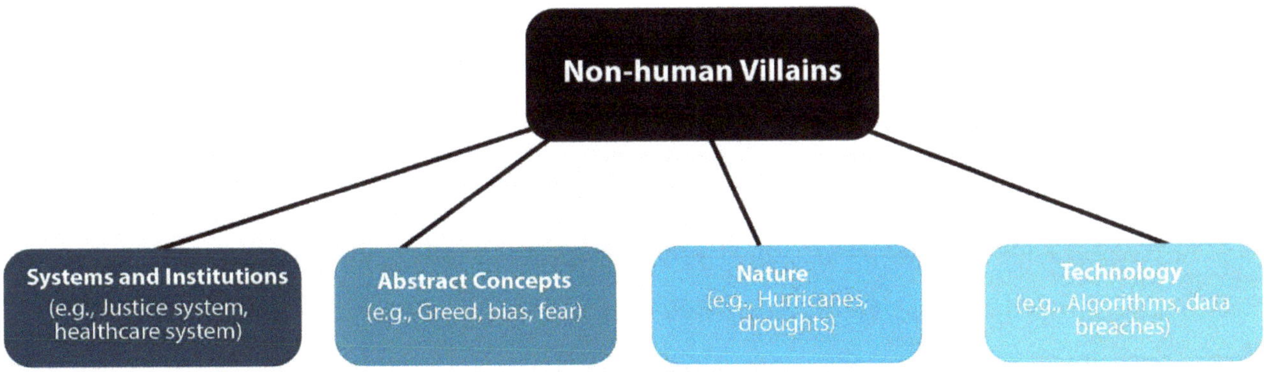

Figure 47: Non-human Villains

Systems and Institutions as Villains

"When systems fail, greed festers, or time runs out, villains emerge that challenge society itself."

Some of the most powerful narratives arise when the villain is a system perpetuating harm. In a wrongful conviction case, the criminal justice system can become the antagonist:

"Once upon a time, the justice system promised fairness. But one day, its obsession with convictions over truth led to innocent lives being destroyed."

Here, the villain isn't an individual but a structure, calling the audience to consider the broader need for reform.

Abstract Concepts as Villains

Abstract forces like greed, prejudice, or fear can be powerful villains when they drive harm. In a workplace discrimination case, institutionalized bias might take center stage:

"Once upon a time, this company valued equality. Until one day, unconscious bias infiltrated decisions, robbing qualified employees of opportunity."

This framing allows the story to confront societal flaws, leaving the audience to ponder their own role in change.

Nature as a Villain

Nature often plays the dual role of victim and villain. In a hurricane insurance case, nature can be framed as an indifferent antagonist:

"Once upon a time, this community thrived along the coast. Until one day, the winds and waves rose, and nature itself unleashed its fury."

This highlights resilience while creating space to critique inadequate human preparation or response.

Technology as a Villain

Technology's promises can turn into nightmares when misused. In a data breach story, algorithms themselves might be the villain:

"Once upon a time, these systems safeguarded privacy. Until one day, they became tools for exploitation, leaving personal lives exposed."

This setup connects deeply in a tech-driven world, making abstract harms relatable and urgent.

Life Lessons: Beyond People

Once upon a time...

I grew up in a world where survival overshadowed success and where systemic inequality shaped the trajectory of our lives. Cultural expectations didn't revolve around aspirations but around survival—working hard, staying quiet, and carrying the weight of generational poverty. There was no room for dreams beyond the immediate need to make ends meet. Yet, even within this, there was an unspoken demand: to carry the dignity of our family's struggle with strength and pride, no matter how heavy it felt.

Every day...

The weight of systemic oppression pressed down on us, dictating where we lived, how we worked, and what futures seemed possible. It wasn't just about individual struggles; it was about navigating a system designed to keep people like us in our place. Success, when it came, felt like a defiance of expectations, but failure felt like a confirmation of every stereotype.

Until one day...

As I began to understand the forces shaping my life, I saw how cultural and systemic dynamics acted like invisible characters in my story. They weren't just part of the backdrop; they were active participants, influencing every decision, every opportunity—or lack thereof. I realized that these forces weren't just my story—they were shaping the lives of so many others as well.

Because of that...

I started to craft narratives that didn't ignore these systemic forces but confronted them head-on. In my work with clients, I framed issues like poverty, bias, and cultural expectations as central elements of the story—antagonists that deserved to be challenged and exposed.

And because of that...

The stories became more than personal—they became universal. Juries, judges, and audiences didn't just see the individual; they saw the systems at play, the cultural forces shaping the conflict, and the courage it took to push back against them.

And ever since that day...

I've committed to crafting stories that include the unseen forces of culture and oppression, turning them from unspoken burdens into characters that can be understood, challenged, and ultimately overcome. Because to tell a story that truly resonates, you must acknowledge every force shaping it—even the ones that don't have a face.

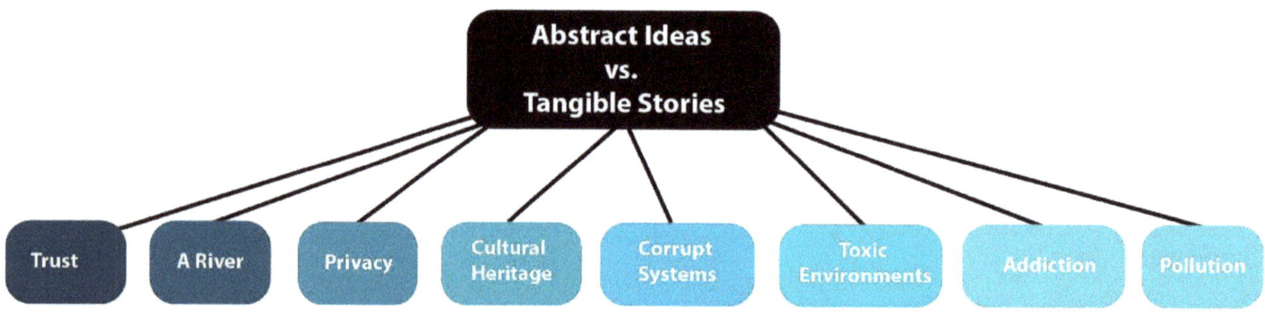

Figure 48: Abstract Ideas vs. Tangible Stories

The Villains Within: Internal and Cultural Forces

Greed and Complacency

Greed can corrupt, and complacency can enable it. In a corporate corruption case, complacency becomes the subtle antagonist:

"Once upon a time, employees believed in speaking up. Until one day, complacency silenced voices, turning blind eyes to unethical actions."

This framing invites audiences to reflect on how inaction can perpetuate harm.

Tradition and Progress

Tradition can be comforting—or stifling. Progress can be transformative—or destructive. In a gentrification case, the villain might be development itself:

"Once upon a time, this neighborhood was alive with culture and history. Until one day, progress arrived, replacing heritage with high-rises."

This narrative challenges the audience to balance preservation with evolution.

Time and Lost Potential

Time is relentless and can become a villain when it exacerbates harm or loss. In an environmental cleanup case:

"Once upon a time, this land held the promise of renewal. Until one day, time ran out, and the damage became irreversible."

This adds urgency, framing time as both antagonist and a call to action.

Non-Human Villains in the Story Spine

When abstract forces collide, stories transcend individuals, shining a spotlight on the systems, values, and connections that bind us all. When you pair non-human victims with non-human villains, the story takes on a richer, more nuanced texture. This combination not only highlights the interconnectedness of harm but also challenges audiences to see conflicts as larger-than-life, often implicating us all in their resolution.

Dynamic Duos: Non-Human Victims and Villains in Action

1. Environmental Impact

- *Victim*: A polluted river.
- *Villain*: Corporate greed.
- *Story Spine Example*:
    - *Once upon a time…* This river brought life to the surrounding communities and wildlife.
    - *Every day…* It sustained farmers, fishers, and families.
    - *Until one day…* A corporation, chasing profits, dumped toxic waste into its waters.
    - *Because of that…* The river grew lifeless, and those who depended on it faced ruin.
    - *Until finally…* Accountability was demanded, and restoration began.

This setup not only shows cause and effect but also underscores the ripple effects of unchecked ambition.

2. Systemic Failure

- *Victim*: The integrity of healthcare.
- *Villain*: A profit-driven model.
- *Story Spine Example*:
    - *Once upon a time…* Patients trusted doctors to prioritize care over cost.
    - *Every day…* People sought treatment with hope and dignity.

- *Until one day…* Profits began overshadowing compassion, and lives were treated as numbers.
- *Because of that…* Patients were denied necessary treatments, and preventable deaths became statistics.
- *Until finally…* Advocates rallied to reform the system, restoring humanity to healthcare.

This framing allows the audience to connect personal experiences with systemic issues.

3. Cultural Erosion

- *Victim*: A historic neighborhood.
- *Villain*: Gentrification.
- *Story Spine Example*:
    - *Once upon a time…* The neighborhood was a vibrant cultural hub.
    - *Every day…* Families, artists, and small businesses thrived in its colorful streets.
    - *Until one day…* Luxury developments replaced affordable homes, and rents skyrocketed.
    - *Because of that…* Lifelong residents were displaced, and the neighborhood's unique identity was lost.
    - *Until finally…* Community leaders fought back, preserving the history while ensuring inclusive growth.

By combining the victim and villain into a shared ecosystem, the stakes feel more tangible and immediate.

Illustrating the Ripple Effect of Harm

Non-human victims and villains create a broader view of how harm spreads. For instance:

- *Victim*: The education system.
- *Villain*: Political apathy.
- *Framing*: "Once upon a time, every child had access to quality education. Until one day, neglected funding turned classrooms into shadows of their former selves."

This narrative demonstrates how a single failure affects generations, prompting audiences to reflect on their role in collective responsibility.

Making Abstract Conflict Personal

Sometimes the most compelling villains are concepts, like fear or misinformation.

- *Victim*: Public trust.
- *Villain*: Misinformation algorithms.
- *Framing*: "Once upon a time, people trusted the news they consumed. Until one day, sensationalism replaced accuracy, spreading doubt like wildfire."

This setup turns an intangible problem into a relatable story with clear stakes.

Driving Emotional Connection Through Symbolism

Symbolic non-human roles evoke strong emotions.

- *Victim*: A child's teddy bear (symbolizing innocence).
- *Villain*: A custody battle's chaos.
- *Framing*: "Once upon a time, this bear was a source of comfort for a little girl. Until one day, it was left behind in the turmoil of her parents' separation."

This subtle storytelling device draws a direct line to the emotional stakes.

Amplifying the Stakes Through Dual Roles

By pairing multiple victims and villains, storytellers can showcase interconnected harm.

- *Victims*: A rainforest and its indigenous people.
- *Villains*: Illegal logging and ineffective regulations.
- *Framing*: "Once upon a time, the forest was a home, a livelihood, and a sanctuary. Until one day, greed and neglect began to chip away at its heart, uprooting lives and erasing cultures."

This layering creates a narrative with widespread implications, showing the scope of the conflict.

Villains Without Boundaries, Victims With Resonance

Combining non-human victims and villains doesn't just expand the scope of storytelling—it shifts the lens through which we see conflict, making it both relatable and revelatory. These narratives remind us that harm isn't always a singular act by a singular person; it's often a tangled web of actions, systems, and values. Sometimes, the line between villain and victim blurs, creating a more nuanced narrative. In a renewable energy case, fossil fuels could play both roles:

- *Once upon a time, fossil fuels powered progress and prosperity.*
- *Until one day, reliance turned into exploitation, leaving the planet scarred and communities struggling to adapt.*

By showing how the villain itself suffers from overuse, the story highlights the interconnectedness of conflict, fostering empathy and a drive for sustainable solutions.

A War Story: Reframing a Case After a Key Development

A few years ago, I was working on a case involving a workplace injury. The original Story Spine we developed focused on my client's perseverance in recovering from her injuries and returning to work. However, midway through the trial, new evidence emerged: the company had ignored multiple safety complaints before the accident.

Suddenly, the story wasn't just about my client's resilience—it was about corporate negligence and accountability. We revisited the Story Spine and reframed the narrative to highlight the systemic failures that had led to the injury. This shift in focus not only strengthened our case but also made it more relevant to the jury, who now saw themselves as protectors of workplace safety. That experience taught me that stories are living entities, and updating them to reflect new realities can transform how they resonate with an audience.

Conclusion

"The most powerful stories don't just describe the world; they ask us to change it."

When you assign non-human roles to victims and villains, you expand the scope of storytelling, transforming abstract issues into relatable, emotionally charged narratives. A polluted river battling unchecked greed or community trust shattered by misinformation becomes more than just a story—it becomes a call to action.

By blending non-human dynamics into your Story Spine, you open up new dimensions of conflict and resolution. These narratives challenge us to look beyond surface-level disputes and confront the systemic, cultural, or environmental forces that shape our lives. They emphasize shared stakes and collective responsibility, reminding us that the harm we ignore today could shape tomorrow.

When we craft stories with non-human victims and villains, we create more than just compelling narratives—we create opportunities for reflection, connection, and change. Because sometimes, the most transformative stories don't just ask, *Who's at fault?* They ask, *What kind of world do we want to leave behind?*

Practice Spines

Ready to experiment? Here are some prompts to help you practice crafting non-human villains:

1. Systemic Negligence Spine

- *Once upon a time…* Healthcare in this community offered dignity and hope.
- *Every day…* Patients relied on the system to heal and protect them.
- *Until one day…* Bureaucratic inefficiency delayed life-saving treatments.
- *Because of that…* People suffered needlessly, families were left devastated, and trust was shattered.
- *Because of that…* Whistleblowers demanded reform, risking their careers for the greater good.
- *Until finally…* The system was overhauled, prioritizing care over red tape.
- *And ever since then…* The community has rebuilt trust in a system that finally works for them.

2. Greed as a Villain Spine

- *Once upon a time…* This company revolutionized the market, creating products that improved lives.
- *Every day…* Customers trusted their innovations to solve everyday problems.
- *Until one day…* Greed took over, leading to cost-cutting measures that compromised safety.
- *Because of that…* A defective product caused widespread harm.
- *Because of that…* Victims banded together, seeking justice and accountability.

- *Until finally…* The company faced consequences, reforming its practices and prioritizing integrity.
- *And ever since then…* It became a cautionary tale of how greed can destroy even the best intentions.

3. Fear as a Villain Spine

- *Once upon a time…* This country welcomed those seeking refuge and opportunity.
- *Every day…* Immigrants brought innovation, diversity, and hope.
- *Until one day…* Fear of the unfamiliar turned compassion into suspicion.
- *Because of that…* Families were torn apart, and dreams were put on hold.
- *Because of that…* Advocates rallied, reminding society of its shared humanity.
- *Until finally…* Policies shifted, restoring fairness and hope for the future.
- *And ever since then…* The nation renewed its commitment to inclusivity and opportunity.

It's Your Turn!

Create your own Story Spine with a non-human villain:

- Who or what is the source of conflict?
- How does the villain embody systemic, abstract, or environmental forces?
- What resolution would feel satisfying and impactful?

"When the villain transcends individuals, stories become mirrors—reflecting not just the characters' struggles but the values and conflicts shaping us all."

Practice Prompt

- *Victim*: Choose an abstract value, place, or object that represents something larger.
- *Villain*: Identify a systemic, cultural, or internal force that threatens it.
- *Craft*: Write your Story Spine using these roles.

Chapter 26
Periodically Updating Story Spines

"A story isn't a snapshot—it's a living, breathing thing that evolves as the world around it changes."

The Living Story

Imagine telling the same story over and over, even as new twists, turns, and revelations come to light. It would quickly lose its spark, right? Stories, especially in the dynamic environment of a trial, need room to grow. With a surprise witness, a new piece of evidence, or a shift in legal strategy, the Story Spine thrives when it's flexible and responsive.

The Story Spine is a narrative roadmap that must be revisited and adjusted as your case develops. New facts emerge, evidence takes center stage, and legal strategies pivot, making updates not just helpful but essential. For trial lawyers, keeping your Story Spine fresh can be the difference between a case that lands with impact and one that falls flat.

For example, maybe the defendant in your case was previously warned about a hazard but ignored it. Suddenly, your personal injury story isn't just about an accident—it's about recklessness. Updating the Story Spine to weave in this detail transforms your argument, making it sharper and more compelling.

As your case evolves, so does its emotional landscape. What stirred hearts at the outset might not hold the same weight midway through. On the flip side, fresh revelations might bring new opportunities to tug at the audience's emotions. For example, in a custody case, early focus on financial challenges might shift to emphasize a parent's sacrifices to protect their children's well-being. Regular check-ins with your Story Spine help ensure it stays emotionally resonant, keeping jurors engaged and invested.

Aligning with Strategy

Your legal strategy can shift gears as the case progresses—and so should your Story Spine. If the focus moves from contesting liability to minimizing damages, the narrative must follow suit. In a defamation case, proving the falsity of statements might initially take center stage, only to pivot to the harm caused once that's established. Adapting your Story Spine ensures your story and strategy march in lockstep, presenting a united and persuasive front.

Opposing counsel's story isn't static, either—and ignoring it is like leaving a door wide open for your audience to wander. If the other side in a product liability case spins a user-error narrative, your Story Spine must counter by refocusing responsibility on design flaws or negligence. Tweaking your narrative to respond to their story keeps you in control, guiding the jury toward your version of the truth.

As the resolution approaches, your Story Spine's final act—"And ever since then"—must deliver the punchline that aligns with your ultimate goal. Maybe you're securing justice for a whistleblower or showing how a verdict can set a precedent for future accountability. A polished and updated conclusion ties everything together, leaving jurors with a message that lingers.

Treating your Story Spine as a living document keeps your narrative dynamic and impactful. Regular updates ensure it aligns with new evidence, strategic shifts, and emotional beats, helping you adapt to challenges without losing the story's core essence. When your Story Spine evolves alongside your case, it becomes a powerful, adaptable tool that ensures your argument remains fresh, relevant, and unforgettable.

Life Lessons: Updating Story Spines

Once upon a time...

When my son Carey was young, he wanted to become the president of the United States. He had no idea what this position entailed, but he instinctively knew that holding the highest office in the land would make him very important. It would mean he mattered. Only 16 years apart, we both pursued law degrees at the same time, our paths running parallel yet distinctly different. But life had other plans for us. Over time, his journey diverged, shaped by his battles with bipolar and by his decision to focus on raising his daughter, Aisleigh.

Every day...

I revisit that story in my mind, seeing how it has since evolved. What once felt like a detour now feels like its own narrative arc—one of resilience, love, and redefined success. The spine of our shared story needed revisiting, updating to reflect the lives we live today.

Until one day...

I realized that stories, like people, grow and change. In courtrooms and in focus groups, I began revisiting old Story Spines, asking whether they still captured the truth or if they needed refinement to stay relevant.

Because of that...

My narratives became more dynamic, better suited to the shifting context of each case. By embracing change, I ensured the stories I told always resonated with current realities.

And ever since that day...

I've committed to periodically updating Story Spines, knowing that the best stories evolve alongside the people and circumstances they represent.

Reflecting Growth and Transformation

A great Story Spine isn't just about what happened—it's about who grew, who changed, and who became something more along the way. Personal growth and transformation breathe life into your story, especially when it comes to your client. As the case unfolds, you might uncover new evidence of resilience, regret, or redemption. These moments are golden opportunities to enrich the narrative.

Picture this: In a criminal defense case, your client isn't just a defendant; they're someone who has taken meaningful steps toward rehabilitation—completing community service, enrolling in school, or even writing letters of apology. These updates bring fresh depth to the "Because of that" and "And ever since then" sections, showcasing your client as a multidimensional person. It's not just their story—it's their journey, and it invites the audience to empathize, root for them, and even see a bit of themselves in the narrative.

Revisiting Themes and Universal Truths

Themes and universal truths give your Story Spine its resonance, but they aren't set in stone. As your case evolves, so might the narrative's emotional focus. For example, a workplace discrimination case might initially be all about fairness. But as evidence of systemic bias emerges, the story might shift to themes of justice and accountability.

Revisiting these overarching ideas keeps your narrative sharp, ensuring it feels as relevant and urgent as the day's headlines. A theme that evolves with the story not only enriches its layers but also keeps your audience interested and eager to see how it all ties together.

Strengthening Connections Between Events

The strength of a Story Spine lies in the impact of its "Because of that" moments. It's the connective tissue that keeps your narrative flowing smoothly. But what happens if new evidence creates a gap or throws off the sequence? You adapt. You strengthen those connections until your story's logic is airtight.

Take a medical malpractice case: Let's say you discover an overlooked error in the treatment timeline. That's a game-changer! You can restructure the sequence to emphasize causation, making it crystal clear how one misstep led to harm. A story with strong, logical connections doesn't just tell the jury what happened; it shows them why it matters.

Incorporating Feedback from Mock Trials or Focus Groups

Mock trials and focus groups are like storytelling boot camps—they help you see your narrative through fresh eyes. If feedback reveals that a part of your story isn't landing, it's time to tweak the Story Spine. For example, in a property dispute, you might learn that your "Until one day" moment isn't pulling its weight. Revise it. Instead of a dry explanation, paint a vivid picture of a family being displaced, their memories packed into boxes, their dreams put on hold. Suddenly, your story has emotional weight, and your audience is connected.

Maintaining Authenticity and Credibility

As your case evolves, so should your commitment to authenticity. If new evidence complicates your original setup, don't ignore it—embrace it. Revising your Story Spine to reflect these nuances makes your narrative richer and more credible. Imagine you discover that your client's "Once upon a time" wasn't as straightforward as you thought. Instead of brushing it aside, embrace it. Adding layers of complexity doesn't just make the story more accurate; it makes it more human. And a human story is one the jury will believe—and remember.

A Story Spine isn't a one-and-done deal. It's a living, breathing framework that grows and adapts alongside your case. By continuously refining your narrative, you ensure it stays relevant, impactful, and authentic from start to finish.

When you update for growth and transformation, revisit themes, strengthen connections, incorporate feedback, and maintain authenticity, your story becomes an unstoppable force. It evolves to meet the moment, captivating your audience and guiding them toward the verdict you seek.

Updating your Story Spine isn't just good housekeeping; it's a strategic power move. Each new discovery or shift in strategy offers an opportunity to elevate your narrative. With every adjustment, you sharpen your focus, align your emotional beats, and maintain control of the courtroom's narrative arc. No case is stagnant, and its story shouldn't be either. Regular updates ensure that every twist, turn, and revelation becomes a meaningful chapter in the journey. It's how you turn a narrative into a movement and a case into a call for action.

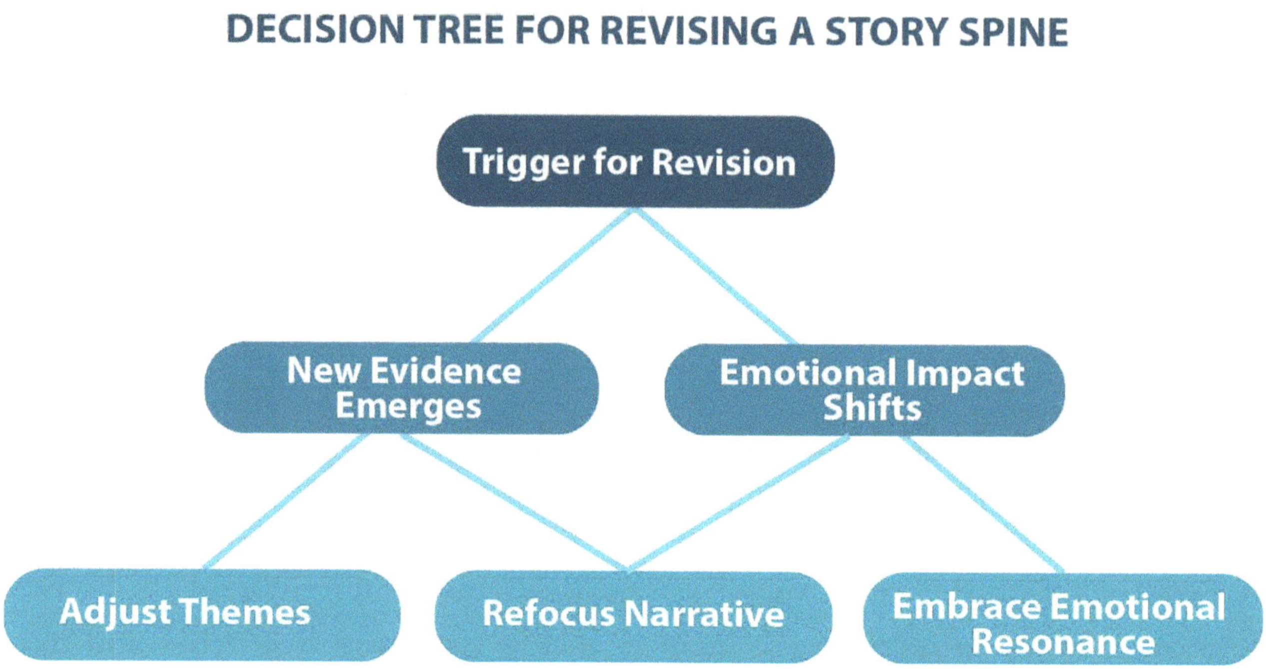

Figure 49: Decision Tree for Revising a Story Spine

A War Story: Discovering the Heart of a Narrative Through Questions

Early in my career, I struggled to find the emotional core of a client's story. It was a personal injury case involving a construction worker who had fallen due to faulty scaffolding. The facts were clear, but the narrative felt sterile and lacked emotional weight.

I decided to ask him a series of questions: "What was the first thing you thought when you fell?" "Who did you call from the hospital?" "What's been the hardest part of your recovery?" His answers surprised me. He spoke about his young daughter, how he'd promised her they'd go to her first softball game that weekend, and how his inability to fulfill that promise haunted him more than the injury itself.

Those answers became the foundation of the case's Story Spine, transforming it into a deeply human narrative about broken promises and the impact of negligence. It reinforced my belief in the power of structured questioning to uncover the heart of a story.

Conclusion

"Periodic updates don't just keep your story fresh—they keep it unforgettable."

Refreshing your Story Spine ensures your narrative remains accurate, compelling, and responsive to the ever-changing landscape of your case. By embracing this process, you transform the Story Spine from a simple tool into a dynamic, strategic powerhouse. It's how you keep your audience connected, your message clear, and your story always ready to deliver its greatest impact. Keep updating. Keep evolving. Keep winning.

Updating Story Spines Checklist

1. Revisit the Core Components Regularly

Periodically assess each part of the Story Spine to ensure it aligns with the most current facts and strategy.

Checklist for Review:

- **Once upon a time:** Does the background still set the stage effectively?
- **And every day:** Is the routine or normalcy still relevant to the audience's understanding?
- **Until one day:** Does the inciting incident remain the strongest entry point into the conflict?

- ❖ **Because of that (x2):** Are the consequences and escalations updated to include new developments?
- ❖ **Until finally:** Does the resolution reflect the current strategy and evidence?
- ❖ **And ever since then:** Does the aftermath capture the latest impacts and stakes?

2. Integrate New Evidence Seamlessly

Each piece of new evidence should either enhance an existing scene or create a new one. Avoid shoehorning evidence without context.

Example: If a security video surfaces showing the exact moment of a breach, update the "Until one day..." scene to showcase this pivotal event. Use descriptive language to make it memorable: "Until one day, the grainy footage captured the defendant bypassing the lock at 11:42 p.m., shattering months of trust in a matter of seconds."

3. Maintain Narrative Coherence

Ensure that updates preserve the logical flow of the story. If new developments shift the narrative, adjust preceding or subsequent sections accordingly.

Example: If an expert witness invalidates a key piece of evidence, ensure that the scenes before and after this revelation are revised to reflect the narrative pivot.

4. Focus on the Audience's Perspective

Keep the audience's understanding and emotional engagement at the forefront. Emphasize elements that connect most with their values, biases, and interests.

Example: In a case involving medical malpractice, if jurors respond emotionally to the patient's suffering, update the "And ever since then..." section to further explore the ongoing impacts on the patient's life.

5. Document Changes Systematically

Maintain a clear record of updates to ensure consistency across all presentations of the case.

Practice Tip: Create a "Living Story Spine" document that tracks each iteration of your narrative. Include the date and reason for each change, along with supporting evidence.

PRACTICE SPINES

Practical Steps for Updating the Story Spine

Schedule Regular Review Sessions

- Set milestones for reviewing and updating the Story Spine during case development (e.g., after discovery, depositions, or pre-trial motions).

Use a Collaborative Approach

- Involve the entire legal team, client, and relevant experts in the review process. Diverse perspectives can uncover overlooked narrative opportunities.

Stress-Test the Story

- Present the updated Story Spine to colleagues or mock juries to identify weak points and gauge emotional impact.

Test for Redundancy

- Ensure that new scenes or evidence do not duplicate existing elements unnecessarily. Each part of the story should serve a unique purpose.

Practice Delivery

- Rehearse presenting the updated story to ensure clarity and confidence in your delivery.

Concrete Example: Evolving the Story Spine in Case Development

Original Story Spine:

- **Once upon a time:** Mr. Brown was a respected landlord managing multiple properties in the city.
- **And every day:** He ensured that all tenants received prompt maintenance and support.

- **Until one day:** A structural defect in one building caused a tenant's injury.
- **Because of that:** The tenant filed a lawsuit, alleging gross negligence.
- **Because of that:** The plaintiff's attorney argued that Mr. Brown ignored prior complaints.
- **Until finally:** The case went to trial, where expert testimony was key.
- **And ever since then:** Mr. Brown's reputation has suffered, and he faces financial strain.

Updated Story Spine:

- **Once upon a time:** Mr. Brown was a respected landlord known for maintaining high standards.
- **And every day:** He made weekly rounds to personally inspect his properties.
- **Until one day:** A tenant's child fell through a damaged railing, sustaining injuries.
- **Because of that:** The tenant filed a lawsuit, claiming negligence.
- **Because of that:** New evidence showed the railing was inspected by an unlicensed contractor hired by the property manager without Mr. Brown's knowledge.
- **Until finally:** The court heard testimony from multiple parties, revealing the contractor's forged credentials.
- **And ever since then:** Mr. Brown has implemented rigorous oversight policies to prevent such incidents, but his reputation remains under scrutiny.

A static story risks obsolescence in the ever-evolving landscape of a trial, where new evidence and shifting perspectives continually reshape the narrative. Embracing the fluidity of your Story Spine—revising it to incorporate fresh insights and unexpected developments—ensures that your narrative remains compelling and relevant.

Always stay attuned to the dynamic currents of your case, allowing your story to evolve with grace and strategic foresight. This commitment to narrative flexibility will not only keep your presentations vibrant but also ensure that they resonate deeply with their intended audiences, leading to more persuasive and effective advocacy in the courtroom.

Chapter 27
Story Spine Intake Questionnaire

"The Story Spine Questionnaire is a mirror for your narrative, reflecting its essence while revealing its hidden depth."

The Building Blocks

The Story Spine Intake Questionnaire is flexible and can be tailored to different storytelling needs. For a courtroom narrative, the questions might focus on uncovering the client's motivations, the opposing party's conflicts, and the key turning points in the case. For a creative project, the focus might shift to character backstories, world-building, and thematic elements. This adaptability makes the questionnaire a versatile tool, no matter the task.

Filling out the Story Spine Intake Questionnaire is not just about gathering information, it's about empowering storytellers to take ownership of their narrative. By breaking the story down into manageable pieces, the process builds confidence and clarity. Storytellers gain a deeper understanding of their material, discovering connections and themes they might not have noticed otherwise. This sense of ownership translates into stronger, more authentic storytelling that captivates and inspires audiences.

This questionnaire is designed to gather information about a story, character, or idea in a way that aligns with the Story Spine structure. Simply answer the questions below, and the responses can be plugged directly into the Story Spine framework.

Life Lessons: Story Spine

Once upon a time...

I was born into a world of poverty, where life was dictated by the grind of survival. My family, poor and uneducated migrant workers, toiled in the fields under the oppressive weight of hard labor and relentless expectations. Opportunities were scarce, conversations about dreams even scarcer. At 13, I left home, carrying the legacy of a teenage mother and soon becoming one myself.

Every day...

The cycle of poverty and limited opportunity pressed down on me like a weight I couldn't escape. There were no guides, no blueprints, no one to help me see beyond the moment. Life felt like a series of disconnected struggles, where survival was the only priority, and meaning was a luxury I didn't know how to find.

Until one day...

Years later, as I began to work with clients whose stories were often buried under layers of hardship and complexity, I saw echoes of my own experience. They came to me with fragmented narratives—filled with pain, confusion, and raw truths they didn't know how to articulate. I realized that, just as I had once struggled to make sense of my own story, they too needed a way to bring their experiences into focus.

Because of that...

I created the Story Spine Intake Questionnaire, a tool designed to uncover not just the facts of a story but the heart of it—the emotions, the struggles, and the moments of resilience that give it meaning. It became a lifeline for those who had been silenced by oppression and circumstance, empowering them to find clarity in their own voices.

And ever since that day...

I've used this framework to help others reclaim their narratives, turning fragmented stories into cohesive, impactful ones. Because I understand what it means to fight for your voice in a world that tries to suppress it. And I believe that every story, no matter how difficult its beginning, deserves to be heard.

Using The Story Spine Is Your Superpower

The Story Spine can be a powerful framework for law firm client intake because it organizes the client's narrative in a clear, logical structure. By mapping a client's situation to the Story Spine, the firm can gather all necessary information, understand the emotional and factual context, and craft a compelling case strategy.

Many clients find it difficult to articulate their situation concisely. The Story Spine prompts them to provide structured, sequential information, ensuring their story is presented in a coherent manner. The Story Spine naturally includes an emotional arc, allowing clients to feel heard and understood. For instance, they can express how specific events impacted them personally, providing the lawyer with insight into the emotional stakes of the case.

The structured nature of the spine reduces confusion. Instead of overwhelming clients with legal jargon, the lawyer can walk them through each step of their story, making the intake process feel approachable and client-friendly.

Example: A client facing a workplace discrimination issue might struggle to explain the timeline of events. Using the spine, they can outline:

- **Once upon a time:** They started working at the company with high hopes.
- **Every day:** They performed well and received positive feedback.
- **But one day:** They were passed over for a promotion while a less-qualified colleague was promoted, and they began noticing discriminatory behavior.

- **Because of that:** They filed a complaint, but the company retaliated.
- **Until finally:** They decided to seek legal assistance.
- **And ever since then:** They've experienced stress and financial hardship.

Benefits for the Law Firm

The Story Spine ensures that the lawyer captures all relevant facts, emotional elements, and potential causes of action in an organized format. It avoids missing crucial details that might emerge only later.

The spine provides a narrative framework that is immediately useful for legal arguments, especially in litigation or mediation. Lawyers can use it to present the client's story compellingly to judges, juries, or opposing counsel. By using the spine to actively listen and structure the intake session, the lawyer demonstrates empathy and professionalism. Clients feel their story is being valued and understood, building trust.

Using the Story Spine as a template standardizes the intake process across the firm. This ensures consistency in the quality of information gathered, making it easier for attorneys and paralegals to review and act on cases.

Example: A workplace harassment case structured with the Story Spine allows the attorney to highlight cause-and-effect relationships and build a timeline that demonstrates the employer's negligence.

Conclusion

"The answers you uncover with the Story Spine Questionnaire don't just build a story—they illuminate its heart."

At its core, the Story Spine is a compass that guides us through the intricacies of storytelling, helping us navigate the delicate interplay of facts, emotions, and meaning. It reminds us that every story has the potential to connect deeply, not just because of its structure but because of the truth and humanity it reveals. When we use tools like the Intake Questionnaire, we're not just building stories; we're fostering understanding and creating bridges between experiences.

Through structured exploration and tools like the Intake Questionnaire, we find the threads that tie a single story to the broader human experience. The turning points and resolutions we discover are not just plot points, they are reflections of the struggles, hopes, and transformations that define us all. This process invites us to dig deeper, to see beyond the surface of events, and to uncover the emotional truths that reach across audiences, cultures, and contexts. In doing so, we don't just tell stories; we honor the shared humanity that makes them meaningful.

By breaking stories down into their essential elements and rebuilding them with purpose, we not only engage our audiences but also evolve as storytellers and individuals. The Story Spine allows us to see our own lives and those of others with fresh eyes, reminding us that every conflict is a chance for growth, and every resolution is an opportunity for reflection.

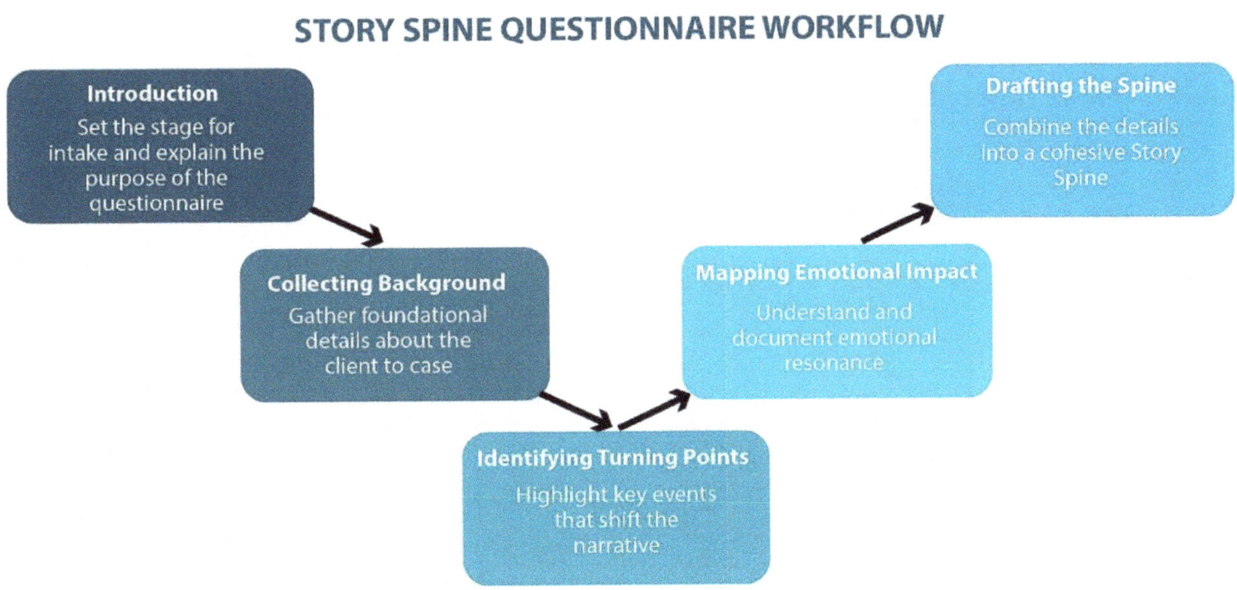

Figure 50: Story Spine Questionnaire Workflow

The Questionnaire In A Nutshell

Section 1: Introduction

- **Who is the protagonist?** (e.g., name, personality traits, motivations, current situation):
- **What is the setting of the story?** (e.g., location, time period, atmosphere, or context):
- **What is the protagonist's normal, everyday life like?** (e.g., routines, struggles, joys, or relationships):

Section 2: Inciting Incident

- **What disrupts the protagonist's normal life?** (e.g., an unexpected event, conflict, or opportunity):

Section 3: Rising Action

- **How does the protagonist initially react to the disruption?** (e.g., immediate actions, emotional responses, or decisions):
- **What new challenges or complications arise as a result of their actions?** (e.g., obstacles, antagonists, unintended consequences):
- **What significant decision or action does the protagonist take to confront these challenges?** (e.g., a bold move, seeking help, or a change in perspective):

Section 4: Climax

- **What is the central conflict or turning point the protagonist faces?** (e.g., a moment of greatest tension or their final challenge):
- **What choice or action determines the outcome of the conflict?** (e.g., how the protagonist resolves the central challenge):

Section 5: Resolution

- **What changes for the protagonist after the climax?** (e.g., lessons learned, relationships transformed, or personal growth):
- **How does the protagonist's world or perspective differ from the beginning of the story?** (e.g., a new normal, enduring consequences, or reflections):

Plugging the Answers into the Story Spine

Once the questionnaire is completed, the responses can be mapped directly into the story spine:

- **Once upon a time...** *(Answers from questions 1–3)*
- **Every day...** *(Answers from question 3)*
- **But one day...** *(Answer from question 4)*
- **Because of that...** *(Answers from questions 5–7)*
- **Until finally...** *(Answers from questions 8–9)*
- **And ever since then...** *(Answers from questions 10–11)*

Optional Add-Ons

- **Theme or Message:** What is the central theme or message of the story?
- **Supporting Characters:** Who are key figures that influence the protagonist's journey?

This questionnaire ensures all necessary elements for a Story Spine are clearly articulated, making it easy to translate ideas into a cohesive narrative.

Chapter 28
Wrapping It All Up

"A great story doesn't end when the last word is spoken—it lingers, resonates, and transforms those who hear it."

Your Narrative Compass

Storytelling is a fundamental part of life, and the ability to tell a clear, compelling story is an invaluable skill. The Story Spine provides a powerful framework for organizing your thoughts, engaging emotions, and delivering impactful narratives.

At its heart, storytelling is about evoking emotion and fostering understanding. The Story Spine encourages you to think beyond surface-level details and explore the emotional stakes of your narrative. Why do these events matter? How do they affect the characters involved? When applied thoughtfully, the Story Spine ensures that your audience not only hears your story but feels it. This emotional resonance is what makes a story memorable and drives people to action.

Mastering the Story Spine doesn't happen overnight; it's a skill that requires practice and intentionality. The more you use it, the more intuitive it becomes, allowing you to craft compelling narratives on the fly. Start with small, everyday stories—explaining a choice, persuading a friend, or recapping an event. Over time, you'll find that the Story Spine becomes a natural part of how you think and communicate. It's not just a tool for big moments; it's a mindset for organizing your thoughts and connecting with others.

Just as a pianist becomes fluent through scales and repetition, mastery of the Story Spine comes through practice. The more you work with this framework, the more it will become your go-to tool for organizing and presenting ideas.

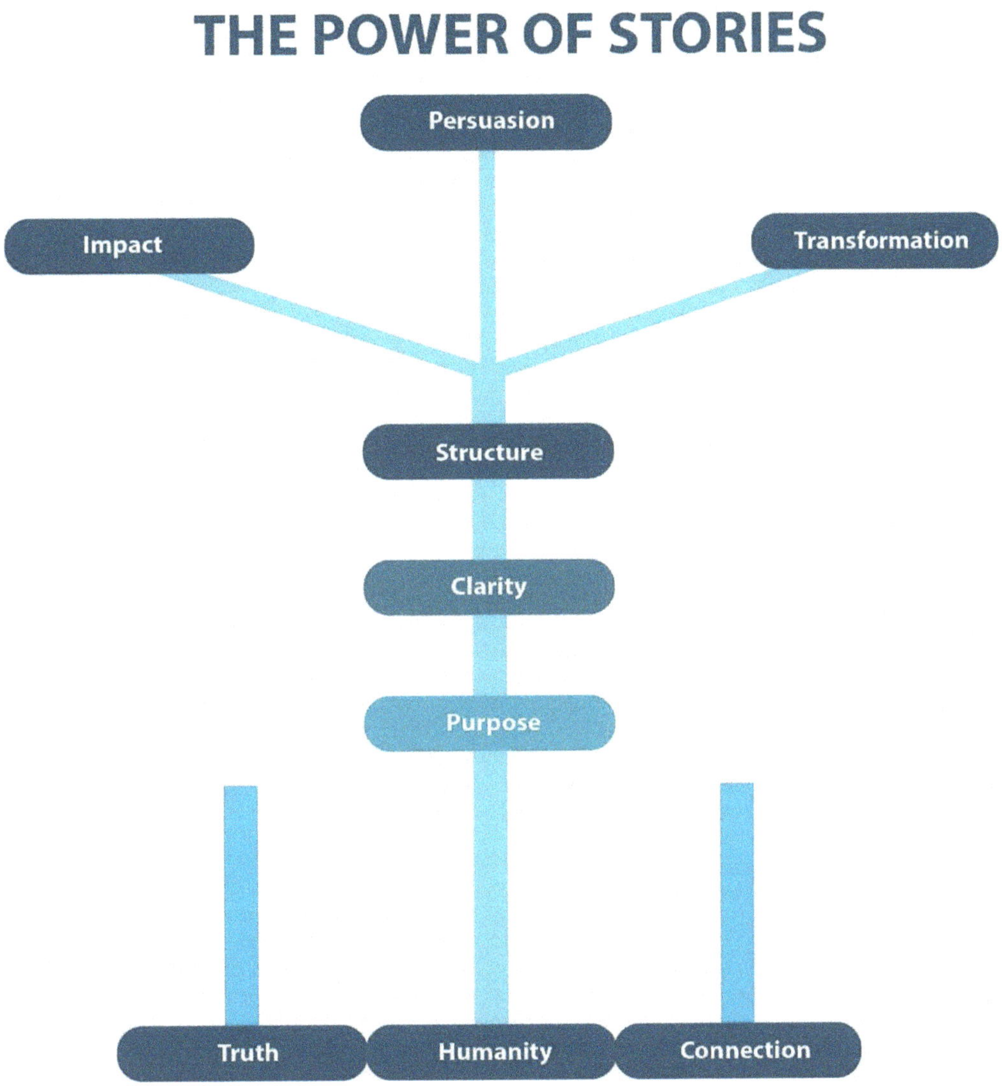

Figure 51: The Power of Stories

Life Lessons: Wrapping It All Up

Once upon a time... After my first major courtroom victory, I went home and sat in silence. The adrenaline of the trial had passed, and I was left with a quiet sense of accomplishment. But as I reflected, I realized the real victory wasn't just the verdict—it was the story we had told, the way it had touched people and brought clarity to chaos.

Every day...I've seen how stories shape lives, from the courtroom to the dinner table. They have the power to transform not just outcomes but understanding, connecting us to each other in ways that transcend the moment.

Until one day...I began teaching others how to use storytelling in every aspect of their work and life. I watched as they found their voices, crafted their narratives, and created their own moments of transformation.

Because of that... The Story Spine became more than a tool—it became a way of seeing the world, of making sense of the complex and finding meaning in the everyday.

And ever since that day...I've embraced storytelling as both an art and a responsibility, knowing that the stories we tell shape the lives we lead and the impact we leave behind.

Here's what to expect as you integrate Story Spine into your routine:

1. Increased Competence

- With consistent practice, you'll build the skill of quickly identifying the key elements of a story:
- The setup (*Once upon a time*).
- The stakes (*But one day*).
- The emotional arc (*Because of that*).
- The resolution (*Until finally*).

2. Better Problem Solving

- The Story Spine is more than a storytelling tool—it's a problem-solving framework. By repeatedly analyzing obstacles, causation, and resolutions, you'll develop sharper critical thinking skills.

3. Greater Confidence

- When you have a framework to fall back on, you'll feel more confident in your ability to communicate under pressure, whether it's answering a judge's question, making a pitch, or explaining a complex idea in everyday conversation.

4. Natural Integration

- Over time, thinking in spines becomes second nature. You'll find yourself instinctively organizing your thoughts, identifying turning points, and crafting compelling conclusions, even in spontaneous conversations.

By mastering this narrative framework, you empower yourself to use storytelling as a tool for influence, empathy, and transformation. In a world increasingly driven by data and complexity, the ability to craft meaningful, relatable stories is a skill that sets you apart and draws people closer.

This book has shown how the Story Spine can transform how you craft stories across legal, professional, and personal contexts, offering clarity and structure to even the most complex scenarios.

As we draw to an end, let's reflect on why the Story Spine is a tool worth mastering and how consistent practice can elevate your storytelling skills, making this framework second nature in your thought process and communication.

Figure 52: Story Spine as Your Compass

A War Story: The Day Storytelling Changed a Life

One of the most memorable moments of my career happened during a pro bono case for a woman facing eviction. Her story was simple yet powerful: a hardworking single mother who had fallen behind on rent due to unexpected medical expenses. Using the Story Spine, I crafted a narrative that highlighted her efforts to stay afloat and her vision of stability for her children.

During closing arguments, I told the jury, "This isn't just about a roof over their heads. It's about a chance for her kids to dream without fear of losing everything." The jury sided with her, and the judge commended her courage. Afterward, she told me, "You didn't just win my case—you saved my life." That moment reminded me of the transformative power of storytelling to not only advocate for justice but to restore dignity and hope.

Conclusion

"Closing a story is like tying a thread in a tapestry; it brings meaning to the chaos and creates a picture worth remembering."

Stories are the currency of human connection, and the Story Spine offers a way to spend that currency wisely. Through its structure, you've learned how to turn facts into meaning, moments into movements, and characters into catalysts for change. This framework equips you to connect deeply and authentically.

But perhaps the most important story you'll craft is your own. By using the Story Spine, you don't just tell better stories; you build a better legacy, one chapter, one case, one moment at a time. Let this be your compass, guiding you to the heart of every story and the impact it holds.

As you take this journey, remember: **Your stories matter. The way you tell them can change minds, move hearts, and make a difference.** Thank you for trusting this book to guide you. Now, go out and tell stories that inspire, persuade, and transform.

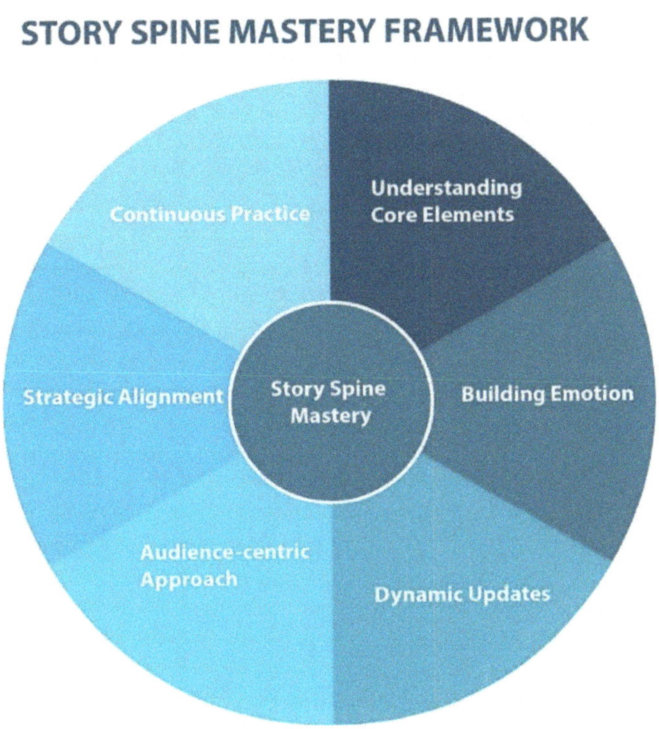

Figure 53: Story Spine Framework

PRACTICE SPINES

A Few Final Exercises to Practice and Reflect

To ensure the concepts in this book stay with you, here are some final exercises:

1. Create a Spine for Every Scenario

Choose three different contexts—a legal case, a professional pitch, and a personal story. Create a Story Spine for each, focusing on the following:

- Highlighting emotional impact.
- Simplifying complexity.
- Connecting to universal truths.

2. Analyze a Famous Story

Pick a well-known legal case, movie, or historical event. Break it down into the Story Spine framework. Reflect on what made it compelling and how you can apply those elements in your own storytelling.

3. Reflect on Your Growth

Set aside time each week to reflect on how you've used the Story Spine. Ask yourself:

- What worked well?
- What could I improve?
- How did my audience respond?

Use these reflections to refine your approach and continue growing as a storyteller.

Chapter 29
Personal Story Spines

"Your life isn't just a story—it's a tapestry of spines, weaving struggle, growth, and triumph into the person you've become."

The Fear of Telling Your Story

For a long time, I was a professional mask-wearer. Lawyer, consultant, teacher—you name it, I had a polished persona for every role. But writing this book? That required a different kind of bravery. It meant taking off the masks, stepping out from behind my bulletproof professionalism, and letting you see the real me. And let me tell you, that was *terrifying*. Every time I put pen to paper (or fingers to keyboard), a voice in my head whispered:

"What if they judge you? What if your story falls flat? What if you're just... ordinary?"

It wasn't until a dear friend called me out—lovingly but firmly—that I realized something important: The most powerful stories aren't the ones wrapped in perfection. They're the messy, honest ones. So I embraced the mess. I let myself write, flaws and all. And you know what I discovered? Vulnerability doesn't weaken us—it liberates us.

Life Lessons: Personal Spines

Once upon a time... When my son Carey and I were both in law school, we would sit together late at night, sharing our fears and hopes. Our paths were different, but our stories overlapped in ways that deepened our bond.

Every day...I've reflected on how personal narratives, with all their twists and turns, connect us to ourselves and to others. The courage to share them—raw and unpolished—can open doors to empathy and understanding.

Until one day...I used the Story Spine to unpack my own journey, discovering patterns and truths that had been hidden in plain sight. Sharing those revelations with others created unexpected connections, turning vulnerability into strength.

Because of that...I began encouraging others to craft their own personal Story Spines, helping them find the power in their lived experiences and the courage to share them authentically.

And ever since that day...I've seen personal storytelling become a catalyst for growth, healing, and connection, proving that our stories—when told with honesty—can be our greatest gift to the world.

Diving Into the Mess

Fear didn't magically vanish when I decided to share my struggles. It was there, front and center, when I wrote about my battles with addiction, my professional missteps, and my moments of self-doubt. That little voice of judgment kept nagging:

"Are you sure you want to admit that? People will think less of you."

But something amazing happened when I stopped fighting the fear and started listening to it. I realized it wasn't just my story I was telling—it was *our* story. Because everyone knows what it feels like to stumble, to doubt, to carry the weight of being human. Sharing those raw, unfiltered moments wasn't just an act of courage—it was an act of connection.

If you see even a glimmer of yourself in my struggles, if you feel a little less alone while reading these pages, then every ounce of self-doubt I wrestled with has been worth it.

A Journey to Authenticity

For years, I hid behind the well-polished and socially acceptable armor of expertise. I taught techniques, shared frameworks, and offered polished advice, but I kept my most vulnerable and embarrassing personal stories locked away. It felt safer that way. But as I wrote this book, I couldn't ignore a deeper truth: The moments that shaped me most weren't the ones where I had all the answers—they were the moments where I stumbled, learned, and grew. The more I wove my own story into these pages, the more I felt connected—not just to the words on the page, but to you dear reader. This book became more than a guide to storytelling to me; it became a testament to the power of showing up as your whole, messy, magnificent self.

A War Story: Finding My Own Story Spine

For years, I told myself I wasn't the kind of person who shared personal stories. I was focused on facts, arguments, and evidence. But one day, while mentoring a young lawyer, I found myself sharing my own journey—how I struggled with confidence early in my career, how I once froze during a critical argument, and how I learned to overcome self-doubt by reframing my internal narrative.

I realized my own Story Spine wasn't just about victories in the courtroom—it was about resilience, growth, and learning to embrace vulnerability. Sharing this story didn't just inspire my mentee; it reminded me of the power of authenticity in connecting with others. Crafting and sharing your own Story Spine isn't just an exercise—it's a way to understand yourself and inspire those around you.

My Personal Story Spines

"Every life is a patchwork of story spines—moments of doubt, triumph, and grit that shape who we are and how we connect with others."

Before Spines vs. After Spines

Before embracing story spines, my storytelling was like assembling IKEA furniture without the instructions: disjointed, incomplete, and occasionally featuring a surprise screw left over. Let's take a quick peek at one example:

Before Spines (Aimless Rambler):

Growing up was... let's just say it wasn't glamorous. We didn't have much—not money, not opportunities, not anything, really. Life had this way of throwing curveballs, one after the other, and most of the time, I wasn't sure which way was up. I always had this vague feeling, like, "I want to help people," but what did that even mean? Sometimes I thought I'd be a teacher, or maybe a doctor, or I don't know—something noble, I guess? But life doesn't hand you a clear roadmap, you know?

Anyway, fast forward through a lot of trial and error—I worked odd jobs, did some soul-searching, probably too much daydreaming—and somehow, I stumbled into law. I mean, who would've thought, right? Me, a lawyer? It wasn't like I had this big plan or anything. It just kind of... happened. And despite everything—despite the messy, chaotic start, despite all the doubts and setbacks—things eventually came together.

After Spines (Heart-Pounding Clarity):

"Once upon a time, I was a migrant worker's child growing up in poverty, surrounded by chaos and loss. Every day, I fought to be heard in a family where silence was survival. Until one day, I realized that my struggles had made me a voice for those who couldn't speak for themselves. Because of that, I dedicated my life to helping the disenfranchised. Finally, I discovered that my own hardships gave me the empathy to connect with people deeply. And ever since then, I've used my voice to amplify the stories of those who need it most."

See the difference? One's a bland recap, and the other? A front-row seat to transformation.

Example: Three Stories, Three Emotions

1. Evoking Hope

"Once upon a time, I thought being a young mother at sixteen meant my dreams were over. Every day, I fought to survive, unsure if I could make a better life for myself or my son. Until one day, I held my baby boy and realized he deserved a future filled with opportunities. Because of that, I earned my GED and clawed my way into college. And because of that, I discovered the strength I never knew I had. Until finally, I built a life for both of us that I'm proud of. And ever since then, I've carried that same hope into every challenge life throws my way."

2. Stirring Courage

"Once upon a time, I was terrified to share my struggles with addiction, convinced it would make me look weak. Every day, I carried the shame like a secret stone in my pocket, letting it weigh me down. Until one day, my son's tear-filled eyes reminded me that I couldn't give up—for him or for me. Because of that, I asked for help and began the grueling climb back to sobriety. And because of that, I found a renewed purpose in helping others who felt as lost as I once did. Until finally, I learned that our hardest battles forge our strongest selves. And ever since then, I've shared my story to remind others that it's never too late to rewrite your ending."

3. Sparking Joy

"Once upon a time, I avoided courtrooms because I thought my passion was "too much" for judges and juries. Every day, I smothered my fire with stiff professionalism, convinced this was what "real lawyers" did. Until one day, during a trial training, I let my authenticity shine through—and saw jurors leaning forward, moved by the raw emotion in my voice.

Because of that, I began walking into courtrooms with confidence, unafraid to be myself. And because of that, I connected with jurors in ways I never had before, turning vulnerability into my superpower. Until finally, I realized that the key to winning wasn't hiding who I was—it was being unapologetically me. And ever since then, I've approached every trial like a stage, ready to bring my whole self to the story."

Transforming Spines Into Scenes

Let's take the spine and turn it into an immersive scene.

Spine: From Crowded Buses to a Clear Voice

Once upon a time, I was a kid crammed onto a school bus so noisy you couldn't hear yourself dream. Every day, I passed big, shiny houses, wondering if life inside them smelled like fresh bread instead of sweaty gym clothes. Until one day, I realized that the fields, the dirt, and the silence at my family's dinner table had given me something the big houses couldn't—a voice shaped by struggle and resilience. Because of that, I learned to tell stories that weren't just mine, but everyone's who'd ever longed for more. Until finally, I stood in a courtroom, speaking not just to be heard, but to connect, to inspire, and to demand justice. And ever since then, I've used my voice to turn dreams into actions and silence into strength.

Scene: The Bus, The Big Houses, and a Bigger Dream

My school bus wasn't just crowded—it was chaos on wheels. There were so many of us being bused to school that it took 3 buses to take us back and forth across the tracks. We pushed, kicked, and shoved, to be the first to get on the buses taking us back and forth to nowhere. Packed to the brim with sweaty, noisy kids, the bus felt like a pressure cooker rolling through the sticky Florida heat. The windows barely cracked open, and the air reeked of sun-warmed vinyl and damp shirts. You couldn't hear yourself think over the yelling, laughter, and occasional scuffles. I held my tattered books close, not as a shield, but as a reminder that they were my ticket out of this world.

The bus route was a cruel tease, winding through neighborhoods that seemed to have fallen straight out of a glossy magazine. Big, pristine houses with manicured lawns and glistening cars in the driveway. I'd press my forehead to the grimy window, daydreaming about the lives lived inside those walls. Did they eat dinner at a real table? Did their parents have soft hands and time to talk about dreams?

My family didn't have time for dreams—or dinners, for that matter. We followed the harvest, chasing oranges, tomatoes, watermelons, and whatever else needed picking. Each season brought a new crop and a new town. The tramp buses herded us from one field to the next, like cattle being shuffled to unseen destinations, their cracked seats and rumbling engines a constant reminder of how trapped we were in their relentless, unfeeling rhythm.

My parents' hands were calloused, their faces lined with quiet determination. They didn't talk much about hopes or what could be; they were too busy surviving and taking care of kids. They got scared when I talked about wanting success, because they knew there was danger in climbing.

Years later, I found myself standing in a courtroom. The faces before me weren't sweaty kids or strangers in passing mansions—they were jurors, lawyers, and a judge, waiting for me to speak. My palms were sweaty, my heart racing, but as I opened my mouth, the words came steady and deliberate. I told the story—not just my story, but the story of people like me, who grew up with dirt under their fingernails and dreams that didn't fit the confines of a field.

For the first time, I saw nods of understanding, not indifference. The courtroom was silent, not because people couldn't hear, but because they were listening. Those years of crowded buses and silent dinners had shaped me into someone who could stand in that room, speak the truth, and hold space for the dreams of every kid who ever stared out a grimy window and imagined something more.

A Call To Action

"Life is made of spines. Some bend, some snap, but the strongest ones grow from struggle."

Personal story spines aren't just for the pages of a book—they're for the moments when you need to understand yourself, connect with someone else, or find strength in your journey. Every triumph and trial we face shapes the narrative we carry, one that can guide, inspire, and change the world. So go ahead, step into your story with open arms. Embrace the messy, the miraculous, and everything in between. Because authenticity isn't just the heart of a great story—it's the heart of being human.

Example: Spinning My Life into Stories

"Behind every triumph, every stumble, and every aha moment is a spine worth sharing—it's the heartbeat of your personal narrative."

Now let's roll up our sleeves and dive into my life's spines, each carrying its own flavor of struggle, growth, and triumph. These stories aren't just examples—they're proof that even the messiest moments can turn into the most compelling tales.

Spine: A Voice for the Voiceless

"Once upon a time, I was the child of an overwhelmed teenage mother, growing up in a world marked by scarcity and upheaval. Every day, I struggled to carve out my own identity in a family where survival often left little room for individual voices to rise above the noise. Until one day, I realized that my childhood without a voice had prepared me to speak for others who couldn't speak for themselves. Because of that, I dedicated my life to helping the disenfranchised and marginalized. Until finally, I found that my personal struggles gave me the empathy to connect with people on a deeper level and to open up new possibilities. And ever since then, I've used my voice to amplify the stories of those who need it most."

Scene: A Voice for the Voiceless

The school bus came to a stop, and I stepped off, already bracing myself for another day. In class, I kept my head down, my hands gripping my pencil tightly. Speaking up felt risky; every word I said felt like it was being measured, judged. At home, words were just as rare—my parents, worn from long days of work, didn't have time for homework, talk, or childhood dreams. But even in the quiet, I knew I wanted more.

I wanted my voice to matter. English was my first language, but growing up surrounded by hard work and survival, it didn't always feel that way. We talked like we were poor and uneducated. Some people called us countrified and undignified. Those were things I didn't want to be. I wanted to be "somebody!" I was hyper aware of the way I sounded. Every sentence felt like a test I wasn't ready for. I hesitated before raising my hand, afraid of being misunderstood, dismissed, or corrected. I didn't want pity. I wanted to be understood. Every now and then, my childhood dialect still spills out in the way I speak, and I cringe.

Years later, I found myself standing in a courtroom, facing a jury, with everyone waiting for me to speak. The nerves were still there, but this time they didn't hold me back—they pushed me forward. I cleared my throat, and instead of hesitation, there was strength. The quiet girl who once struggled to be heard was now speaking for others who couldn't.

The challenges of my childhood hadn't silenced me; they had shaped me. They taught me how to listen with empathy and to speak with purpose. In that courtroom, I wasn't just an advocate—I was proof that struggle can be transformed into strength. My words weren't just my own; they were for everyone who had ever felt unheard. This was my voice, finally doing what I had always wanted: making a difference.

Becoming a Mother at Sixteen

Story Spine:

"Once upon a time, I was a teenager with no direction, lost in the crises of leaving home too young. Every day, I struggled to survive, wondering if I'd ever find my way. Until one day, I became a mother, holding my son in my arms and realizing he deserved better than the life I was living. Because of that, I joined the military the moment I turned 18, determined to create a stable future for both of us. And because of that, I gained discipline, purpose, and the tools to reshape our lives. Until finally, I built a life of stability and opportunity, proving to myself and my son that we could overcome any challenge together. And ever since then, I've carried the belief that with determination and love, no obstacle is insurmountable."

Make it a Scene:

The room was dim, a single bare bulb casting harsh light over the cluttered dresser and crumpled clothes on the floor. I sat cross-legged on the thin mattress, holding my newborn son close, his tiny body wrapped in a blue blanket. He was so small, so fragile, yet his presence was overwhelming. I felt a deep sense of love and obligation as I stared at him, his small fingers curling and uncurling. "I can't let this be his life," I whispered. The weight of every bad decision I had ever made, and every missed opportunity crushed down on me. I could still hear the echoes of arguments from the home I'd left behind, I could feel the sting of nights spent afraid and taste the bitterness of hopelessness.

But as my little boy lay innocently sleeping in my arms, a fierce determination burned through the haze of despair. I pressed my lips to his forehead, inhaling the soft, warm scent of his skin. "You deserve better," I vowed.

The following month, I stood in front of the military recruiter's desk. The room smelled faintly of coffee and paper, and the crisp uniforms displayed on the wall seemed almost impossibly far from my reality. I filled out the forms, my heart pounding with a mix of fear, hope, and purpose. I proudly served both my country and my son in the United States Air Force. I see my son Carey as the reason I became who I am.

The Lessons of Failure

Story Spine:

"Once upon a time, I was on top of the world as an air traffic controller, earning good money and feeling invincible. Every day, I carried myself with pride, believing nothing could bring me down. Until one day, I suffered from burnout. I lost my job, my confidence, and my sense of purpose all at once. Because of that, I spiraled into despair, questioning everything I thought I knew about myself. And because of that, I learned that failure isn't the end—it's the beginning of resilience. Until finally, I used that lesson to rebuild my life, going to college, and forging a new path. And ever since then, I've embraced failure as a teacher, one that prepares us for the victories yet to come."

Scene: The Lessons of Failure

The headset sat on the desk, mocking me with its silence. It used to feel like an extension of me—my connection to a world that demanded precision and control. Now, it was nothing more than plastic and wires, a reminder of everything I'd lost. The phone call that ended my career echoed in my head, sharp and final, like a door slamming shut.

At first, I tried to shake it off, telling myself it was just a bad patch. But days turned into weeks, and the pride I used to carry with me felt like a distant memory. The mirror became my enemy; I couldn't stand to see the face of someone who no longer knew where they belonged. One afternoon, in the middle of a particularly heavy silence, I grabbed a notebook from the cluttered coffee table. My hand trembled as I wrote these words across the blank page: **"What's next?"**

I stared at the question for what felt like hours. It wasn't a grand epiphany, but it was a flicker of something I hadn't felt in a while: possibility. That tiny spark propelled me to research college programs, and fill out an application before my fear could talk me out of it. The path wasn't easy. Classes were filled with students who hadn't yet tasted failure the way I had. But each paper I wrote and every exam I took chipped away at the doubt, building something stronger in its place.

For the first time in years, I wasn't trying to outrun my past—I was using it to push me forward. Standing in my cap and gown on graduation day, I thought back to that quiet afternoon with the notebook. "What's next?" had been my question, but now I had the answer: resilience, growth, and a future I'd earned one step at a time. Failure hadn't broken me—it had built me. And I knew I'd be ready for whatever came next.

Battling Addiction to Rewrite My Story

Story Spine:

"Once upon a time, I was lost in the grips of addiction, certain I had fallen too far to ever recover. Every day, I battled the shame and self-loathing that told me I was unworthy

of a second chance. Until one day, I realized that my son needed me to fight—for him and for myself. Because of that, I sought help, fighting my way back to sobriety one step at a time. And because of that, I found not just recovery but a renewed purpose to help others who felt as broken as I once did. Until finally, I learned that our hardest battles can become our greatest triumphs. And ever since then, I've used my story to remind others that no matter how far you've fallen, you can always rise again."

Scene: Battling Addiction to Rewrite My Story

The shelter's fluorescent lights buzzed overhead, a dull, relentless reminder that this was rock bottom. The walls were beige, the kind of beige that made you feel invisible, like the world had already written you off. I sat on the edge of a cot that creaked with every movement, staring at the worn-out sneakers by my feet. They'd carried me through more bad decisions than I cared to admit, and now they were about to carry me somewhere new.

My son's face flashed in my mind—his hand clutching mine the last time I saw him, his eyes asking questions I didn't have answers for. That thought was my shove off the edge. I grabbed a crumpled flyer from my pocket: **"NA Meeting, 7 PM."**

The meeting was in a musty church basement, the kind where the coffee tasted like regret, and the folding chairs had seen better days. I sat in the back, trying to make myself small. The room filled with people who didn't look like me, didn't sound like me, but somehow felt exactly like me. When they started sharing, their words cracked open something I thought I'd buried for good: hope. "Hi, my name is—" I could barely choke out the words. But I did. And when I said it, heads nodded, hands clapped, and someone whispered, "Keep coming back."

I didn't just keep coming back—I threw myself into it. Ninety meetings in ninety days. A sponsor who didn't let me off easy. Journals full of truths I'd spent years running from. Each step felt like climbing out of quicksand, but with every pull, I got closer to solid ground.

Months later, I stood in that same basement, holding my first chip in my hand. The room erupted in cheers, but the only thing I could hear was my son's laughter in my memory.

This wasn't the end—it was the start of a new chapter. Sobriety wasn't just about staying clean; it was about becoming the person my son could look up to and the person I'd forgotten I could be. Every meeting, every hard conversation, every step forward—it all brought me here, not just standing tall but reaching out. If I could climb out of the darkness, maybe I could light the way for someone else.

Finding Strength in Cancer's Shadow

Story Spine:

"Once upon a time, I sat in a doctor's office, hearing the words no one wants to hear: "You have breast cancer." Every day, I faced the physical toll of chemo and the emotional weight of uncertainty, wondering if I had the strength to keep going. Until one day, I realized that the strength I needed was already within me, built from a lifetime of overcoming. Because of that, I kept moving forward, even on the hardest days. Until finally, I finished treatment and reclaimed my life, piece by piece. And ever since then, I've shared my journey to inspire others to find their own strength."

Scene: Finding Strength in Cancer's Shadow

The doctor's words had hit me like a freight train: **"You have breast cancer."** I nodded like I understood, but inside, it was chaos—a thousand thoughts colliding at once. I walked out of that office holding a stack of pamphlets I'd never read and a diagnosis I wasn't ready to own. Fast-forward weeks later, and there I was, sitting in the chemo chair, trying to ignore the cold prickle of the IV drip.

The room was too quiet, except for the beeping machines and the whispers of nurses. I caught a glimpse of my reflection in my phone screen—bald, ashen, but still me. That's when it hit me: Cancer didn't get to write this story. I was the author here. When I got home that day, I didn't crawl into bed like I wanted to. Instead, I grabbed my phone and made a playlist of every fight song I could think of—

survivor anthems, empowering ballads, even the cheesy ones that made me laugh. I cranked up the volume, blasting it so loud the neighbors probably thought I was throwing a party.

And maybe I was—because in the middle of my kitchen, scars and all, I danced. Not gracefully, mind you—chemo doesn't exactly leave you with much rhythm. But I spun, stomped, and swayed, tears streaming down my face, mixing with laughter I didn't even know I had left. It wasn't pretty, but it was real. It was defiance wrapped in joy, a declaration to the universe that I was still here.

That dance didn't cure the cancer, but it reminded me of something more important: I was still me. The woman who had faced hard things before and found a way through. The woman who could make a choice—every day—to fight, to laugh, to live.

Months later, when I rang the bell to signal the end of my treatment, I didn't just feel relief. I felt victorious. Because this wasn't just about survival—it was about reclaiming the parts of me cancer tried to steal. And now, every time I share my story, I hope it does for someone else what that playlist did for me: reminds them that no matter how hard the fight, there's always a reason to dance.

Writing This Book

Story Spine:

"Once upon a time, I dreamed of writing a book to share everything I'd learned about storytelling and story spines. Every day, life seemed to get in the way, with trials, personal struggles, and self-doubt delaying the process. Until one day, after battling cancer and finding my strength again, I decided it was time to tell my story. Because of that, I poured myself into these pages, determined to create something real, authentic, and useful. Until finally, I realized that storytelling isn't just about crafting narratives—it's about living them. And ever since then, I've embraced the belief that every story has the power to change a life."

Scene: Writing This Book

The blinking cursor on my screen felt like it was taunting me. Every time I tried to start, the doubts crept in. **"Who are you to write a book?"** they whispered. **"What if no one cares?"** I sighed, glancing at the notes scattered across my desk—scraps of ideas, half-formed sentences, and a coffee-stained Post-it that read: **"Just start."** I thought about shutting my laptop, but then a memory hit me like a jolt—a client, sitting across from me, their hands unsteady as they shared their story for the first time. I remembered the look in their eyes when they realized someone was truly listening. That was it. That was why I needed to do this. Not for perfection. Not for applause. For them.

I started typing. The words came out hesitant at first, like a faucet that hadn't been used in years. But then, something shifted. The sentences began to flow—not polished or pretty, but honest. I wrote about failure, about resilience, about the moments when I felt like I'd hit rock bottom and somehow found a way to climb back up.

Before I knew it, hours had passed. The blank screen had transformed into a messy, glorious tapestry of truths I'd been too scared to tell. I read back the first paragraph and smiled—it wasn't perfect, but it was mine.

That night, I closed my laptop with a sense of peace I hadn't felt in years. This wasn't just a book; it was a lifeline. A way to reach people I might never meet but who needed to hear: **"You're not alone. Your story matters."** And as I drifted off to sleep, I realized something even bigger: writing this book wasn't just about helping others—it was about healing myself.

Conclusion: We Are All Spines in Progress

"The truest stories aren't told—they're lived, with every messy, beautiful, and human moment that makes us who we are."

These aren't just stories—they're my life distilled into moments that shaped who I am. You and your cases have them too. Your spines are waiting to be written, shared, and celebrated. So pick up your pen (or keyboard), and start spinning. Your story matters. Your case matters. Your voice matters.

If you take anything from this chapter—or this book—I hope it's this: *Your story matters*. Not the polished, highlight-reel version, but the unvarnished truth. The doubts, the triumphs, the failures—all of it. Because in those moments, you'll find the threads that connect you to others.

Chapter 30

Ethics- Responsibility- and the Weight of Storytelling

"Stories are powerful, and with great power comes great responsibility—not just to entertain or persuade, but to honor the truth and protect those we serve."

Use These Methods With Care:

As you reach the final chapter of this book, you've likely realized that storytelling is more than just a skill—it's a craft, an art, and sometimes a lifeline. But like any powerful tool, storytelling must be used responsibly. The ability to shape narratives and connect with emotions carries ethical obligations, especially when the stakes are high and lives hang in the balance. This chapter isn't about technique—it's about heart. It's about understanding the profound responsibility you carry as a storyteller. Because when you tell someone's story—or even your own—you're doing more than speaking; you're shaping how others see the world.

Life Lessons: The Weight of Storytelling

Once upon a time...

When I was young, stories were not a luxury we could afford. My family, poor migrant workers, lived under the constant weight of survival. But in rare moments of pause, my grandmother would share pieces of our family history. These weren't the whimsical fables of fairy tales—they were raw and real, stories of struggle, resilience, and sacrifice. She spoke deliberately, often pausing to remind us, "Speak the truth," she'd say, "even when it's hard."

Every day...

I've carried her words with me, understanding that storytelling is more than an act of expression—it's a duty. Stories shape how we see ourselves, how others see us, and how we move forward. They can build bridges or create divides, heal wounds or deepen them. The weight of that responsibility is something I've never taken lightly.

Until one day...

In the courtroom, I faced a difficult choice: craft a story that exaggerated the truth for dramatic impact or stay faithful to the facts, even if they felt less compelling. My grandmother's voice echoed in my mind. I chose truth. The story I told was harder, more nuanced, but it was honest—and it resonated deeply because of it.

Because of that...

I've come to understand that the ethical responsibility of storytelling isn't just about avoiding lies; it's about honoring the humanity of everyone involved. It's about ensuring that the stories we tell don't exploit, diminish, or harm but instead elevate and connect.

And ever since that day...

I've approached storytelling as both an art and a sacred responsibility. Whether crafting a narrative for a case, guiding a client through their story, or reflecting on my own, I hold myself to the standard my grandmother set: speak the truth, even when it's hard. Because the stories we tell shape the world we leave behind, and the weight of that is something we must all carry with care.

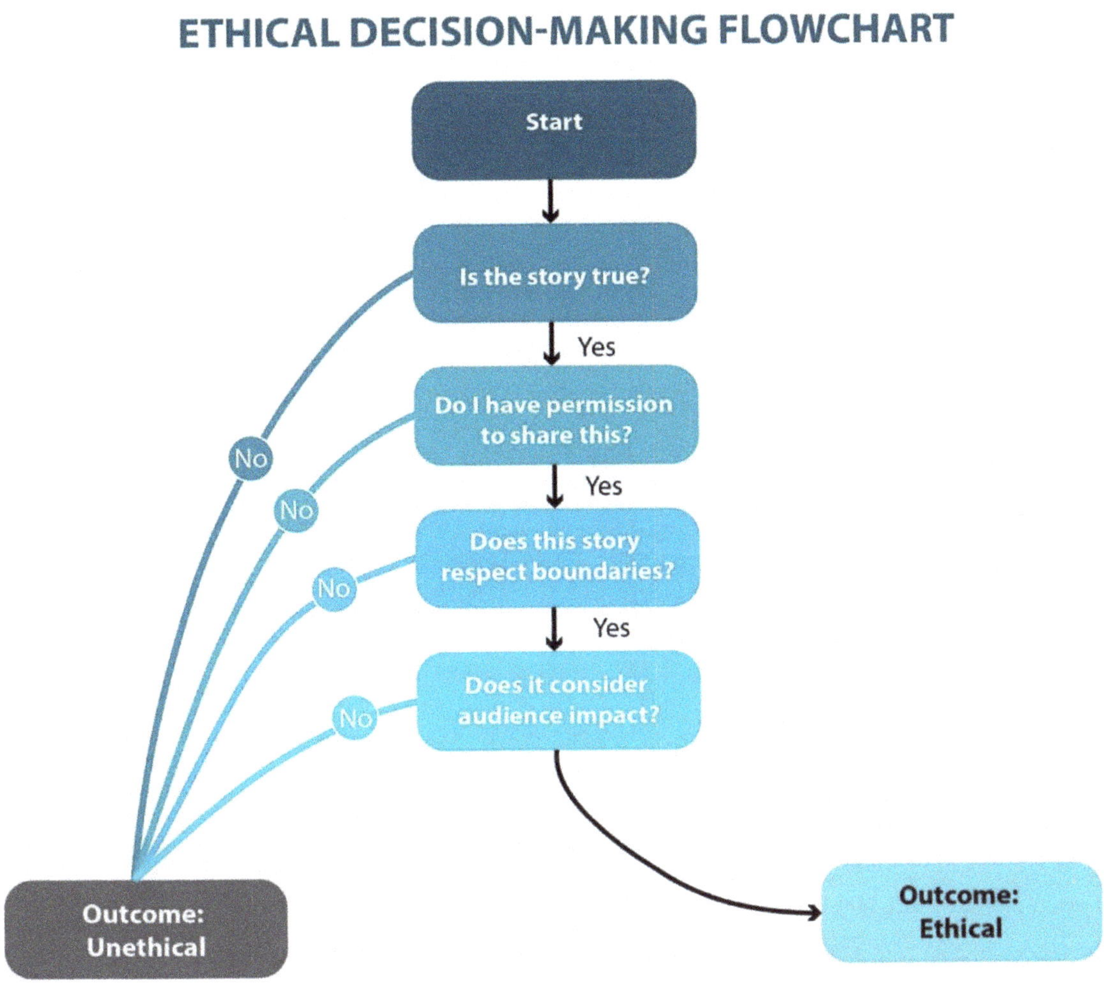

Figure 54: Ethical Decision-Making Flowchart

Truth Telling: The Bedrock of Storytelling

Let's start with the most important rule: **Tell the truth.** That doesn't mean you can't highlight certain aspects of a story or use creative structure to engage your audience. But it does mean that your narrative must remain anchored in honesty. The moment you twist facts or invent details to suit your agenda, you undermine not just your story but your credibility—and once that's lost, it's almost impossible to regain.

Remember, truth doesn't have to mean perfect. Stories often connect more when they reveal vulnerability, complexity, and contradiction. People don't need polished heroes; they need real ones. And truth, even when it's messy, always lands more powerfully than a lie wrapped in glitter.

The Weight of Psychodrama

If you've explored tools like psychodrama—stepping into roles to uncover deeper truths—you know how transformative they can be. But these tools aren't toys. Psychodrama requires care, sensitivity, and respect for boundaries.

When working with clients, colleagues, or yourself, ask:

- **Am I qualified to lead this exercise?**
- **Is this the right tool for this moment?**
- **Am I prioritizing their emotional safety over the story I want to tell?**

If you ever feel out of your depth, don't be afraid to pause. Call in a professional—a therapist, counselor, or trained psychodrama practitioner. There's no shame in knowing your limits; in fact, it's one of the greatest responsibilities you carry as a storyteller. Sometimes, the best thing you can do is listen and refer someone to the help they need.

Know Your Boundaries

It's tempting to lean into the rawest parts of someone's story—it's where the emotion lives, right? But stories are not yours to mine. They are entrusted to you, and with that trust comes the duty to honor the storyteller's boundaries.

Before diving into sensitive topics, ask yourself:

- **Have I sought permission to share this?**
- **Am I telling this story to serve them or to serve myself?**
- **Have I considered the potential impact on everyone involved?**

When in doubt, err on the side of caution. A story withheld is better than a story misused.

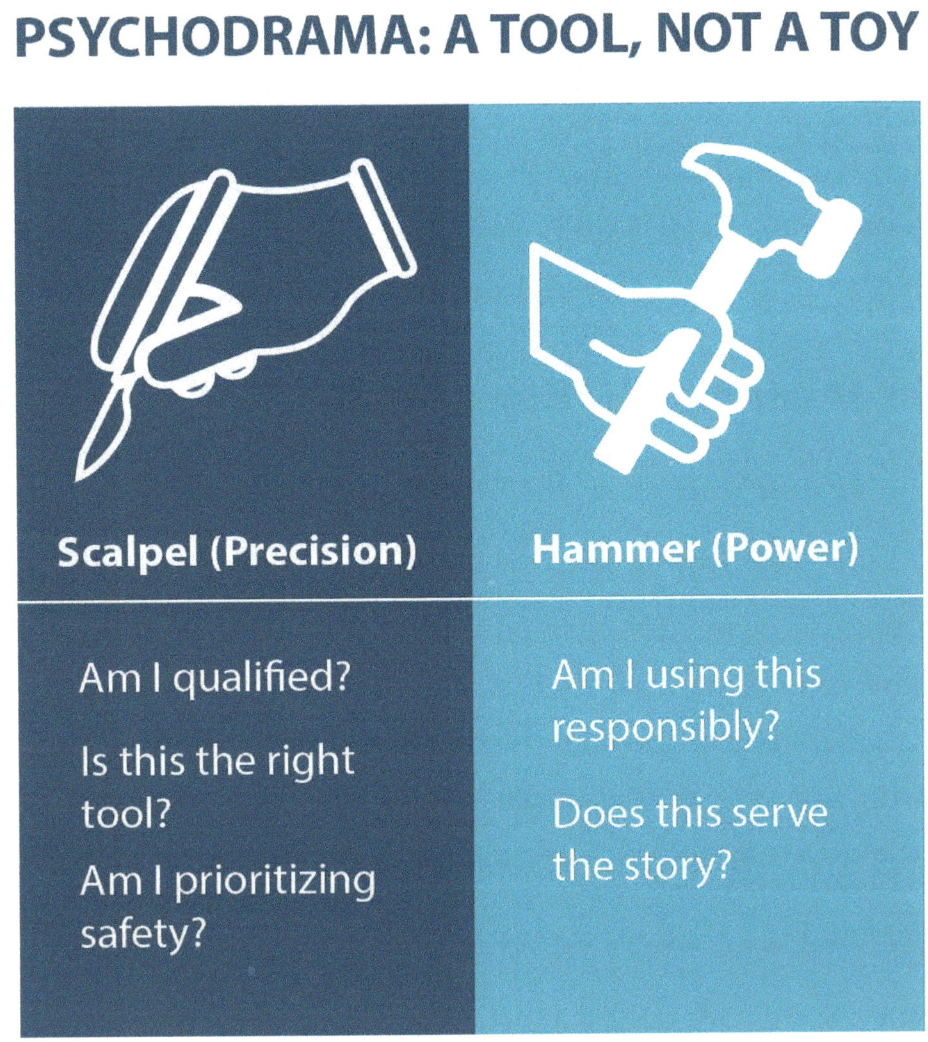

Figure 55: Psychodrama: A Tool-Not a Toy

Respecting the Role of the Listener

As a storyteller, it's easy to focus on the story you're telling and forget about the audience receiving it. But listeners carry their own histories, emotions, and triggers. A powerful story can evoke deep responses, some of which you can't predict.

Be mindful of this by:

- **Preparing your audience** for sensitive material when appropriate.
- **Providing context** so listeners can ground themselves in the narrative.
- **Acknowledging their reactions** and leaving space for reflection.

When to Step Back and Let Others Speak

Storytelling isn't always about you. Sometimes, the most ethical thing you can do is step back and let someone else share their truth. Amplify their voice instead of speaking for them. Hand over the mic. Your role as a storyteller is not to dominate the stage but to create a platform where all voices can be heard.

Advice for Mastering the Story Spine

1. Start by Immersing Yourself in the Structure

Before you can wield the Story Spine like a pro, you need to understand its bones. Each phrase—from "Once upon a time" to "Ever since then"—has a job to do, so take time to explore what each part accomplishes. Think of it as a map: you need to know where you're starting, the twists and turns ahead, and the destination you're heading toward. Read sample spines, practice breaking down familiar stories, and make sure you know how each phrase contributes to the bigger picture.

2. Make It Personal

The Story Spine works best when you infuse it with authenticity. Use it to reflect your unique voice and perspective. When practicing, draw from your own experiences and challenges to craft stories that evoke genuine emotion. A story about overcoming odds hits differently when it's rooted in truth. If you're building a courtroom argument, a pitch, or a personal anecdote, grounding your spine in real emotions and stakes will make it unforgettable.

3. Lean Into the Emotional Arc

The Story Spine isn't just about what happened, it's about why it matters. Pay special attention to the emotional journey you're creating. The turning point ("Until one day") should shift the audience's perspective, and the resolution ("Until finally") should give them a sense of closure and meaning. If your story feels flat, ask yourself: Am I making them feel something? Emotions are the glue that makes stories stick, so don't be afraid to tug at the heartstrings.

4. Use It as a Creative Lens

Once you're comfortable with the structure, use the Story Spine to see narratives everywhere. Look at news stories, famous cases, or even daily challenges through its lens. How did the "Once upon a time" set the stage? What was the "Until one day" that created conflict? Using the spine to break down and analyze existing stories sharpens your instincts and inspires fresh ideas for your own.

5. Practice, Reflect, and Refine

Like any skill, mastering the Story Spine requires repetition. Write spines for different scenarios, test them on friends or colleagues, and gather feedback. Pay attention to what lands and what falls flat. Did your resolution leave them nodding in satisfaction, or were they still waiting for the "aha" moment? Each attempt is a step toward making the Story Spine a seamless, natural tool in your storytelling arsenal.

A War Story: The Fine Line Between Advocacy and Exploitation

In a case involving a family who lost their son in a tragic accident, I was faced with a dilemma: how far could I go in telling their story without exploiting their pain? I wanted to honor their loss while ensuring the jury understood the depth of their suffering.

I decided to let the family lead. Instead of emphasizing the graphic details of the accident, I focused on who their son was—his love for music, his plans for the future, the laughter he brought into their lives. I used their words, their perspective, and their boundaries to guide the narrative.

The jury connected with the story, not because it was shocking, but because it was honest and human. That experience reinforced my belief that storytelling is a profound responsibility. It's not just about winning cases—it's about honoring the truth and respecting the dignity of those whose stories we tell.

Conclusion

"A story is only as strong as the storyteller who crafts it—so make your spine the foundation of something unforgettable."

The Story Spine is your storytelling superpower. Use it to cut through chaos, find the heart of any narrative, and leave your audience wanting more. Captivating a jury, inspiring a team, or sharing a personal moment, the Story Spine is your guide to crafting unforgettable stories. As you go out into the world armed with this framework, remember that storytelling is more than an art form; it's a profound act of connection. Done well, it can heal wounds, build bridges, and change lives. Done poorly, it can exploit, harm, and divide.

So tell your stories boldly—but with care. Speak your truths—but with empathy. And above all, honor the humanity in every story you touch. Because at the end of the day, the greatest responsibility of a storyteller is not just to move hearts but to leave them whole.

Now, go tell stories that make the world better—one spine, one soul, one moment at a time.

SIDE EFFECTS: MAY CAUSE LIFE-CHANGING EPIPHANIES

Handle this book responsibly! Side effects may include:

- Sudden bursts of creativity.
- An uncontrollable urge to tell everyone your life story (even in line at the grocery store).
- Enhanced ability to make people laugh, cry, or both—sometimes in the same sentence.
- Overuse of the phrase "Once upon a time…" in meetings, emails, and text messages.
- Unexpected moments of self-reflection that lead to major personal breakthroughs.

Important Dosage Instructions:

- **Do** use the Story Spine to craft memorable tales.
- **Do** wield your newfound storytelling superpowers for good, not manipulation.
- **Do not** attempt to "psychodrama" your roommate's love life without proper training—it's a story, not therapy.

Warning Labels:

- **Not for use while driving.** (Seriously, the emotional resonance might distract you.)
- **Consult a professional if symptoms of overconfidence or excessive metaphors persist.**

- **Keep away from audiences that are not emotionally prepared for your newfound authenticity.**

Remember, with great storytelling power comes great responsibility. Now go forth and spin spines, but tread carefully—stories this good can move mountains, melt hearts, and maybe even start revolutions.

📚 YOU HAVE BEEN WARNED. 📚

References and Acknowledgments

"Behind every great story is a chorus of voices that helped shape it—here's to the legends, teachers, and cheerleaders who made this book possible."

References

1. **Adams, Kenn.**

   How to Improvise a Full-Length Play: The Art of Spontaneous Theater.

   A foundational work that introduced the world to the Story Spine framework. Kenn Adams' brilliant insights inspired much of the storytelling structure explored in this book. His innovative approach to narrative is a gift to storytellers everywhere.

2. **Friedman, Rick.**

   Rules of the Road: A Plaintiff Lawyer's Guide to Proving Liability.

   Rick Friedman's groundbreaking techniques for crafting trial narratives shaped how legal professionals use storytelling to connect with jurors. His emphasis on simplicity and clarity is a touchstone for any advocate.

3. **Trial Lawyers College.**

   Trial Lawyers College Training Materials.

   The Trial Lawyers College has been instrumental in blending storytelling with trial advocacy. Their dedication to empowering attorneys with tools like psychodrama and story structure deeply influenced this book's approach to legal narratives.

4. **Ethos Advocacy.**

   Ethos Advocacy Training Curriculum.

A comprehensive program that marries the art of authenticity with the science of persuasion. Ethos Advocacy's focus on authentic connection provided invaluable insights into making stories resonate in high-stakes environments.

5. **Brown, Brené.**

   Daring Greatly: How the Courage to Be Vulnerable Transforms the Way We Live, Love, Parent, and Lead.

   Brené Brown's work on vulnerability and connection is a reminder that storytelling isn't just about the narrative—it's about the heart behind it. Her lessons on authenticity echo throughout these pages.

6. **Neimeyer, Robert A. (Ed.)**

   Techniques of Grief Therapy: Creative Practices for Counseling the Bereaved.

   This book informed the delicate use of psychodrama and storytelling in emotionally charged situations, underscoring the importance of ethical responsibility when engaging with vulnerable clients or audiences.

7. **Heath, Chip, & Heath, Dan.**

   Made to Stick: Why Some Ideas Survive and Others Die.

   A masterclass in crafting messages that resonate, this work provided valuable guidance on the "sticky" elements of a memorable story.

8. **Campbell, Joseph.**

   The Hero with a Thousand Faces.

   Campbell's exploration of the hero's journey reminds us that storytelling is as much about shared archetypes as it is about individual experience. His work is a timeless compass for narrative structure.

Acknowledgments

"It takes a village to raise a storyteller—and an entire galaxy to write a book."

1. **Kenn Adams.** For your invention of the Story Spine, which transformed storytelling into a simple, elegant art form. Your brilliance gave this book its foundation.

2. **Gerry Spence, Rick Friedman, and the Trial Lawyers College.** Thank you for teaching that a well-told story is the most powerful tool in the courtroom. Your lessons gave depth and purpose to this book's mission.

3. **Ethos Advocacy.** To the team that reminds us why connection is the essence of persuasion—your guidance shaped how this book approaches storytelling in professional contexts.

4. **Friends and Family.** For being the first audience to my stories, for encouraging me when I doubted myself, and for reminding me that every story worth telling starts with love.

5. **Readers, Learners, and Storytellers.** This book is for you. For everyone brave enough to tell their truth and connect with others through the messy, beautiful, transformative art of storytelling.

www.ingramcontent.com/pod-product-compliance
Lightning Source LLC
LaVergne TN
LVHW071343210926
848486LV00003B/217